Thomas Heywood

Twayne's English Authors Series

Arthur F. Kinney, Editor

University of Massachusetts, Amherst

TEAS 388

A
WOMAN
KILDE
with Kindneſſe.

Written by Tho: Heywood.

PRV
DEN
TIA

LONDON
Printed by William Iaggard dwelling in Barbican, and
ate to be ſold in Paules Church-yard.
by Iohn Hodgets. 1607.

Title page of the 1607 edition of *A Woman Killed with Kindness*
Reproduced from the unique copy in the British Library

Thomas Heywood

By Barbara J. Baines

North Carolina State University

Twayne Publishers · Boston

Thomas Heywood

Barbara J. Baines

Copyright © 1984 by G. K. Hall & Company
All Rights Reserved
Published by Twayne Publishers
A Division of G. K. Hall & Company
70 Lincoln Street
Boston, Massachusetts 02111

Book Production by Marne B. Sultz

Book Design by Barbara Anderson

Printed on permanent/durable acid-free
paper and bound in the United States of
America.

**Library of Congress Cataloging in
Publication Data.**

Baines, Barbara J. (Barbara Joan)
   Thomas Heywood.

   (Twayne's English authors series; TEAS 388)
   Bibliography: p. 168
   Includes index.
   1. Heywood, Thomas, d. 1641 —
Criticism and interpretation.
I. Title.   II. Series.
PR2577.B35 1984   822'.3   84-10768
ISBN 0-8057-6874-2

For my father, in loving memory

Contents

About the Author

Barbara J. Baines received her B.A. and M.A. degrees at the University of Oklahoma and her Ph.D. at Ohio University, where she worked under the direction of Calvin G. Thayer. She is at present an Associate Professor in the English Department at North Carolina State University. Her publications include *The Lust Motif in the Plays of Thomas Middleton* (Salzburg, 1973) and articles on Jonson, Shakespeare, Beaumont and Fletcher, Kyd, Marlowe, and Marston.

Editor's Statement

Thomas Heywood has long been studied as the author of an *Apology for Actors* (which alone ascribes *The Spanish Tragedy* to Thomas Kyd) and honored as the writer who saved Marlowe's *Jew of Malta* from oblivion. Now, in a lucid and persuasive study, Barbara J. Baines argues that Heywood was also the finest bourgeois playwright of the English Renaissance while also the most prolific. The author of more than two hundred plays, Heywood is the representative writer of his time, yet "he did not merely reflect [a middle-class] sensibility but consciously shaped it in a positive way that has had permanent cultural significance." By tracing Thomas Heywood's major works by mode and through a detailed analysis of *A Woman Killed with Kindness,* the most significant domestic tragedy of the English Renaissance, Baines demonstrates how this writer has been seriously underrated. Her study should mark the beginning of renewed critical and scholarly interest in one of the most important minor playwrights of his time.

— *Arthur F. Kinney*

Preface

Our understanding of Renaissance drama is so influenced by Shakespeare that we inevitably perceive his fellow playwrights in the somewhat blinding light of his genius. However unfair or inappropriate the Shakespearean yardstick may be, we continue, perhaps unconsciously, to measure with it and are thus obliged to contend with Charles Lamb's stigmatic labeling of Thomas Heywood as a "prose Shakespeare." From the start, then, we must concede the prosaic nature of Heywood's dramatic verse, the general absence of a figurative language that functions organically with character and action. With few exceptions, the best we can say of Heywood's verse is that it is fluid and graceful—that it never gets in the way. As one comparison and concession leads to another, we also acknowledge that Heywood's characters are, for the most part, stereotypes. If, however, we look for the playwright who is most representative of the values of his age, of the practice of his art, and of the taste of the average London playgoer, we find no one better than Thomas Heywood. The most prolific of Renaissance playwrights, he wrote from the full flowering of the drama before the turn of the century until shortly before the closing of the theaters in 1642. His success, like Shakespeare's, is in part attributable to his experience as a professional actor as well as a playwright. Although he found his audience primarily in the middle-class London citizens who were merchants, tradesmen, and apprentices, he was able on occasion to please the more refined audiences at the Globe, the Blackfriars, and the court.

Obliged throughout his dramatic career to delight the less sophisticated audiences of the Curtain, the Red Bull, the Cockpit, and the provinces, Heywood never lost sight of another obligation: to teach as well as to please. "Aut prodesse solent, aut delectare" became the motto on the title pages of most of his works and in the signatures of his addresses. An adaptation of Horace's "Aut prodesse volunt aut delectare poetae," this motto is an accurate reflection of Heywood's achievement. He gave to his "unlettered" audiences the classical myths and legends as well as Roman and British history, and he instilled in those audiences a feeling of nationalism, patriotism, and respect for the established church and state. In his plays of domestic middle-class life he defined middle-class morality and taste. As a playwright whose professional circumstances dictated that he cater to a bourgeois audience and as one who willingly accepted this necessity, Heywood has been of interest to the modern critic primarily as a means of defining the Elizabethan bourgeois sensibility. It is important, however, to acknowledge that he did not merely reflect this sensibility but consciously shaped it in a positive way that has had permanent cultural significance. The values, virtues, and ability that Heywood ascribes to the common man were crucial to the fashioning of the identity or self-image of the class for which he wrote. The objective of the present study is not only to affirm this cultural achievement but also to demonstrate the artistic skill with which it is accomplished. Heywood has been too long dismissed as a careless hack who just happened to write one good play.

A comprehensive study of Heywood's extant plays is burdened with numerous problems, such as determining the canon and the dates of composition of most of his plays. His best plays were written at unpredictable intervals throughout his long career: *A Woman Killed with Kindness* in 1603, *The Ages* around 1610, *The English Traveller* between 1624 and 1627, *Love's Mistress* in 1634. The best of these is the earliest, a fact that creates serious difficulties for anyone who would attempt to chart a chronological development of the playwright's skill. The fact that he was not, as Shakespeare was, ensconced in the most esteemed and lucrative company in London surely explains in part the unpredictable quality as well as the prodigious quantity of his production. Financial need must in large part explain such mediocre works as *The Late Lancashire Witches* and *A Maidenhead Well Lost,* which were written at a time when the old playwright was capable of a work as fine as *Love's Mistress.*

The problems of dating the plays and of tracing the development of the playwright's skill are matched by still another problem: generic classification. If ever a writer demonstrated the Renaissance love of the mixed genre, it was Thomas Heywood. His practice would defy the refined classification of any Polonius. Despite this resistance, I have attempted generic classification for convenience of discussion and for a clearer understanding of the nature of each play. Various plays, like illegitimate offspring (Heywood's own metaphor for plays that came to light without his permission), are reluctant to conform to legitimate categories or insist upon belonging to more than one.

The final problem for a study of Heywood's plays is the selection of texts. The principle followed here, despite the inconveniences that result, is to use the best available text for each play. The standard edition of the plays is still *The Dramatic Works of Thomas Heywood,* edited, presumably, by R. H. Shepherd for John Pearson in 1874. Many of the plays are still available only in this six-volume edition. Since there are no line numbers in the Pearson edition, citations are located by volume and page numbers in parenthesis. Whenever possible I have used, as the notes indicate, modern editions made available in the Malone Society series, the new Garland series, the Regents Renaissance Drama series, the Revels series, and elsewhere. Needless to say, we need a new standard edition of the complete works of Thomas Heywood. Heywood's nondramatic works, of which there is an astonishing quantity, are rarely read and, in most instances, inaccessible. Although these works are beyond the scope of this study, I have tried to provide some information about them, particularly as they pertain to the plays.

Barbara J. Baines

North Carolina State University

Acknowledgments

This study was facilitated by a semester of release from my teaching obligations and by financial assistance from the North Carolina State University research fund. To Arthur F. Kinney, Renaissance field editor of the Twayne series, I give special thanks for the opportunity to do this study and for his careful and constructive editing. My thanks also to Emily McKeigue, associate editor of Twayne Publishers, and her colleagues for expeditious work and kind correspondence. For lessons in the past that prevail after many years, I remember with gratitude my teacher and mentor, Calvin G. Thayer of Ohio University. For the lessons of the present and particularly for numerous constructive readings of this study, I am most deeply indebted to my husband, A. Leigh De-Neef of Duke University.

Chronology

1612   1 and 2 *The Iron Age* (pub. 1632).

1619   Queen Anne's death and approximate date of Heywood's retirement as an actor.

1624   *The Captives* (pub. 1885). *Gunaikeion, or Nine Books of Various History Concerning Women* (pub. 1624).

1625   Death of King James I and Heywood's *A Funeral Elegy*.

1627   *The English Traveller* (pub. 1633).

1631   2 *The Fair Maid of the West* (pub. 1631). Begins series of seven Lord Mayors' pageants, the last written in 1639 (pub. 1631). *England's Elizabeth: Her Life and Troubles, During her Minority, from the Cradle to the Crown.*

1632   Revival and publication of Marlowe's *The Jew of Malta* (with Heywood's prologue and epilogue). *A Maidenhead Well Lost* (pub. 1634).

1633   Second marriage, to Jane Span.

1634   *The Late Lancashire Witches,* with Brome (pub. 1634). *Love's Mistress, or The Queen's Masque* (pub. 1636). *The Challenge for Beauty* (pub. 1636).

1635   *The Hierarchy of the Blessed Angels* (pub. 1635). *Pleasant Dialogues and Dramas* (pub. 1637).

1641   Heywood's burial in the Church of St. James, Clerkenwell, a London suburb.

Chapter One
Life and Works

Little is certain about Thomas Heywood's birth, family background, or formative years. His principal biographer, A. M. Clark, has presented convincing evidence that he was born in 1573 to the Reverend Robert Heywood and his wife Elizabeth, members of a poor but respectable Lincolnshire family.[1] Heywood was thus approximately the same age as his chief rivals, Thomas Middleton, Thomas Dekker, and Ben Jonson, and ten years younger than the great poets he obviously admired, Marlowe and Shakespeare. In *An Apology for Actors* Heywood refers to the years he spent at Cambridge, where the performance of plays was an important part of the university education. He probably attended the university from 1591 until 1593, when the death of his father obliged him to begin his career as a professional writer and actor in London. A voracious reader with an astounding memory, Heywood made good use of his Cambridge years to acquire a thorough classical education and the skills of a competent translator, both of which served him well throughout his long career.

His first literary achievement, an Ovidian imitation much in the fashion of Shakespeare's *Venus and Adonis,* is *Oenone and Paris,* published in 1594.[2] At this time he appears to have begun a rigorous apprenticeship in the public theaters with the Lord Admiral's company under the financial control of Philip Henslowe. His first experience as playwright was limited to patching or revising old plays and minor collaborations. By 1596, however, he had received payment from Henslowe for a complete play. In 1598 Henslowe recorded payment for Heywood's *War Without Blows and Love Without Strife,* one of approximately two hundred plays that did not survive the author. That his talent as an actor was equally important to Henslowe and to the Lord Admiral's company is evident in the contract that Heywood made with the company to perform exclusively with them from 1598 to 1600. This contract did not, however, prohibit him from free-lance work for other companies, for it was during this period that he wrote two of his earliest extant plays, 1 and 2 *Edward IV,* for the Earl of Derby's company. Of the twenty-four extant plays safely attributed to Heywood, only 1 and 2 *Edward IV* and *The Four Prentices of London* can confidently be assigned to this early period of his career, 1594–1599. Nevertheless, by

1598 Heywood had obviously written a substantial number of plays with sufficient appeal for him to be mentioned in Francis Meres's *Palladis Tamia* as among "the best for Comedy."[3] In 1601 his popular appeal won him a position as actor and sharer with the Earl of Worcester's company, renamed in 1603 the Queen Anne's company. The success of this company can be attributed to the skill and industry of Heywood. Henslowe's diary indicates, for example, that Heywood at the height of his production was averaging a play and a half per month over an extended period. His facility was essential because the Worcester-Queen Anne's company was in demand not only at the Rose and the Curtain, and later at the Red Bull and the Cockpit, but also at court and throughout the provinces.

To the first decade of the seventeenth century belong the Heywood plays most familiar to the modern reader, 1 *The Fair Maid of the West* and *A Woman Killed with Kindness*. The first part of *The Fair Maid* has for many modern critics a distinctly Elizabethan quality that suggests a date of composition perhaps as early as 1600.[4] Certainly the play was written no later than 1609. *How a Man May Choose a Good Wife from a Bad* and probably *The Royal King and the Loyal Subject* immediately precede *A Woman Killed with Kindness*, which was written in 1603 and published in 1607. It is likely that the last four extant plays written before *Troia Britannica*, his verse narrative of Greek mythology and the matter of Troy, were 1 and 2 *If You Know Not Me, You Know Nobody* (1603–04), *The Wise-Woman of Hogsdon* (1604–05), and *The Rape of Lucrece* (1607). Supporting E. K. Chambers, Clark contends that *An Apology for Actors* was also written in 1607,[5] at approximately the time of Heywood's excellent translation of Sallust and a year before *Troia Britannica*. It is possible, however, that *An Apology for Actors* was written, at least in part, shortly before its publication in 1612. After *Troia Britannica* Heywood resumed his production of plays with *Fortune by Land and by Sea* in 1609 (published posthumously in 1655), followed by a five-part dramatic sequence known as *The Ages* and consisting of *The Golden Age, The Brazen Age, The Silver Age,* and 1 and 2 *The Iron Age*. Although *The Golden Age* was published in 1611 and *The Silver Age* and *The Brazen Age* in 1613, Heywood delayed publication of parts 1 and 2 of *The Iron Age* until 1632.

After part 2 of *The Iron Age* Heywood wrote nothing else for the stage until 1624, the date of composition for *The Captives*, a tragicomedy performed by the Lady Elizabeth's company. This ten-to-twelve-year hiatus in Heywood's productivity has never been explained adequately, but it is perhaps related to the gradual decline of the Queen Anne's company. From 1612 until its total demise in 1619, the company faced financial problems exacerbated by numerous law suits. In addition, on March 4, 1617, the apprentices, whom Heywood had so often pleased, partially destroyed the company's new playhouse, the Cockpit. Heywood may have spent part of this period engaged in the popular controversy over women that had been revived through a misogynistic diatribe by one Joseph Swetnam. In 1619 Heywood's company gave women their revenge in a play called *Swetnam, the Woman-hater Arraigned by Women*, possibly written by Heywood.[6] However, his major defense of women, *Gunaikeion, or Nine Books of Various History Concerning Women*, was not published until 1624. We might be inclined to think that the 466 folio pages of this prose work would account for a considerable part of the poet's energy between 1614 and 1624, but Heywood's Latin colophon declares that the work was devised, begun, finished, and published in seventeen days.[7]

With the accession of Charles I in 1625, Queen Henrietta's company was formed primarily from the Lady Elizabeth's company. Although Heywood was not officially a member of either company, he wrote occasionally for both. Two tragicomedies, *The Captives* and *The English Traveller*, were written between 1624 and 1627. In 1630–31 he wrote a prose history, *England's Elizabeth: Her Life and Troubles, During Her Minority, from the Cradle to the Crown*, and 2 *The Fair Maid of the West*; and in 1631 he saw parts 1 and 2 of that play through the press. Perhaps the sustained popularity of *The Four Prentices*, reflected in a second edition in 1631, was responsible for the haberdashers' choice that year of Heywood to write the Lord Mayor's pageant, *Londoni's Ius Honorarium*. This first effort pleased the tradesmen so well that Heywood was commissioned to write six more pageants between 1632 and 1639. Sixteen thirty-two is also the likely date of *A Maidenhead Well Lost*. Fortunately, Heywood's interest in the publication of plays during the 1630s was not restricted to his own work. When the Queen Henrietta's men revived and performed for the court Marlowe's *The Jew of Malta*, Heywood provided a prologue and epilogue and saw the play through the press.

The year 1634 was a particularly productive and gratifying one for Heywood: he wrote at least three plays and probably began his most ambitious nondramatic work, *The Hierarchy of the Blessed Angels*. He also no doubt felt personally vindicated by the legal punishment of William Prynne, who had attacked the theater, plays, and players (with specific reference to Heywood) in his *Histriomastix*.[8] In the prefatory letter of *A Maidenhead Well Lost*, published in 1634, Heywood alludes to the punishment of Prynne. His next play, *The Late Lancashire Witches*, was written with Richard Brome for the King's men at the Globe. Also for the King's men at the Blackfriars and probably in 1634, Heywood wrote *A Challenge for Beauty*. But it was for the Queen as a special court performance by her company in honor of the King's birthday that he wrote *Love's Mistress: or, the Queen's Masque*. The success of this masque-play is apparent in the fact that it was performed three times before Charles I and the Queen. Part of that success, as Heywood graciously acknowledges in the epistle to the reader, was a result of the elaborate scenery and stage machinery of Inigo Jones. Encouraged by this achievement, Heywood presumed to dedicate *The Hierarchy of the Blessed Angels* to Queen Henrietta Maria. The work, perhaps because of its dullness, failed to win him the patronage he wished and thus did not alter the course of his career in any positive way. Nevertheless, with its abundance of commendatory verses and costly plates paid for by his friends, the work is a testament of the love and respect Heywood had earned. *The Hierarchy* is also of particular interest to the biographer because in it Heywood looks back with a poignant regret at a lifetime of writing that left him in poverty despite his popularity and amazing industry:

> It grieues vs now, although too late, at last,
> Our Youth in idle Studies to haue past;
> And what a folly 'tis, we now haue found,
> To cast our Seed in an vnfaithfull Ground:
> That in our Youth we haue layd up no store,
> Which might maintaine vs when our heads be hore;
> And that our shaken Vessell, torne and thin,
> Can finde no easie Port to harbor in.
> Then Barren *Muses,* seeke some other Friend,
> For I henceforth a Thriuing Course intend.[9]

With *The Hierarchy* Heywood did indeed abandon the muses of the stage, but a "Thriuing Course" he did not find. In 1635 he put together an odd collection called *Pleasant Dialogues and Dramas,* published in 1637. The labor of his final years, from 1635 until his death in 1641, provides us with an image of a journalistic writer who was trying to eke out a living with whatever he could hastily turn out or salvage from earlier years. For example, to this period belong *Philocothonista, Or, The Drunkard, Opened, Dissected and Anatomized* (1635), *The Wonder of this Age: or The Picture of A Man Living, who is One Hundred Fifty-two years old, and upward* (1635), *The Three Wonders of this Age* (1636), *A True Description of His Majesty's Royal Ship, Built this Year 1637, at Woolwich* (1637), *A Curtain Lecture* (1637), and *The Exemplary Lives and Memorable Acts Of Nine The Most Worthy*

Women Of The World (1640). *The life and death Of Queen Elizabeth, From the womb to the Tomb, from her Birth to her Burial* (1639) tells once again, and this time in couplets, the story of Elizabeth. She is also included in *Exemplary Lives and Memorable Acts Of Nine The Most Worthy Women Of The World: Three Jews. Three Gentiles. Three Christians. Written by the Author of the History of Women* (1640). Although Clark has shown Heywood's hand in numerous obscure pamphlets of this late period, the only other work of note is *The Life of Merlin, Surnamed Ambrosius. His Prophecies, and Predictions Interpreted; and their truth made good by our English Annals, Being a Chronographical History of all the Kings, and memorable passages of this Kingdom, from Brute to the Reign of our Royal Sovereign King Charles* (1640). The long list of hackwork and self-plagiarism is a poignant confirmation of Heywood's promise to the reader of *The Hierarchy* that time "will neuer suffer our braines to leaue working, till our pulses ceas beating."

Although much about the life of Thomas Heywood must remain conjectural, the prefatory letters, prologues, and epilogues to his plays and the self-reflecting digressions in the nondramatic works provide valuable information about his attitude toward his profession and about his sense of achievement.

The playwright's attitude toward the publication of his plays shifted gradually over the years from indifference to concern as he witnessed either the inept and unauthorized printing of his plays or the loss of them altogether. In the prefatory letter to *The Rape of Lucrece* Heywood prides himself on the fact that he is a faithful servant of the stage and does not profit from "a double sale" of his plays, first to the players and then to the printer. He adds that he is obliged to authorize publication of *The Rape* in order to prevent an inaccurate printing. In the address to the readers of 1 and 2 *The Fair Maid of the West* he draws a comparison between himself and other playwrights, probably Ben Jonson and Shakespeare: "my plays have not been exposed to the public view of the world in numerous sheets and a large volume but simply (as thou seest) with great modesty and small noise." A similar comparison is made in the 1633 preface to *The English Traveller*, but with some indication of the price to be paid for such modesty: he tells us that there were "two hundred and twenty, in which I haue had either an entire hand, or at the least a maine finger" and then accounts for the disappearance of most of these plays:

True it is, that my Playes are not exposed vnto the world in Volumes, to beare the title of Workes, (as others) one reason is, that many of them by shifting and

change of Companies, haue beene negligently lost, Others of them are still
retained in the hands of some Actors, who thinke it against their peculiar
profit to haue them come in Print, and a third, That it neuer was any great
ambition in me, to bee in this kind Volumniously read.

Dedication to the stage subjected Heywood not only to the tastes of
his audiences, but also to the insatiable demand for novelty. In the
Prologue written for the 1637 publication of an old play, *The Royal
King and the Loyal Subject,* Heywood expresses his pride in the ingenuity requisite for a lifetime of writing for the theater:

> To give content to this most curious Age,
> The gods themselves we' have brought down to the Stage,
> And figur'd them in Planets; made even Hell
> Deliver up the Furies, by no spell,
> (Saving the *Muses* rapture) further, we
> Have traffickt by their helpe; no History
> We have left unrifled, our Pens have beene dipt
> As well in opening each hid Manuscript,
> As Tracts more vulgar, whether read, or sung
> In our domesticke, or more forraigne tongue.

The Epilogue to *The Royal King and the Loyal Subject* suggests that
the poet in his waning years had come to terms with the problem of
meeting the changing taste of his audience and could finally submit his
works to the passage of time. He states simply, "That this Play's old 'tis
true . . . what's now out of date, Who is't can tell, / But it may come in
fashion, and sute well."

However diversely Heywood's contemporaries may have judged the
moral or artistic values of his works, none could doubt his erudition
and his love for poets ancient and modern.[10] It is unfortunate that one
of his chief ambitions—to write a life of all the poets up to his own
time—was never realized. Even so, he contributed substantially to our
understanding of his fellow playwrights, for it is through Heywood's
An Apology for Actors that we confidently ascribe *The Spanish Tragedy* to Thomas Kyd,[11] and it is through his revival and the subsequent
publication of *The Jew of Malta* that we now possess the text of
Marlowe's play.

Throughout his career Heywood revealed a concern for accurate as-
cription and accurate printing. His rare outbursts of anger and protest
concern the surreptitious publication of his plays "not one word true,"
the theft of his translations of Ovid by one Austin (exposed by Heywood in the preface to *The Brazen Age*), and Jaggard's unscrupulous

publication of Heywood's love epistles under the name of Shakespeare. Heywood's castigation of Jaggard reveals not only a concern for accuracy and recognition for his own work, but a rather amazing consideration for the reputation of the superior poet, Shakespeare. Referring to Jaggard's theft in a letter appended to *An Apology for Actors,* Heywood remarks: "but as I must acknowledge my lines not worthy his patronage, under whom he hath publisht them, so the Author I know much offended with Mr. Iaggard (that altogether unknowne to him) presumed to make bold with his name." Heywood's respect for his fellow poet and his consistent concern for accuracy and proper acknowledgment are traits very hard to reconcile with Clark's contention that Heywood is responsible for interpolations in *The Jew of Malta.*[12]

Equally difficult to reconcile with the facts of Heywood's life and the image of the man that emerges from his works is Clark's argument that in the last years of his life Heywood was an ardent Puritan, specifically a Presbyterian.[13] In refuting this argument, Allan Holaday has accurately defined the significant and constant religious and political convictions of the poet as mainstream Anglican and royalist.[14] Conversion to the Puritan camp in the decade preceding the civil war would have meant a betrayal of the theater that had been Heywood's livelihood and identity, of his theatrical friends and noble patrons, and of all the royalist-Anglican values that pervade his works. Holaday suggests that confusion about Heywood's religious and political positions derives from a broader confusion over terminology. Heywood, however, tells us exactly what he means by the crucial terms. In his pamphlets "The Rat-Trap," published in the critical year 1641, and "Reader, Here You'll Plainly See," Heywood makes clear that "Protestant" (the term he applies to himself) means Anglican and that "Puritan" means Presbyterian or Separatist. Heywood thus carefully distinguishes himself from the extremes of Irish Papism on the one hand and Scots Puritanism on the other. It was not, therefore, inconsistent with his loyalty to both the crown and the Church of England that he spoke out for reform and for the dignity of the common man. Heywood ended his career as the true protestant he had always been; he represented and spoke for a spirit of reform and accommodation to the times that could have saved the royalist establishment had its leaders been equally alert to the demands of the changing "audience."

Chapter Two
The History Plays

Throughout his long career as a writer of nondramatic works and plays Heywood demonstrated his love and knowledge of history. His serious interest in history as a literary mode is evident in his translation of the fourth chapter of Jean Bodin's *Methodus ad facilem historiarum cognitionum* (*Method for the Easy Comprehension of History*), a work that he published with his translation of Sallust in 1608. Like Machiavelli, Bodin believed that through a study of history one could discover the universal laws that govern political institutions and thus master the art of ruling wisely and successfully.[1] Bodin's fourth chapter, "De historicum delectu," attacks the idea that the historian, because of his aesthetic concerns, is justified in his use of extreme rhetorical devices, such as feigned orations and eloquent expressions. Bodin insists instead upon the value of clear, truthful narrative that allows events to speak for themselves.[2]

Bodin's argument here strikes us as an essentially modern attitude toward history and the obligations of the historian. As such, it is difficult to reconcile with Heywood's practice as a writer of dramatic and nondramatic histories, for he was in every sense conventional, if not old-fashioned. Heywood is, for example, perfectly representative of the medieval and Renaissance convictions that the primary value of history is the moral it presents and that the chief obligation of the historian is to illuminate that moral. Like his immediate predecessors and his contemporaries, Heywood saw as his objective to hold up the mirror of the past for the political and moral edification of his reader. The purpose of history was not primarily to present the truth about the past, but to "use the past for didactic purposes."[3] The private and public virtues of his historical figures are for the most part inseparable, and the private virtues of the individual determine the well-being of the commonwealth. For Heywood, history is essentially biography, and it is also the unfolding of events according to a providential order. The historical perspective that E. M. W. Tillyard defines as the "Tudor Myth," consisting of "a scheme fundamentally religious by which events evolve under a law of justice and the ruling of God's Providence,"[4] is exemplified perfectly in the history plays of Thomas Heywood.

1 and 2 *King Edward the Fourth*

Although 1 and 2 *King Edward the Fourth* were published anonymously in 1599, there is little doubt that they were written by Heywood.[5] It is possible that part of this work existed as early as 1594 as *The Siege of London,* a play belonging to the Lord Admiral's company.[6] Like many of his plays, 1 and 2 *Edward IV* consist of multiple plots that appear at first glance to be loosely connected. Part 1 presents three episodes: the Falconbridge rebellion, the king's relationship with Hobs the Tanner, and Edward's courtship and conquest of Jane Shore. Part 2 continues the political conquests of Edward and depicts the rise of Richard III, but it is primarily concerned with the Shores. Despite the diversity of this material, these plays are carefully structured and thematically unified, as the following analysis will show.

The problem of unity that does exist resides not so much in the matter or the structure as in the divergent styles of parts 1 and 2. In part 1, for example, the verse is fluid and natural, thus promising the achievement of Heywood's mature works. The pace is brisk with careful attention to scene variation and dramatic juxtaposition. The realistic detail that lends verisimilitude to the best of his domestic scenes of later years is evident here in part 1, particularly when the disguised king comes to dinner at the home of Hobs the Tanner. We are made aware of Nell's clean apron, Mother Whetstone's ale, the coarse but clean sheets, even the chamber pot. The dialogue of part 2, on the other hand, is rather wooden by comparison; it is marked by repetitive, self-conscious turns of phrase and persistent rhyme. The pace is all too frequently broken to allow the moral emphasis and directness of a sermon. The stylistic differences between parts 1 and 2 are significant enough, in fact, to cause one critic to see part 2 as the work, at least in part, of another playwright.[7] These differences could, however, result from a greater dependence upon Thomas Churchyard and the ballad lament, as the playwright focuses in part 2 upon the consequence of Jane's fall. To some extent, then, stylistic differences between parts 1 and 2 are appropriate to, if not necessitated by, a shift in the dramatist's perspective. Part 1, depicting the solidarity of the nation and the beneficial influence of middle-class citizens like Hobs and Jane upon the English monarch, constitutes an acknowledgment of temporal achievement in a modern world. In part 2, the temporal triumph of Edward over the French is but a prelude to his sudden death, to the rise of Richard III, and to the progress toward death of Jane and Matthew Shore. The shift, in short, is from *gloria mundi* to *contemptus mundi.*

Like Heywood's other history plays, 1 and 2 *Edward IV* fulfill perfectly the objectives of the English chronicle play as Heywood defines them in his *An Apology for Actors:*

> to teach the subiects obedience to their King, to shew the people the vntimely ends as such as haue moued tumults, commotions, and insurrections, to present thē with the flourishing estate of such as liue in obedience, exhorting them to allegeance, dehorting them from trayterous and fellonious stratagems.
>
> ([F4v])

But the specific didactic function of 1 and 2 *Edward IV* is considerably more complex than this quotation suggests. The middle-class London citizens that Heywood depicts are clearly models for the living counterparts that constituted the majority of his audience. Through these characters Heywood shaped and affirmed the values and aspirations of the London citizens and delineated for them their place in a changing social and economic structure.[8] The tradesmen of London were shown their noble heritage and exhorted to uphold it, just as the apprentices of part 1 are spurred to heroic action by the examples of their predecessors recorded in the English chronicles. Heywood and his audience favored Edward among the English monarchs despite his faults because he was traditionally associated with the middle class and with its achievement of a place in English history. With his predilection for the simple life and ordinary people, Edward makes it possible for Hobs the Tanner to affirm his importance, and thus the importance of all men like him, by asking the King, "Dost thou not know me? . . . Then thou knowest nobody" (Pearson 1:42). When the citizens come to the rescue of their king, city, and nation, Edward gladly acknowledges both their courage and their beneficence. As Michel Grivelet notes, Edward is the image of the modern, as opposed to the feudal, sovereign whose power resides in the noble virtues of the middle class.[9] His reign and the events associated with it provide the opportunity for a celebration of that power which is founded upon the middle-class virtues. The established accounts of Edward's intimacy with ordinary citizens also provided Heywood with the opportunity to treat the subject for which he is best known — the unfaithful wife. His dramatization of the fall and redemption of Jane Shore defines the moral integrity and strength of the class she and her husband represent.

That Jane Shore, traditionally an embodiment of frailty, could be used by Heywood to define the integrity of the middle class indicates the synthesis and significant alterations that he made in his sources and thus one aspect of his originality and moral vision. In the version that came to Heywood from Sir Thomas More's *History of Richard III,* from Churchyard's *Mirror for Magistrates,* and from the English chronicles, Jane is a victim of an arranged marriage and of the imperious will of the king. When she becomes the king's mistress, her husband (whose name in earlier accounts is William, not Matthew) disappears from the story; there is no reconciliation between Jane and Shore after Jane's public penance. Most critics have assumed that Heywood drew his altered version of the Shore story from a ballad attributed to Thomas Deloney.[10] Whether the ballad or the play came first, there are significant similarities between them that are not to be found in other versions. The ballad tells of Mistress Blague's evil council and subsequent cruel rejection of Jane. In the ballad, however, Mistress Blague does not eventually share in Jane's disgrace and poverty and is not forgiven by Jane. Unlike the earlier sources, the ballad tells briefly of a young man (unnamed) who is hanged for giving succor to Jane. Like the play, the ballad asserts that Shoreditch takes its name from the tragic events that occurred there. Assuming that the ballad is a source for some of Heywood's details, we see that the differences in the account in the play and in the ballad are more significant than the similarities and thus reveal again the playwright's originality. It is clear, for example, that in Heywood's version Jane's sin is not simply adultery, but the destruction of an ideal marriage, that state wherein mankind experiences a bliss second only to his prelapsarian condition or heaven itself. In his development of Mistress Blage (Heywood's spelling) and young Aire, the friend who is hanged, and in the final reconciliation of Shore and Jane, Heywood explores in his own distinct manner the magnanimity of the human spirit.

   1 *King Edward the Fourth.* A brief description of the plots of part 1 will give some indication of the artist's task and strategy for providing form and unity. In part 1 Heywood had three stories to tell: the citizens' support of Edward through the defeat of the rebel Falconbridge; Edward's discovery and playful manipulation of the simple virtues of Hobs, the tanner of Tamworth; and Edward's wooing and winning of the goldsmith's wife, Jane Shore. In the first of these episodes the citizens of London successfully defend the city and Edward against two attacks by Falconbridge and his rebel army. The leader of the citizens is the Lord Mayor of London; the self-effacing hero of the day is the goldsmith, Matthew Shore. Loyalty to Edward extends beyond the city into the provinces, as Edward discovers in the second episode. Taking advantage of the fact that Hobs the Tanner does not recognize him, Edward presents himself as Ned the butler. Behind this disguise, he tests the loyalty of the simple tanner, accepts Hobs's hospitality, and then invites Hobs to visit him at court and to enjoy the king's generosity. When Hobs's son is arrested for theft, Hobs calls upon Ned to use his influence with the king. The situation offers Edward great amusement as well as the opportunity to show his gratitude to the simple tanner. As Edward attempts to show his gratitude to the Lord Mayor and Shore for their parts in the defeat of Falconbridge, he meets and falls in love with Shore's wife. Thus begins the third episode. When Jane makes the painful decision to submit to the king's desire, Shore manifests his loyalty by a self-inflicted exile.

Heywood forges an obvious link between the episodes by giving Shore a major role in the defeat of Falconbridge[11] and by defining the significance of Jane's fall through its effects upon the abused husband. A similar link is evident between the rebellion of Falconbridge and the loyalty of Hobs the Tanner when the disguised Edward uses Falconbridge's argument for the Lancastrian cause to test Hobs. The king's use of a disguise to establish his relationship with Hobs and Jane is another link between episodes. The unity of part 1, however, does not depend primarily upon these superficial connections but upon the prevailing concern with political and private loyalty. In all three plots the theme of loyalty is explored through examples of fidelity and betrayal, gratitude and ingratitude. The social placement and displacement of the characters is directly related to their ability or failure to manifest some form of loyalty. The unifying figure of various forms of disloyalty, betrayal, and ingratitude in all three episodes is the thief. Although the loyalty of subject to king is obviously important in this history play, the ultimate loyalty manifested here is to a belief in the intrinsic worth of the ordinary individual. This loyalty is expressed in the mercy and forgiveness that make possible spiritual regeneration.

Heywood opens part 1 by presenting a monarch who will obviously require considerable forgiveness. The Duchess of York, Edward's mother, does well to admonish her son, for she is the only character who can voice such a reprimand without appearing disloyal. Through her Heywood announces the negative traits of Edward that will determine much of the action: his lack of responsibility, his capitulation to his private needs at the expense of his public obligation. His casual attitude toward the serious business of choosing a wife and queen prepares us for his later wanton self-indulgence with Jane Shore. Clearly, it is not the personal merits of Lady Elizabeth Gray that are at issue here. Heywood allows her a humility and mildness that contrast favorably with the aristocratic pride of the duchess. Thus, as he introduces Elizabeth Gray, Heywood lays the foundation for her later generosity and magnanimity toward her rival, Mistress Shore. What is most important here is the carefree attitude of the king — a quality dangerous however appealing.

With significant juxtaposition, Heywood interrupts this scene of strife within the royal household with the news of Falconbridge's rebellion and with the introduction of Falconbridge and his henchmen, Spicing, Smoke, and Chub. Falconbridge's oration in which he argues the Lancastrian cause of the deposed Henry VI is undercut by the disorder and violence of his henchmen and by his own promises to the mindless rabble:

> We will be Masters of the Mint ourselues,
> And set our stamp on the golden coin.
> We'll shoe our neighing coursers with no worse
> Then the purest siluer that is solde in Cheape.
>
> (10)

Fired by these promises, Spicing, Smoke, and Chub anticipate the gratification of their appetites at the expense of London's haberdashers, vintners, goldsmiths, and grocers. Falconbridge and his motley crew are thus as much a threat to the hard-working tradesmen of London and to the social and economic order of the realm as they are to Edward IV. Through the dramatic juxtaposition of what would be the first two scenes if the play had scene division, Heywood makes apparent the analogy between Edward's failure at self-governance and the Falconbridge rebellion. This dramatic juxtaposition figures forth the familiar concept of the king as a microcosm of the state, and it does so in terms hardly complimentary to Edward.

From the nobles at court and the rebels in the countryside the scene shifts to the heart of London and a delineation of the moral strength and courage of its citizens. Cosby, the Lord Mayor, Matthew Shore, Urswick the recorder, and Josselin lead their fellow tradesmen and apprentices in the fortification of the city. The mayor's first words are an indication of the poet's pervasive didactic goal: "This is well done. Thus should good Cittizens / Fashion themselues as well for warre as peace" (11). Through the model that these characters constitute Heywood fashions the values and aspirations of his middle-class audience.

These citizens, loyal to the king that *is*, manifest little interest in the ancient quarrel between the houses of Lancaster and York that Falconbridge would rekindle. Shore speaks for his class in his support for Edward:

> Nay, then, I tell thee, bastard *Falconbridge,*
> My lord *Maior* bears his sword in *his* defence,
> That put the sword into the arms of *London.*
> Made the lord maiors for euer after knights,
> *Richard,* depos'd by *Henry Bolingbroke,*
> From whom the house of *Yorke* doth claime their right.
>
>   (15)

Through Edward's reliance upon them the valor of the citizens is manifested as it was in Richard's reign. Cosby thus exhorts his tradesmen to carry on the ancient custom of their fathers through heroic service to the king. The noble tradition is reiterated by the First Apprentice:

> Nay, scold vs not that we are prentices.
> The Chronicles of *England* can report
> What memorable actions we haue done,
> To which this daies achieuement shall be knit,
> To make the volume larger than it is.
>
>   (18)

The citizens thus achieve a dignity and self-respect that derive from a knowledge of their own class heritage, and it is precisely this kind of knowledge that the play itself offers its audience.

Although an avid historian committed to teaching history through his chronicle plays, Heywood is no more concerned with the ancient debate between the houses of Lancaster and York than are his onstage citizens. In this respect he could not be farther from Shakespeare, who gave us that great argument from the reign of Richard II through that of Richard III. However well Falconbridge articulates the Lancastrian position, his base motives negate that position and define his eloquence as destructive. He is hanged later as a traitor, not only for his assaults on London but for his "confederacy with *France*" (54). The product of a breach of moral law, Falconbridge is what the Renaissance epithet *bastard* connotes: he has no legitimate place in the social-political hierarchy. In turn, he attracts to his cause those men who threaten the social and economic order of London:

> . . . those desperate, idle, swaggering mates,
> That haunt the suburbs in the time of peace,
> And raise vp ale-house brawls in the streete.
>
>   (18)

In Smoke's words, these are men who "liue by honest filching and stealing" (19). As the organizer of a band of thieves to whom he promises the riches of the city as the spoils of war, Falconbridge is the ultimate thief. He would steal Edward's crown, London's gold, and London's goldsmith's wife.

Into this quarrel between the rebels and the loyal citizens Heywood thus skillfully introduces the figure of Jane Shore. As Matthew Shore speaks out against the rebel cause, Falconbridge identifies him and claims Jane, who is famous throughout London for her beauty, as his victory trophy. Shore, therefore, fights for king and city, but also for the honor of his wife and for the sanctity of his home.

Like the Greek dramatists who retold the ancient legends most familiar to their audience, Heywood begins his account of Jane Shore by capitalizing on the dramatic irony made possible by his audience's familiarity with her story. He heightens the irony in the initial scene between Jane and Shore by altering an important detail of the story as his audience knew it. In the familiar accounts, running from More's history through the ballads, Jane is the victim of an arranged marriage and thus feels no love for her husband. Heywood, in contrast, defines Matthew Shore as an ideal young husband whom Jane dearly loves. In Heywood's scene of conjugal bliss Jane professes in absolute terms her love, devotion, and fidelity to Shore. She assures him,

> Were I by a thousand stormes of fortune tost
> And should indure the poorest wretched life,
> Yet *Jane* will be thy honest loyal wife.
> The greatest prince the Sunne did euer see,
> Shall neuer make me proue vntrue to thee.
>
> (24)

Of course, at this moment she has not yet encountered that glorious son of York and thus ironically continues in a confident comparison of herself to the ultimate model of chastity, Lucrece: "These hands shall make this body a dead corse / Ere force or flattery shall mine honour stain" (24). The irony derived from the audience's knowledge of the course of future events does not call into question the innocence or sincerity of Jane at this moment; rather, it underscores the painful disparity between the ideal Jane holds and the reality she will live. This disparity and Heywood's skillful development of it is the essence of his tragedy of Jane Shore. This scene of perfect devotion between husband and wife is essential to our understanding of what a falling off there is in Jane's subsequent behavior, and to our understanding of the necessity of her suffering in part 2.

Once more unto the breach with his rebels and citizens, Heywood develops the unscrupulous dimension of his rebels and the threat they

pose to order. Spicing, as his name suggests, is fiery and humorous to
the extreme. In Tamburlaine fustian he anticipates what it will be like
to "ride in triumph through *Cheape* and *Pauls*." And, in a manner
reminiscent of Falstaff, Spicing asks a boon of his young lord to be
granted when Falconbridge comes into power: "That I may haue the
knighting of all these rogues and rascals" (26). Again there is a deceptive oratorical display as Falconbridge tries once more to move the citizens to his cause. His hollow arguments contrast with the valor and
conviction of the citizens and with the incoherent ramblings of Josselin, whom Falconbridge in disgust describes as "this parenthesis of
words" (29). With the defeat of the rebels after the second battle, the
Lord Mayor can proclaim the triumph of the class he represents:

> That twice, without the help either of King,
> Or any but of God and our own selues
> We haue preuail'd against our countries foes.
>   (31)

Where, indeed, has the king been during these two battles in which
so much was at stake? We do not know, but he now appears in time at
least to express his gratitude to the citizens who have fought for him.
And instead of fulfilling Spicing's wish to knight rogues and rascals,
the king knights the leaders of his army of tradesmen and apprentices.
Only Matthew Shore, out of a refined sense of order and degree and an
acknowledgment of his humble place, refuses the king's honor. The
king then promises, "some other way / We will deuise to quittance thy
deserts" (33). The irony of this promise is fully appreciated later by
Shore, as well as by the audience.

We next see Edward doing what he does best—amusing himself at
another's expense. As the second plot of the play begins, we inevitably
wonder how the playwright will bring his diverse material together.
The apparently unrelated plots of the Falconbridge rebellion, the
king's game with the tanner, and the seduction of Jane present a significant challenge. That Heywood is conscious of the challenge is indicated first by the fact that he introduces his simple, honest Hobs in the
midst of a royal hunt. Hobs, who knows only one kind of deer and hart
(what is dear to his own heart), is somewhat alarmed as the queen and
duchess approach him. He says to himself, "Put vp, John Hobs: money
tempts beauty" (39). His apprehensions alleviated, he speaks to the
queen with a bold familiarity because she looks so much like his daughter Nell and his neighbor Mistress Ferris. He even remarks to himself,
"I had rather than a bend of leather she and I might smouch together"
(40). Hobs's breach of social decorum is quickly rectified once the

queen is identified; he knows and gladly accepts his social place. Thus, the opening of this second episode presents an initial failure to recognize royalty, a fear that something will be stolen, and an amorous inclination that violates all sense of social propriety—all of which constitutes a parodic foreshadowing of the king's theft of Shore's wife, the matter of the third episode.

Perhaps the more obvious parallels between the Hobs-Shore episodes is that in each Edward's objectives require his use of disguise. In both episodes the disguise is essential to a testing pattern in which the loyalty and honesty of Hobs and Jane are made manifest. But the testing process also holds up a mirror in which may be seen the weaknesses of the king. Let us examine first the way the testing pattern works in the episode of Hobs the Tanner.

Initially, Edward's disguise, like that of Henry V on the eve of the battle of Agincourt, seems designed to allow him a free exchange with common men and thus an opportunity to know their true sentiments about him. Edward wastes no time before he casually inquires of Hobs, "I prithee tell me, what say they of the King?" Hob's response, "Of the Kings, thou meanst," confronts the issue directly. Edward learns that King Henry is devout and that King Edward "is a frank franion, a merry companion, and loues a wench well. They say he has married a poor widow, because shes faire" (44). Putting Hobs's loyalty directly to the test, Edward declares, "I think Harry is the true King" (45). Hobs merely asserts, "Harrys of the old house of Lancaster; and that progenity do I loue." But he adds, "I am just akin to *Sutton* Windmill; I can grind which soe're the winde blow. If it be *Harry*, I can say, Well fare *Lancaster.* If it be *Edward*, I can sing, *Yorke Yorke*, for my mony." To love both houses well and to be indifferent to the quarrel between them does not preclude a loyalty to the king that *is*. Therefore, when Edward in his disguise asserts, "*Edward* is but an vsurper, and a fool, and a coward," he draws fire from Hobs: "Dost thou not speake treason?" Hobs proceeds to tell this young butler to the king, "Thou art the arranter knaue to speake ill of thy master" (46). Little as he knows of politics, he recognizes an abuse when he hears one: he speaks freely against the "letters patent" and declares, "Faith, 'tis pity that one subiect should haue in his hand that might do good to many through the land." He speaks, in other words, against the very abuse that Jane, as the king's mistress, will attempt to correct. The conversation is edifying for Edward, and through the king's tribute to Hobs, Heywood pays tribute to the class he addressed throughout his career:

> I see plain men, by obseruation
> Of things that alter in the change of times,

> Do gather knowledge; and the meanest life
> Proportiond with content sufficiency,
> Is merrier then the mighty state of kinges.
>
> (47)

To be plain Ned and pass the time with the tanner is a luxury Edward can scarcely afford. The king's refusal to know himself and to accept his proper role is punctuated by Hobs's assumption that his daughter Nell would be a proper match for Ned, provided he had an occupation (50), and by Hobbs's offer to help Ned get a start in the leather trade. Ned's idleness and fine clothes remind Hobs of his own son, who is a thief, and the thought occurs to him that perhaps Ned has stolen from his king. The disguise clearly figures forth that aspect of the king's nature that rebels against and robs him of his majesty. When Hobs comes to London to find his son, he finds Ned instead and addresses him as "rogue," "rascal," "villain," and "merry hangman" (86). We cannot fail to recall that Falconbridge's men are rogues and rascals and that one of them, Chub, becomes a merry hangman (38).

Hobs's affectionate but approbrious epithets for the king (in the guise of Ned) prepare for and pass judgment upon the rebellion of Edward's heart and the theft of Shore's wife. Edward's first encounter with Jane indicates a temptation that even he conceives of in terms of rebellion:

> . . . what, and thou traitor heart,
> Wouldst thou shake hands in this conspiracy?
> Down, rebel; back, base trecherous conceit;
> I will not credit thee. My *Besse* is fair,
> And *Shores* wife but a blowze, compared to her.
>
> (60)
>
> . . . .
> Yet, idle eye, wilt thou be gadding still?
> Keep home, keep home, for feare of further ill.
>
> (61)

The conflict between the private and the public man is skillfully dramatized as Edward contemplates Jane's beauty while he appears to read the letter from the Duke of Burgundy and the Constable of France. The opportunity to claim his right to France through the assistance of these two disaffected noblemen is the opportunity to repeat the heroic achievement of his greatest ancestors. But in Edward's case it is "A womans aid, that hath more power than *France* / To crowne vs, or to kill vs with mischance" (61).

With a delicate balance between censorship and sympathy Heywood thus introduces his final and most important plot, the seduction of Shore's wife. Disguised as a jewel merchant, Edward seeks out Shore's shop at the sign of the Pelican in Lombard street (64). Here, he says, in the nest of the Pelican is the phoenix, "Oh, rare perfection of rich Natures work!" More to the point of his disguise, here is the perfect diamond that he must "cheapen." Heywood plays upon the word *cheap* or *cheapen* with the double meaning "to bargain for" and "to diminish the value of." Failing to recognize the king in his disguise, Jane at first innocently assumes he has come to bargain for the shop's finest jewel, which she happens to be wearing. Although she learns quickly enough that she is the "fairest jewel" this stranger seeks, she enjoys the metaphoric compliments that allow her the exercise of her own wit. When the king discovers himself, the courtship through the jewel metaphor abruptly ends as Jane kneels and declares, "Whateuer we possesse is all your highness; / Only mine honour, which I cannot grant." Edward's response is equally direct: "Only thy loue, bright angel, Edward craues" (66). An example of Heywood's superb sense of dramatic timing is Matthew Shore's entrance at this moment. Jane closes the intimate dialogue: "But here comes one to whom I only gaue it; / And he, I doubt, will say you shall not haue it." With this "it" of multiple referents — love, honor, and the jewel of chastity betokening both — the king resumes his disguise and his role as a jewel merchant. Jane now takes a crucial step toward her fall: she becomes an accomplice to the king's deception of her husband. When Shore recognizes the king behind the disguise, she pretends to be ignorant of his true identity. She reassures her husband, "You are deceiu'd, sweetheart. Tis not the King / Thinke you he would aduenture thus alone?"

It is consistent with the character, as Heywood has thus far delineated it, that Jane should contend with the king's persistence by confiding in and seeking the advice not of her kind and wise husband but of Mistress Blage. To her friend Jane complains of the king's passion: "He, he it is, that with a violent siege / Labours to breake into my plighted faith" (73). These lines are reminiscent of Shakespeare's Lucrece as she names her assailant, "He, he fair lords, 'tis he" (*The Rape of Lucrece*, 1. 1721). The echo is reinforced by the fact that in Shakespeare's poem Tarquin's rape is defined repeatedly as a violent siege and Lucrece as the broken or defaced temple. The borrowing here serves to underscore with irony Jane's blindness and weakness as it calls to mind her earlier Lucrecean declaration that she would choose suicide to avoid dishonor. Jane's metaphor of violent siege asserts once again the parallel between personal and political rebellion.

In Mistress Blage, Jane finds the rationale for a much less heroic yet more tragic solution to her dilemma than the choice of Lucrece:

> You know, his greatness can dispense with ill,
> Making the sin seem lesser by his worth;
> And you yourself, your children, and your friends,
> Be all aduanced to worldly dignity;
> And this worlds pomp, you know is a good thing.
>   (74)

In the same vein, she argues that with the power of her influence over the king, Jane will be able "to quit the guilt one small transgression brings." Paving the way for Edward, Mistress Blage is present when he arrives to press and win his suit. Assuming a loving but imperative stance, Edward makes the decision easier for Jane by allowing her to avoid responsibility. To his "Thou must" she can reply, "If you inforce me, I haue nought to say; / But wish I had not liued to see this day" (76).

Leaving her home with the pathetic resolve to "learn how to be repentant," Jane is apparently innocent of the obvious sins of incontinence or desire for power. Her sin of marital infidelity derives from a more basic infidelity: she places the will of her temporal king above that of the spiritual King. To Jane's crucial question, "How if the Host of Heauen at this abuse / Repine? who can the prodigy excuse," Edward responds with casual blasphemy: "It lies within the compasse of my power, / To dim their enuious eyes, dare seem to loure" (76). At no point are we led to believe that Jane loves Shore and her simple life with him any less as a result of the king's love for her. Instead, she is much like Chaucer's Criseyde, "slydynge of corage." Because her spiritual weakness is fear, the promise of king's protection is the ultimate temptation.

Jane's decision to surrender to the king is dramatically juxtaposed with Shore's suspicions expressed to Jane's kinsmen, the Lord Mayor and Fraunces Emersley (76–78). When the kinsmen come to Jane's defense, Shore explains, "Though I misdeeme not her, yet give me leaue / To doubt what his sly walking may entend." The goldsmith adds that the king is one "Whose greatnesse may guild ouer vgly sinne." Fraunces doubts that the king would come disguised to Shore's shop "In this serious busie time" when his citizens are reaching deeply into their purses and his lords are in "day and nightly turmoile" to prepare for Edward's war with France. But the operative word for the king—Shore uses it twice—is "sly," and Shore's suspicions are confirmed by the timely entrance of a messenger who informs him that the king has sent for Jane. Shore must now by his example of patience console and calm Jane's dishonored kinsmen. Well might Shore and the Lord Mayor, Edward's chief defenders against Falconbridge, rage against the treachery and ingratitude of their king. But Shore, Heywood's embodiment of loyalty, insists that "To note offences in a mightie man / It is enough" (79). As he thus rejects a course of revenge, Shore establishes the pattern of Heywood's other injured husbands, lovers, and friends. By patiently enduring his injury, he relinquishes Jane to the regenerative power of her penance and thereby makes possible the final reconciliation with her at the end of part 2.

The play concludes with two parallel scenes of recognition. One is the comic denouement of the Hobs episode; the other is the tragic denouement of the Shore episode. As each of these episodes evolves out of the disguises of Edward in pursuit of his pleasure, so the conclusion of each begins with a form of disguise that must be penetrated. Jane's metamorphosis from goldsmith's wife to king's mistress is signified by her altered appearance. When Shore encounters her as he is preparing to set sail, she is "lady-like attired," complete with mask. Shore observes, "This is not she, that once in a seemely blacke / Was the chaste, sober wife of *Matthew Shore*" (82). Preoccupied with her expiatory good works, Jane does not recognize Shore, whose appearance is equally altered by his suffering and by his sea-faring attire. He thus has the opportunity to observe her as she wins the sympathy of all but one Rufford, who seeks through Jane the king's license to sell corn to the enemy. The image of Jane's power through her "honorable shame" is reflected in the mirror that Shore holds for her: "For now thou art nor widow, maide, nor wife" (84). She is as displaced, in other words, as her husband who now prepares for exile. Confessing that she "yeelded vp the fort" under the king's strong siege, she contritely offers to return to Shore as his servant rather than as his wife. This offer, contrite as it is, indicates Jane's inability to grasp fully the consequence of her action. Through her adultery she has forever displaced Shore, who of all the citizens knows best his humble place. With a loyalty punctuated by irony and bitterness, he refuses Jane's offer to return:

> Thou go with me, *Jane?* Oh God forbid
> That I should be a traitor to my King!
> Shall I become a felon to his pleasures,
> And fly away, as guilty of the theft?
> No, my dear *Jane*, I say it may not be.
> Oh, what haue subiects that is not their kings,
> Ile not examine his prerogatiue.
>
> (84–85)

In a play that presents in many forms a testing pattern, Shore proves the model of restraint and the prototype of Heywood's loyal subject.

Shore's moral achievement is underscored by this king who, though unworthy in many respects, is nevertheless the King. Shore's sacrifice is contrasted in the final scene with Edward's playfulness as he makes himself known to Hobs the Tanner. Edward's return to his disguise as Ned the butler is ironically appropriate, for it reveals the negative dimension of his character. The tanner's terms of familiarity ("mad Rascal, Villain, made rogue") are closer to the king's real identity than he or the king realizes. Surely Heywood's judgment is not lost upon the audience even in the final joyful moments of the play when Edward wins "the widows mite" with a single kiss. The king's mock courtship of the widow brings the play full circle, for in this action we have a parodic reflection of the opening scene in which this king of charm has won a widow as his bride.

2 *King Edward the Fourth.* Part 2 of *King Edward the Fourth* is in terms of its unity a disappointment after part 1. The action is divided by a chorus into two parts, unequal in length and in dramatic interest. The first section of the play, presenting Edward's triumph over the French, puts aside the earlier perspective in part 1 of his human weaknesses. Instead there is a patriotic portrait of English majesty: imperious, resolved, courageous, and wise.[12] Edward quickly penetrates the rather obvious treachery of the Constable of France and the Duke of Burgundy. As they betrayed the King of France, they betray Edward and finally each other. When Lewis, King of France, conveniently capitulates to Edward's uncompromising demands, the two kings join together to expose the perfidy of their mutual adversaries, the Duke and the Constable. The playful nature of Edward emerges once more, this time to his and his nation's credit. Demonstrating again his love for the theatrical, he contrives a play at the expense of the Constable and Duke, with Lewis as a hidden audience. All conspiracies and counterconspiracies are dramatically revealed with the proper humiliation of the villains and with the glorification of the all-seeing English monarch. With the aid of the chorus, the audience is then carried across the channel and into the matter that was obviously more interesting to the poet — the tragedy of Shore's wife and the rise of Richard III.

In depicting Jane's power, her fall from favor, and Richard's ascension to power, Heywood creates in part 2 what is essentially a *de casibus* play. As such, the play highlights, through an almost endless series of situations, the unexpected shift in human fortune and the necessity of acceptance and endurance. This pattern allows Heywood to dramatize the efficacy of suffering that leads to wisdom, particularly to an understanding of mercy, forgiveness, and love.

The central figure in this pattern of spiritual enlightenment is the man more sinned against than sinning, Matthew Shore. Homesick, he returns to England from his long sea voyage with the less than charitable hope that Jane is dead and that he will be able to hide his disgrace under his assumed name, Flud. With his characteristic bad luck, he is arrested and sentenced to death along with the equally innocent captain and crew of the ship that brought him home. Jane, on her customary charitable rounds to the prisons, attempts to rescue the disguised Shore and his companions but is prevented when she is herself arrested by the queen's son, Dorset. Shore thus prepares for death as Jane prepares for the fearful encounter with the woman she has wronged. He attempts the requisite forgiveness of Jane that will clear his own soul, but what we hear is a note of resentment: "Yet will not I, poore *Jane*, on thee exclaim, / Though guilty thou, I guiltlesse suffer shame" (Pearson 1:125). As he sees her arrest as the first stage of her fall, she becomes the subject of his sermon and the object of his pity:

> O, see weake womens imperfections,
> That leaue their husbands safe protections,
> Hazarding all on strangers flatteries,
> Whose lust allaid, leaues them to miseries.
> See what dishonour breach of wedlock brings
> Which is not safe, euen in the arms of kings.
> Thus do I *Jane* lament thy present state,
> Wishing my teares thy torments might abate.
>
> (126)

Jocky's interruption of Shore's scaffold speech (128) emphasizes that, despite this sympathy, Shore has much to learn: "Sirrah, ye that preach, come down . . . Mistress Shore brings a new lesson for you." Until the final reunion with Jane, Shore's sympathy is coupled with expressions of his wounded pride:

> But twenty deaths I rather wish to die,
> Than liue beholding one minutes breath
> To him that liuing, wounded me with death.
>
> (138)

His response to Jane's saving his life (not once, but twice) is marked, accordingly, by resentment rather than gratitude. The lesson that Mistress Shore brings, unfolded in the subsequent action of the play, is the meaning of humility and genuine forgiveness.

This point is begun as Jane's efforts to save Shore from the executioner are interrupted by her interview with the queen who has as much cause for resentment and revenge as Shore. The queen, who obviously shares her husband's love of theatrically contrived tests, finds in Jane a degree of contrition and humility that inspires not only total forgiveness but love (126–31). The queen's charity evokes from Edward gratitude and wonder; from Jane, however, it evokes a keener awareness of her transgression:

> In this bright christal mirror of your mercy
> I see the greatnesse of my sinne the more,
> And makes my fault more odious in mine eyes.

Like her later counterpart, Heywood's Anne Frankford, Jane is almost killed with kindness:

> Your princely pity now doth wound me more
> Than all your threatnings euer did before.
>   (129)

Jane's interview with the queen concludes with an emblematic image of perfect reconciliation and loyalty: "*As Jane kneels on one side the King, so the Queen steps and kneeles on the other*," according to the stage direction (130). Through his observation of the suffering of Jane, Shore will eventually be able to show that he, like the queen, has indeed forgiven her. He, Jane, and Aire will thus eventually form their own perfect three-in-one union, emblematically represented as Jane and Shore sit beside, embrace over, and die upon Aire's coffin (183).

But before this union can take place, Shore must witness Jane's acceptance of suffering as just punishment for her sins. This acceptance comes gradually; for Jane, like Shore, tries at first to escape her identity as the king's concubine. She pleads with Dorset to allow her to avoid the queen, and with Edward's death she hopes to escape the hatred of Richard by retiring from court to the friendship of Mistress Blage. Through the ingratitude and betrayal of Blage, Jane's own ingratitude and betrayal are requited. In a white sheet with her hair disheveled, her feet bare, and a candle in her hand, Jane becomes an emblematic spectacle of her sin. As she glosses this spectacle, she comes to understand its moral:

> And therefore in derision was I wrapt,
> In this white sheete; and in derision bore
> This burning taper to expresse my folly,
> That hauing light of reason to direct me,
> Delighted yet in by-wayes of darke error.
>
> (165)

She avoids the spiritual pitfall of trying to rationalize her sin by blaming the king or the friend who gave her bad advice and subsequently betrayed her. By accepting total responsibility for her fall, she is able to forgive and embrace Mistress Blage when the two women meet again as outcast beggars. In the crystal mirror of Jane's mercy, manifest in her forgiveness of Blage, Shore finally sees his own pride and his own proper course of action.

Richard's ordinance against rendering assistance to Jane provides the ultimate test of love and forgiveness for Shore. He is offered a model of Christian love in the young Aire, whose life Jane saved as she twice saved Shore's. When Aire is arrested for giving his purse to Jane, Shore comes forward to imitate the act of charity and to face arrest with Aire. Shore's act forces him to reveal his identity and to claim the right of a husband to aid his wife. In doing so, Shore acknowledges his wife and thus confronts his own wounded pride. This confrontation constitutes the most dramatic and psychologically complex moment of the play. Perversely delighting in Shore's struggle between love and pride, Richard defines the terms by which Shore may assist his wife without penalty:

> Vpon condition thou forgiue her fault,
> Take her againe, and vse her as before;
> Hazard new hornes; how saiest thou, wilt thou, *Shore?*

When Shore has difficulty accepting these terms, Richard gleefully presses the point: "Then neuer feede her whom thou canst not loue" (179). Shore then tries to draw a distinction between the charity that feeds and the love that weds; it is charity that now moves him. He admits, "I neuer can forget so great a wrong" (179).

The lesson of true love and forgiveness is played out before Shore as he witnesses as an onstage audience the execution of Aire. This scene, of course, is reminiscent of the earlier one in which Shore himself faced execution and attempted to make his peace. What Shore now overhears, in contrast to the "sermon" which he offered his audience, is an expression of the truly magnanimous spirit—that quality which Aire's name suggests. The grace with which Aire gives his life for the woman Shore cannot quite forgive brings Shore to a renunciation of the world and of his pride that belonged to it. He can then make known his identity to Jane, sincerely forgive her, and accept her as his wife. Thus they are both restored to their proper places as husband and wife at the same time that they are prepared for their eternal homecoming.

The reunion of Shore and Jane does not, therefore, mark a new beginning in this world. As they place themselves on either side with their hands joined across Aire's coffin, they renounce the world of the flesh for the life of the spirit. In this emblematic tableau of contempt for the world Heywood shows little concern for verisimilitude; Jane and Shore die suddenly not from any explicable ailment or injury, but because they are spiritually prepared for death. Their long suffering and enlightenment constitute the pattern of preparation. The closure of this two-part history is perfectly consistent with Heywood's unifying moral design and dramatic objectives. Parts 1 and 2 *Edward the Fourth* recounts and celebrates the glory and the human appeal of an English monarch whose reign brings a special dignity to the London citizen. Balancing this image of glory is the perspective of human weakness and vulnerability. Despite his winning ways with his citizens and with France, Edward cannot preserve himself, his queen, his mistress, or his innocent young children. The disaffection of Buckingham and the threat of Richmond in the final moments of the play signal the turn of Fortune's wheel as well as the fall of Richard. The prevailing vision of the play is summarized in Shore's lament: "O world, what art thou? man, euen from his birth, / Finds nothing else but misery on earth" (181). Nevertheless, the common grave of Aire, Shore, and Jane remains a lasting monument to human love and forgiveness:

> The people, for the loue they bear to her
> And her kind husband, pitying his wrongs,
> For euer after meane to call the ditch
> *Shores* Ditch, as in memory of them.
>
> (186)

1 and 2 *If You Know Not Me, You Know Nobody*

For his next chronicle play Heywood turned to the reign of his own Queen Elizabeth. Parts 1 and 2 *If You Know Not Me, You Know Nobody* were most likely written shortly after 1603, the year of Elizabeth's death. Since both parts were entered in the *Stationer's Register* in the fall of 1605, a reasonable date for composition is 1604–05. The eight editions between 1605 and 1639, plus the revival at the Cockpit,[13] attest to the popularity of part 1. Part 2 appeared in four editions, the first in 1606, the last in 1634.[14]

The eight editions of part 1, published by Nathaniel Butter or his associates, provide us with an example of the literary piracy to which the playwrights of the age were continually subjected. For the revival of part 1 at the Cockpit, Heywood wrote a prologue in which he lashed out at the unscrupulous theft through shorthand and subsequent publication of his play, "scarce one word true." He included this prologue, along with an epilogue, in his *Pleasant Dialogues and Dramas*, published in 1637. Far from being shamed by the playwright's accusation of piracy, the printer attached the prologue and epilogue to his next edition (1639) of the play to lend it an air of authenticity.[15]

1 *If You Know Not Me, You Know Nobody.* From a modern perspective, part 1, or *The Troubles of Queen Elizabeth*, is not one of Heywood's best dramatic works. Our first objective, then, should be to account for the tremendous seventeenth-century appeal that warranted eight editions and a revival. Obviously, this appeal lies to a considerable degree in the fact that the play about Elizabeth is specifically designed to capitalize on the myth of and the nostalgia for the late monarch.[16] But to the conventional glorification of Elizabeth, Heywood succeeded in bringing a degree of novelty by dramatizing her troubles during the reign of Queen Mary. The material was indeed so appealing that Heywood would use it repeatedly, and rather shamelessly so, in four later works: *Gunaikeion, or Nine Books of Various History Concerning Women* (1624), *England's Elizabeth* (1631), *The Life and Death of Queen Elizabeth* (1639), and *Exemplary Lives and Memorable Acts of Nine the Most Worthy Women of the World* (1640).[17] In short, the story of Elizabeth's early years was Heywood's staple, rendered in dramatic verse, nondramatic verse, and prose. The prose history, *England's Elizabeth*, is so similar to the play that it was once thought to be its source. R. G. Martin, however, has shown that Heywood's source for both the play and the history was the *Acts and Monuments of John Foxe*, specifically the section entitled "The Miraculous Preservation of the Lady Elizabeth, now Queen of England," with a few details taken from Holinshed's retelling of Foxe.[18]

Because Foxe's own narrative is inherently dramatic, Heywood follows it very closely. To achieve a sense of dramatic unity he excludes Foxe's preliminary account of Elizabeth's birth and education and begins instead with Mary's defeat of the Wyatt conspiracy and the suspicion of complicity that falls upon Princess Elizabeth. The following is Foxe's version, repeated by Holinshed and dramatized by Heywood. At the advice of her Chancellor, Winchester, Mary orders members of

her council to transport the princess from her country residence in
Ashbridge to Westminster for interrogation. The urgency of their com-
mission requires that the noblemen break in upon Elizabeth in the
middle of the night and, though they find her seriously ill, order her to
prepare immediately for the arduous journey. At Westminster she is
rigorously questioned and declares her innocence of any involvement
with the conspirators. She is then stripped of her household and ordered to the Tower of London, despite the lack of evidence against her.

After many weeks, Elizabeth is placed in the custody of Sir Henry
Beningfield and transported from the Tower to Woodstock Castle. At
Woodstock she is again held under the close and humiliating watch of
her "jailor" Beningfield. She is urged to submit to the queen, that is,
to plead guilty and beg for clemency; but Elizabeth refuses, insisting
instead upon the letter of the law. At Woodstock numerous attempts
are made upon her life, but she is miraculously saved. Finally, she is
allowed to write to her sister and shortly after is ordered to appear at
Hampton Court. Here she is again interrogated and urged to submit,
but she stands firm in her innocence. At last, late at night, she is suddenly sent for by the queen, before whom she declares her innocence
and manifests her humility. The queen, although sullen in her responses, is apparently satisfied and orders the release of the princess
and her return to her country residence, where she remains under
guard until the queen's death. For the final details of his history, the
good news of Elizabeth's accession and the acknowledgment of the
court and the city, Heywood turns to Holinshed or to his own imagination.

What Heywood saw in the Foxe account as thus outlined was, first of
all, the drama of a young princess caught between faith and fear. He
saw also the ways in which Foxe's narrative of her suffering illuminates
the qualities for which Queen Elizabeth was especially loved by the
middle class long after her death: her clemency, piety, humility, patience, and courage. Accordingly, these qualities are significantly
heightened as Heywood adapts Foxe's narrative to the stage. Still more
important is the emphasis that Heywood places on Elizabeth as the
defender of the Protestant (and for Heywood this means Anglican)
faith. For example, in Heywood's dialogue Elizabeth's arch-adversary,
Stephen Gardiner, Bishop of Winchester and Mary's Lord Chancellor,
repeatedly refers to the princess as a heretic. He persecutes her because
he sees her as a threat to the Catholic political establishment and to the
Catholic faith in England. Elizabeth's Protestant faith is dramatically
defined by her knowledge of and reliance upon her most treasured possession, an English Bible. Heywood takes the single reference by Foxe

to "her book"[19] and makes of it a dynamic stage property and symbol of the faith that Elizabeth embodies.

The playwright begins with a significant rearrangement of the material in his source. The Dodd episode sharply defines the ingratitude, pride, and tyranny of Queen Mary. These negative qualities of the queen are then immediately contrasted with the virtues of the Princess Elizabeth. Mary's first act as queen is to break the promise she made to the brave men of Suffolk, who defeated the Wyatt rebels for her. Dodd, as representative of the Suffolk men, reminds the queen of her agreement:

> Twas thus concluded that we your liegemen
> Should still enioy our consciences, and vse that faith
> Which in King Edwards daies was held Canonicall.
> (83–85)

The queen affirms Winchester's response, "May't please your highness note the Commons insolence / They tye you to conditions, and set lymits to your liking," by setting Dodd in the stocks to demonstrate her contempt for the citizens. This contempt extends also to noblemen when Sentlow intercedes on behalf of Elizabeth and is banished from the court. Persecuted by Winchester as a heretic, Elizabeth is a potential martyr for that same faith embraced by the commons of Suffolk (332–43). Thus the commons "shew their loue that want the remedy" (514–15) and noblemen like Sussex "sorrow / For her sorrow" (550–51). While Queen Mary punishes those who fail "to frowne when we frowne, smile on whome we grace" (123), Elizabeth sets about her "huswiffry" ministering to the poor in the Tower (808–9) and is grateful for the nosegay and the cup of cold water that are offered by the simple citizen (844–46).

Heywood again departs from Foxe's narrative and expands Holinshed's by presenting the arrival of King Philip of Spain and the formal betrothal of Philip and Mary (237–76). This marriage of great powers contrasts dramatically with the suffering and vulnerability of the princess, who, despite her sympathizers, has no source of strength other than her faith and patience. Surrounded by the symbols of her temporal power — the purse, the mace, the scepter, and the crown — Mary anticipates her royal bridegroom; Elizabeth, with her prayerbook and her English Bible, anticipates death in the Tower. This contrast is established to prepare for one of Heywood's later inventions, the dreams of Elizabeth and her lady Clarentia. Elizabeth dreams

> . . . her sister was new married,
> And sat vpon a high Emperiall throne,
> That she her selfe was cast into a dungeon,
> Where enemyes enuiron'd her about,
> Offering their weopons to her naked breast.
>   (1346–50)

Clarentia also dreams "of weddings, and of flowers" and of a bride who goes "to happynes eternall" (1355, 1362). The dreams of a wedding are indeed prophetic of death, as Elizabeth fears, but of Mary's death rather than her own. With the denouement, the fates of the two royal sisters are reversed as Elizabeth is instated and Mary goes to her eternal bridegroom.

Mary's temporal bridegroom offers yet another example of Heywood's substantial expansion upon his source. The playwright makes clear that the malice of the Catholic prelates who surround the queen is not characteristic of Catholics in general. Upon his arrival to claim the hand of Queen Mary, Philip kindly requests the presence of the Princess Elizabeth. The English lords (Chandos, Thame, Sussex, and Howard) who are sympathetic to Elizabeth find in Philip a crucial ally in their efforts to soften the heart of the queen. In Heywood's dumb show (672–82) Philip intercedes with the queen on behalf of the nobles and their princess. When Winchester fails to find Elizabeth guilty of treason, he attempts to secure a warrant for her execution by deceiving Philip. The warrant is slipped in among the routine papers on Philip's "sealing day" (1140). The deception is revealed by the king's agent, Thomas Gresham, the hero of part 2. The discovery of this treachery moves Philip to order Elizabeth's release from Beningfield and her appearance at Hampton Court, "There to attend the pleasure of the Queene" (1174). Thus, in Heywood's version, Philip is responsible for the interview between the sisters that results in Elizabeth's release. Once his task as peacemaker is accomplished, Philip exits from the play; with his departure the queen's fortune begins to turn.

For Foxe, for Holinshed, and certainly for Heywood, this reversal of fortune is not the manifestation of Fortune's wheel in a temporal world of mutability. It is rather a result of Elizabeth's Christian patience and faith in the will and the Word of God. Her faith, clearly Protestant, is dramatically defined by the prayerbook and the Bible that defend and preserve her throughout her imprisonment. Departing completely from his text, Heywood presents a dumb show that depicts divine protection through faith in this Bible. In the dumb show Elizabeth's enemies approach her while she sleeps and are prevented from killing her by two angels (1049–53). One angel then opens the Bible and places it in the hand of the sleeping princess. Elizabeth awakens to read, "Whoso putteth his trust in the Lord, / Shall not be confounded." The scriptural promise is fulfilled when Elizabeth is finally allowed to see the queen and to defend herself. Mary concludes their conversation, "What ere we thinke aryse and kiss our hand, / Say God hath rais'd you frends" (1294–95). Elizabeth responds, "Then God hath kept his promise . . . To rayse them frends that on his word relie." In the final scene Elizabeth, newly crowned and surrounded by the symbols of her temporal power, is approached by the Mayor of London who brings two gifts from her faithful citizens—a purse and a Bible. Although the purse is accepted with gratitude, it is the Bible that moves the queen, for it is the Word that has set her free. Her tribute to the English Bible is worth quoting in full because it not only makes clear the basis of Heywood's idealization of Elizabeth, but it also reveals the deep religious feeling of the poet:

> This is the Iewell that we still loue best,
> This was our solace when we were distrest,
> This booke that hath so long conceald it selfe,
> So long shut vp, so long hid; now Lords see,
> We here vnclaspe, for euer it is free:
> Who lookes for ioy, let him this booke adore,
> This is true foode for rich men and for poore,
> Who drinkes of this, is certaine nere to perish,
> This will the soule with heauenly vertue cherish,
> Lay hand vppon this Anchor euery soule,
> Your names shalbe in an eternall scrowle;
> Who builds on this, dwel's in a happy state,
> This is the fountaine cleere imaculate,
> That happy yssue that shall vs succeed,
> And in our populous Kingdome this booke read.
> (1582–96)

As Elizabeth attributes her physical and spiritual salvation to the Bible, she also draws an analogy between her recent history and that of the Bible. Like the princess during her imprisonment, this book during Mary's reign has been "So long shut vp, so long hid." As the Word has made her free, she now sets free under her protection this English Bible: "We here vnclaspe, for euer it is free." As the virgin Queen, she is like the Book, a "fountaine cleere imaculate," and the book is the "happy yssue" that will succeed her.

Written after Queen Elizabeth's death, 1 *If You Know Not Me* cannot be dismissed as an attempt to gain royal favor through compliment. In fact, this play reveals not what the prince can do for the poet, but what the poet (even a modest one) can do for the prince. Through Foxe and Holinshed to Heywood, we have a myth in the making and, especially in the play, a valuable insight into the cult of Elizabeth that survived long after her reign. The play makes clear what it was in the received image of Elizabeth that inspired Heywood to elevate her to virtual sainthood. He saw in that image the archetypal Christian pattern of ordeal and triumph. In her miraculous survival of "the troubles" Heywood's faith in Christian Providence was affirmed. Since Elizabeth's claim to the throne was dependent upon the Protestant faith, modern historians are inclined to conclude that as queen she had no choice but to become the defender of that faith. From the perspective of the myth that Heywood helped create, the relationship between temporal power and religious faith is reversed: from faith comes power.

   2 *If You Know Not Me, You Know Nobody.*   Part 2 is singularly deficient in plot and is thus aesthetically disappointing. There is no dramatic progression in the action centering on the three main characters, Thomas Gresham, Hobson the Haberdasher, and young John Gresham. Instead, a series of isolated vignettes provides a kaleidoscopic view of London life, a brief excursion into a French brothel, followed by an attempt upon the life of Elizabeth and the defeat of the Spanish Armada.[20] Despite the absence of both probability and progression in the action, the play does achieve some sense of coherence through its thematic unity. Clearly aware of the social and economic changes resulting from the rise of capitalism, Heywood asserts the moral obligations of the newly rich. The play is one long argument that charity identifies the Christian and makes possible the Christian community.

   A summary of the play's events—one can hardly call them plots—will make apparent its primary deficiency and provide the necessary details for a discussion of its virtues. The play opens with the grand monetary adventure of the wealthy London merchant, Thomas Gresham. Rushing in where kings have feared to tread, Gresham concludes an agreement to pay the King of Barbary ninety thousand pounds for a sugar monopoly, an agreement that is valid only as long as the Barbary king lives. Gresham then turns his attention to personal matters: first, to his spendthrift nephew John; second, to his quarrel with Sir Thomas Ramsey. Hobson comes to Gresham's aid by accepting the wayward nephew as his apprentice and by settling the ancient quarrel. When the joyful reconciliation between Gresham and Ramsey is suddenly dampened by a rain storm in the open Market of Lombard

Street, Gresham resolves to build a grand bourse for the London merchants. John, meanwhile, steals a hundred pounds from his uncle, places the blame on Gresham's clerk, Timothy Thinbeard, and then departs for France to work as Hobson's factor.

As Gresham goes about the building of his bourse, Hobson tends his shop. His generosity extends from pedlar to queen, as he freely loans the queen's pursuivant two hundred pounds. During the grand ceremony of the opening of the bourse, news comes that the Barbary king is dead and that his heir has sent Gresham a dagger and slippers instead of his ninety thousand pounds paid to confirm the monopoly. At this moment a jewel merchant offers at the exchange a priceless pearl. Undaunted by his loss of the monopoly, Gresham buys the pearl, has it crushed into a powder, and drinks it in a toast to the queen. The ceremony is capped by the appearance of the queen, who names the bourse "the Royal Exchange" and knights its founder.

The action then shifts to Hobson, who wanders out on a morning walk, gets lost, and discovers John Tawnycoat, who laboriously tills the soil in a futile attempt to pay his debts to Hobson. The kind haberdasher cancels the debts and reinstates the pedlar in his trade. At this point he also learns of young John Gresham's relationship with a French prostitute and dashes across the channel to rescue the profligate. Hobson, like Timothy, is bested by the witty prodigal but succeeds in bringing him home. Back in London, John crowns his audacity by making love to the now-widowed Mrs. Ramsey. Although he does not win her hand, he does win her purse and is able to pay off his debts and begin a new life. Before the resolution of this episode, however, the play provides us with another gratuitous and surprising event: Dr. Parry's attempt upon the life of Queen Elizabeth. Still more incongruous are the final scenes of the play, depicting, through a series of messengers, the defeat of the Spanish Armada.

The failure of these diverse episodes to provide any sense of probability or dramatic progress is only one cause for complaint. Equally serious is the inadequacy of the moral perspective inherent in Heywood's treatment of certain characters. Gresham's gesture of drinking the priceless pearl, apparently designed to show his cavalier indifference to money, is downright idiotic — an example of bad taste on the part of Heywood as well as his character — and morally problematic in a play that posits charity as the ultimate virtue. Gresham's attitude toward and treatment of his prodigal nephew is even more objectionable. Heywood begins his account of the uncle-nephew relationship with a conflict that appears to be forgotten rather than resolved. In the first scene of the play Gresham defines himself as a father to the prodigal son by chastising him for his "bad husbandrie / Carelesse respect, and prodigall expence" (91–92). The position with Hobson is an opportunity for John to show that he can reform and thus become a "new man" (134). John accepts this obligation, but with a reminder: "I haue seru'd my prentiship alreadie, but bind me againe and I shall be content . . ." (150–51). His true intentions, however, are expressed in an aside: "and I doe not shew you the right tricke of a Cosin afore I leaue England, ile giue you leaue to call me Cut, and cosen me of my patrimonie as you haue done" (169–71). John's accusation against the heroic entrepreneur is never again mentioned, but it is not the only detail that calls into question the moral integrity of the uncle. When John tricks Timothy by having him arrested and then absconds with one hundred pounds, Gresham's response is delight at his nephew's wit (950–62).

John's knavery is given full dramatization in the French brothel scene (1750–2013), one of the longest in the play. The scene begins with a prolonged and rather salacious exchange between John and his courtesan in which she compliments his English virility (1757–66). The dialogue abounds with bawdy double entendres that attest to the crude wit of both prodigal and playwright. Far from being found out and made accountable for his debauchery, John manages to entrap and intimidate the innocent haberdasher to the extent that Hobson agrees to say nothing of John's French enterprise. Young Gresham never suffers for his knavery or for his lechery.[21] Having won his uncle's good will through cleverness, he is never thereafter obliged to give an account of himself. The only penalty for his decadent behavior is the inconvenience of his demanding creditors once he returns to England. This unpleasant problem he solves by easily winning the favor of the widowed Lady Ramsey, who is so taken with the bluntness of his wooing that she pays all of his debts. Having thus with amazing impunity "all [his] wilde oates sowen" (2532), John can now "grow rich" and, we assume, responsible. Heywood's treatment of this character is precisely the sort of thing the Puritans must have had in mind when they charged that plays of the period encouraged sexual immorality.

Heywood's permissive attitude toward this prodigal son (here nephew) can be explained to some degree as part of his affirmation of faith in the goodness of human nature and as part of his concern with charity. This concern gives the play what form and moral validity it possesses. Young Gresham is given by his Christian society every opportunity to reform—in the religious sense, to "proue a new man." In Thomas Gresham, Heywood has made a hero out of the "new man" that came into power with the rise of capitalism in the last half of the

sixteenth century.[22] Gresham embodies the wealth, power, and growth
of the middle class through prudent use of capital in trade and industry. Clearly Heywood's play is a celebration of this social and economic
change; but it is also an affirmation of the medieval Christian values
that are endangered by the new profit motives of capitalism and the
great wealth of the financiers.

Despite Gresham's good deeds, his charity is tainted by self-glorifi-
cation. For Heywood's true image of Christian charity we must turn to
the literary descendant of Hobs the Tanner, namely, Hobson the Haberdasher.[23] It is Hobson's common sense and faith in the reasonable
nature of man, more than the sermons of Dr. Nowell, that move
Gresham and Ramsey to end their longstanding quarrel. It is Hobson,
not Thomas Gresham, who accepts responsibility for and endures the
abuse of the prodigal John Gresham. Tawnycoat, who exhausts his own
resources helping the needy and who then cannot pay his debt to the
haberdasher, is given a fresh start by Hobson and thus eventually becomes Master of the Hospital (2130). Lady Ramsey offers testimony to
Hobson's charity:

> I haue knowne old *Hobson*,
> Sit with his neighbour *Gunter* a good man,
> In Christs Church morne by morne, to watch poore couples
> That come there to be married, and to be
> Their common fathers, and giue them in the Church,
> And some few Angels for a dower to boot,
> Besides they two are cal'd the common Gossops
> To witnesse at the Funt for poore mens Children,
> Nor they refuse that on their helpe doe call,
> And to speak truth, they're bountifull to all.
> (2136–45)

Even the hypocrite Puritan, Timothy Thinbeard, is saved by the charity
of Hobson when Timothy is sentenced to be executed for having stolen
from his employer, Gresham. As Hobson rushes off to prevent the execution, he declares the basic values by which he lives:

> A hundred thousand pound cannot make a man:
> A hundred shall not hang one by my meanes:
> Men are more worth than monie . . .
> (2179–81)

As Hobson gives to the least of these, he also gives to the greatest in
her time of need. When Elizabeth's pursuivant comes to Hobson's

shop for a loan for the queen, he receives double the sum requested. Hobson is, in short, the spirit of generosity that justifies his assertion, "Knowest thou not mee Queene? then thou knowest nobody" (2071–72). That the queen does indeed know Hobson — knows, that is, the charity that he personifies — is evident in the episode of Dr. Perry's attempt upon her life. Heywood goes to considerable lengths to point out that the queen has already shown great clemency to Perry by forgiving him for a previous attempt of murder. She is ready again to forgive him when Leicester steps forward to rescue the good queen from her own benevolence. The reward for such virtue is her miraculous preservation from enemies within and without, as the Armada episode shows.

Unlike his grand bourgeois counterparts, Gresham and Ramsey, Hobson never loses sight of his humble origin and "rising." His direct contact with the suffering of the poor is the source of his wisdom and compassion. He overhears Tawyncoat's lament as he attempts to dig a living from the land:

> Though I be stirring earelier then the Larke,
> And at my labour later then the Lambe,
> Towards my wife and childrens maintenance,
> I scarsely earne me three-pence by the day.

Hobson responds,

> Alas the while, poore soule I pittie them,
> And in thy words as in a looking-glasse,
> I see the toyle and trauell of the countrey,
> And quiet gaine of citties blessednesse.
> (1678–81)

Heywood's celebration of the profit motive of the new capitalism must be seen in light of the deliverance made possible by it. This play makes clear, however, that the hope that the playwright places in the new affluence of the middle class is firmly anchored in the obligations and proper attitudes that must accompany this affluence. His own play, despite its manifold weaknesses, is just such a looking glass for his middle-class audience.

Chapter Three
The Comedies

Heywood's versatility and durability are evident when we compare the earliest of his comedies, *The Four Prentices of London*, with the latest, *A Maidenhead Well Lost*. His comedies reflect perfectly the variety of literary influences that shaped and enriched the comedy of the Renaissance: the romance, the English morality play, the continental novella, and the New Comedy. Although the amalgamation of this literary legacy complicates the task of classifying Heywood's comedies, three categories emerge: comedies of adventure-romance, comedies of domestic life, and comedies of intrigue.

The Four Prentices of London and 1 and 2 *The Fair Maid of the West* belong to the category of adventure-romance. Written in the early and in the late stages of his long career, these plays reflect the sustained interest of the Renaissance audience in this type of literature. Although the primary objective of *The Four Prentices* and *The Fair Maid* was to entertain a middle-class audience, the plays were also designed to affirm the old moral verities as well as the new spirit of English patriotism. Like the history plays, these comedies attest to the dignity of the ordinary English citizen. A prevailing characteristic of the three plays is the improbable plot, an unlikely sequence of events that results from a benevolent providence working in strange and wondrous ways to reward virtue and punish vice within the temporal order. Using this criterion, we could very well include *Fortune by Land and by Sea* in this category; however, other salient characteristics commend this play as domestic comedy.

To the category of domestic comedy belongs *How a Man May Choose a Good Wife from a Bad*, as well as *Fortune by Land and by Sea*. At the heart of all domestic drama are family relationships of ordinary men and women, particularly the relationships of father and son and of husband and wife. As demonstrations of prodigality, penance, and patience, domestic comedies derive from the native homiletic tradition, particularly from the English morality play. For Heywood, the family is a microcosm of, as well as the foundation for, the Christian community of mankind. Sexual love, patterned on the love of Christ for man, is the source of domestic felicity rather than of romantic ecstasy. The ability to capture the essence of everyday life — the skill of the realist — is manifest in these domestic comedies, as well as in Heywood's fine domestic tragedy.

The definitive characteristics of the plays of the final category, comedies of intrigue, are deception and wit. To this category belong *The Wise-Woman of Hogsdon* and *A Maidenhead Well Lost*.[1] Unlike the domestic comedies, these plays are not concerned with everyday domestic relationships, but with the process of creating and overcoming obstacles to the pairing-off of the right young man with the right young woman. Clever and ingenious schemes, rather than fortune or patience, bring about the comic resolution. The debt to Plautus is fairly obvious.

Comedies of Adventure-Romance

The Four Prentices of London, with the Conquest of Jerusalem. The date of *The Four Prentices of London* is uncertain; it appears to have been written in either 1594 or 1599–1600. The argument for the earlier date has been made by Otelia Cromwell and more recently by Mary Ann Weber Gasior.[2] Of the many accounts of the Nine Worthies of the World that were popular in the Renaissance, the one that is probably most relevant to the play is the Latin history of William of Tyre, composed between 1163 and 1183. William Caxton in 1481 translated the first one hundred pages into English and published them as *Godeffroy of Boloyne, OR The Siege and Conqueste of Jerusalem*. Caxton's work inspired the narrative romances of chivalric exploits in the Holy Lands, but it was probably Richard Johnson's *Nine Worthies of London* that had the most direct influence on Heywood's *Four Prentices*. The last four heroes in this narrative are apprentices who gain fame and honor through heroic deeds.[3] During the same period London citizens also enjoyed numerous ballads that celebrated the heroic adventures of apprentices in foreign lands. In this early dramatic effort Heywood thus succeeded in capitalizing on the citizens' love of adventure-romance, pseudohistory, and self-aggrandizement.

The play begins with the Earl of Boulogne's account to his daughter, Bella Franca, of the circumstances and history of the family. He tells her that while fighting for William the Conquerer he lost his estate and is now forced to live in London where, as a result of his poverty, he has apprenticed his four noble sons. Godfrey, his eldest, is a mercer; Guy, a goldsmith; Charles, a haberdasher; and Eustace, the youngest, a grocer. They are "all high borne, / Yet of the Citty-trades they have no scorne" (34–35). The old Earl has called together his four sons and daughter to give them his blessing prior to his departure for the Holy

Land to fight in the First Crusade. Although the four sons assure their father that learning a trade is an honorable and useful endeavor, they too seize the opportunity to enlist with Robert, Duke of Normandy, and follow their father in pursuit of fame and glory in the Holy Land. Not to be left out, Bella Franca disguises herself and follows her brothers.

From a chorus and a series of dumb shows we learn that the four brothers are shipwrecked en route to the Holy Land. Godfrey is washed ashore in Boulogne, his father's homeland, where his heroic endeavors quickly gain him his father's lost title. Guy surfaces somewhere in France, where the French Princess (no name provided) immediately falls in love with him and her father makes him a great officer in his army bound for the Holy Land. Charles is "Borne on a Planke as farre as *Italy*" (305), where he becomes the leader and reformer of the mountain banditti. Eustace, washed ashore on the Irish coast, makes his way into the mountains of Italy before we see him again. Fortune that casts the family apart then begins quite miraculously to bring it back together. Charles finds his old father with and rescues him from the banditti. Told that his other three sons drowned in the shipwreck, the old earl sets out again for the Holy Land only to be set upon by two of the unrehabilitated bandits and then rescued by Eustace. Charles and Eustace, although they do not recognize each other, join forces as outlaw brothers and co-leaders. Bella Franca, disguised and pursued by an outlaw, shows up, and Charles and Eustace both fall in love with her because she reminds them of their sister back in London. An Italian prince, Tancred, interrupts the rivalry between brothers, joins forces with them, and takes Bella Franca (whom he, too, instantly loves) into protective custody until the war is over. The two remaining brothers now enter the scene, quarreling and challenging each other. Peace is made between Godfrey and Guy by Robert of Normandy.

After what seems an endless repetition of challenges, boasts, and fights between these brothers — who resolutely refuse to recognize one another because each assumes the others drowned — they agree to turn their hostilities toward the Soldan and the Sophy. Again, however, fighting breaks out between Guy and Eustace, and both are banished for this disorderly conduct. Bella Franca, the object of much of this rivalry, decides to escape from the pressure by running off into the woods. With her goes the French princess, disguised as a page in the service of her beloved Guy. When Charles and Robert wander into the woods in search of Bella Franca, they are captured by the Soldan, then rescued by the banished Guy, then captured by the Soldan, and rescued again by Eustace. At last, Eustace learns that this beautiful lady who looks so much like his sister is, in fact, his sister. But as the identity of one woman becomes clear, that of the other becomes all the more obscured: the French princess, disguised as a page, disguises her disguise by dressing as a woman.

The rivalries and complications arising from the failure to identify each other finally give way to the serious business of conquering Jerusalem. Before the final combat a grand recognition scene occurs in which father and sons are joyously reunited. Against impossible odds, the Christians triumph and attribute their victory to God. Bella Franca then reveals her identity to crown the joy of her old father, and the French princess comes out of her disguise to claim her willing lord, Guy. With their war trophies divided amongst them, the Christian victors and their ladies go to visit the tomb of Christ.

The deficiencies of this play mark it as a product of the playwright's apprenticeship. Its salient characteristic is improbability. Most of the action depends upon the repeated and bizarre failure of the various family members to recognize one another. Equally contrived is the inclination of the brothers to fight with each other at the slightest provocation. If fight scenes were crowd-pleasers, there was much here calculated to please, from the single combat of brothers reenacting Hector and Achilles to the prolonged siege of Jerusalem. Without the badges which serve as a constant reminder of their trades back home the four brothers would be indistinguishable. The female characters are only slightly more defined, but just as improbable. The convention of disguise which is strained throughout reaches a new level of absurdity when the French princess, already disguised as a page, further disguises herself as a lady. The dialogue is as repetitious and wooden as the action and serves only to complete the mechanical quality of the characters. It is, in fact, an understatement to note, as Gasior does, that "what is perhaps [Heywood's] finest quality, his lucid prose style, is missing."[4]

Perhaps the ultimate hurdle in this play of improbabilities is the first one: the identity of the four main characters. The heroic endeavors of these young men are in keeping with their noble blood. What is novel and of special appeal to Heywood's middle-class audience is that they are apprentices in the major trades of London. As such, they embody a fusion of aristocratic, chivalric aspiration with middle-class pragmatism toward work and love. Godfrey articulates a work ethic that cuts across class barriers:

> I praise that Citty which made Princes Trades-men:
> Where that man, noble or ignoble borne,

> That would not practise some mechanicke skill,
> Which might support his state in penury,
> Should die the death; not sufferd like a drone,
> To sucke the hony from the publicke Hive.
> I hold it no disparage to my birth,
> Though I be borne an Earle, to have the skill
> And the full knowledge of the *Mercers* Trade.
> And were I now to be create a new,
> It should not grieve me to have spent my time
> The secrets of so rich a trade to know,
> By which advantage and much profites grow.
>
> (67–79)

The knowledge of a trade is for Guy the ultimate protection against the fickleness of fortune:

> Say I be borne a Prince, and be cast downe
> By some sinister chance, or fortunes frowne:
> Say I be banisht: when I have a Trade,
> And in my selfe a meanes to purchase wealth,
> Though my state waste, and towring honours fall,
> That still stayes with mee in the extream'st of all.
>
> (84–89)

Guy's response to the French princess's delineation of the role of the courtly lover is perfectly in keeping with his pragmatism and self-reliance. Concerning the service of such a lover—the weeping, sighing, sonnet writing, and loss of all powers in pursuit of love—Guy observes, " 'Tis pretty for some foole that could endure it" (410).

The middle-class qualities of these class hybrids are far more convincing than their aristocratic qualities. This achievement is a reflection of Heywood's early and continuing talent for realistic delineation of middle-class life. The opening scene set in London provides a vivid image of apprentice life that is as convincing as the rest of the play—the chivalric action—is exotic and farfetched. In the opening frame Eustace, who is the Earl's youngest son and the quintessence of youth, makes clear the meaning of being *bound* to a trade. His complaint provides an additional perspective on the life of the London apprentice and his master and thus serves as a complement to what we have seen in the shop of Hobson in 2 *If You Know Not Me*.

After the performance of *The Four Prentices*, the real apprentices in Heywood's audience returned to their shops with, no doubt, a renewed dedication to their trades. Through the play that fashioned 'prentices into knights, their perceptions of themselves were refashioned and the dignity of their place in the social structure affirmed. Through the myth-making process of play-making, Heywood did for the London apprentice what he did for the English prince.

1 *The Fair Maid of the West, or, A Girl Worth Gold.* Although arguments have been made for 1604 and for 1609 as the date of composition for 1 *The Fair Maid of the West,*[5] the most recent opinion is that the play belongs to the reign of the queen it compliments. Robert K. Turner and Michel Grivelet find 1600 to be the most probable date of composition.[6] The play captures the spirit of patriotism, conquest, and adventure that prevailed at the end of the century, following Essex's defeat of the Spanish at Cadiz (1596) and at Fayal in the Azores (1597). In Heywood's complimentary treatment of Essex there is no hint of the rift between him and the queen that led to Essex's revolt and execution in 1601. As the play opens on the eve of the Islands Voyage, the streets of Portsmouth swell with the pride of English gallants who are ready to gain honor and treasure under the leadership of the noble Essex.

Within this historical context Heywood creates his most delightful female character, Bess Bridges, the girl worth gold. Although she is a barmaid and a tanner's daughter, her literary ancestry is to be found in popular folk legend, particularly in the ballads of Mary Ambree and Long Meg, and in the 1590 pamphlet, "The Life and Pranks of Long Meg of Westminster." Bess, in fact, sees herself as reenacting the feats of these legendary superwomen (II.iii.13). For the more exotic characters, Mullisheg and Joffer, Heywood was most likely indebted to Peele's *Battle of Alcazar* (1588-89) and to the anonymous *Captain Thomas Stukeley* (1596). The adventures of Stukeley are explicitly mentioned in 2 *If You Know Not Me* and it is quite possible that Heywood had a hand in this early play.[7]

As an adventure-romance 1 *The Fair Maid* is in every respect a radical improvement over *The Four Prentices* and is probably the best play of its kind in the Renaissance. Despite the improvements, generic resemblance to Heywood's earlier adventure play is obvious: the action of *The Fair Maid* is highly improbable and episodic. In this more mature work, however, a unifying theme binds and shapes both character and action. In the opening scenes heroine and hero are initially defined in terms of honor, and it is this honor that is illuminated and tested by the play's action and mirrored in its subordinate characters. The wholesome Elizabethan concept of honor that governs characterization and action is a primary reason for the play's sustained popularity. Here, too, Heywood demonstrates what William Hazlitt identified as his most important literary achievement, the "unembarrassed facility of style."[8] Diction and syntax are immediately accessible and graceful. Despite the fairy-tale contexts in which the characters appear, they achieve validity in what they feel and how they speak.

As the play opens, Heywood quickly defines the integrity and unique appeal of his heroine, Bess Bridges. Although she is a tavern maid, she has preserved her chastity in the midst of all the young gallants who gather at the tavern in Plymouth where she dispenses wine and good company. Among her devotees is a wealthy gentleman named Spencer, who, recognizing her virtue, has won her affection. When an arrogant, aristocratic character named Carrol tries to deprive Bess of her place at Spencer's table, Spencer defends her honor, and a quarrel ensues. Carrol gives the lie to Spencer and is fatally wounded in the fight that results. Spencer is then forced to escape the authorities by immediately departing for the Azores.

On her own, Bess proves a superb businesswoman and triumphs over the cowardly bully, Roughman, who becomes her loyal servant. Spencer, meanwhile, reaches Fayal in the Azores only to receive a near-fatal wound while trying to break up a fight between two captains who have come to blows over their share of honor in the recent attack on Fayal. Goodlack, Spencer's friend, promises to return to England and fulfill the last wishes of Spencer concerning his Bess. Provided that Bess has preserved her honor, Goodlack is to return her ring as a sign of Spencer's death and to give her Spencer's fortune. If, on the other hand, Bess should prove unchaste, Goodlack is to inherit Spencer's wealth. As Goodlack sets sail for England, he receives word that a man named Spencer has just died. There happens, of course, to be more than one wounded gentleman in Fayal named Spencer, and our hero, unlike the more unfortunate Spencer, recovers to meet up with his friend and his betrothed at a later date. This contrived case of mistaken identity allows for further testing of the heroine's virtue. Finding Bess not only chaste but prosperous, Goodlack attempts to break her patience and faith in Spencer's love. When he fails, the reformed Goodlack joins Roughman and Clem in loyal service to Bess.

On the high seas and in foreign lands Bess shows the same commanding presence that she showed in the tavern; she even leads her men in triumphant battle against a Spanish ship of war. Amidst the golden spoil of this conquest is an English merchant and, as fortune would have it, her own Spencer. Seeing her in captain's garments, Spencer does not trust his powers of recognition, and Bess concludes that what she has seen is Spencer's ghost. Thus the lovers are separated once more only to meet as fortuitously in the final episode at the court of Mullisheg, King of Fez. Like most men who come in contact with the beautiful Bess, Mullisheg begins with base intentions but is soon reformed by the forcefulness and integrity of this versatile heroine. Her constancy and love for Spencer are finally matched by the king's honor and generosity as he plans to celebrate the marriage of the faithful, long-suffering lovers.

As this summary indicates, Heywood presents in 1 *The Fair Maid* an ideal of honor in man and woman. The rare combination of beauty and chastity merits for Bess the love of Spencer even though she is far beneath him in social station. What is particularly refreshing and truly human about Bess is that her virtue is not defined exclusively in terms of honesty (that is, chastity), but in terms of courage, charity, industry, and Christian patience. Bess belongs to that category of women described in one of Heywood's dedications to the *Exemplary Lives and Memorial Acts of Nine the Most Worthy Women of the World*: "we shall find them to parallel men, as well in the liberal Arts, as in high Facinorous Acts," women who possess "masculine and heroick spirits."[9] As her beauty attracts, so her virtue refines all who come in contact with her.

Although we see Spencer primarily through the eyes of Bess, the few scenes that focus on him reveal that his sense of honor is crucial and complex. When we first see him, he declares to Goodlack his motive for joining the Islands expedition:

> Pillage, Captain?
> No, 'tis for honor; and the brave society
> Of all these shining gallants that attend
> The great lord general drew me hither first,
> No hope of gain or spoil.
>
> (I.ii.8–12)

Although Spencer assumes when Carrol gives him the lie that his honor necessitates a duel, he later realizes that there is no honor in the private quarrel that leads to another's death. What he learns from his mistake he tries to share with the two enraged captains at Fayal. Wounded in the fray as he attempts to separate the two captains, Spencer tells them,

> I killed a man in Plymouth and by you
> Am slain in Fayal. Carrol fell by me
> And I fall by a Spencer. Heav'n is just
> And will not suffer murder unreveng'd.
> Heaven pardon me, as I forgive you both.
>
> (II.ii.55–59)

Spencer is Heywood's ideal hero because his sense of honor is tempered by humility and reverence for life. Through the wisdom that comes with his tragic experience, Spencer, like Bess, is the worthy recipient of a benevolent providence working through the vagaries of fortune.

Presumption and the resulting inadequate notions of honor become the basis of humor in Heywood's treatment of his fools, Roughman and Clem. Roughman is a parodic inversion of men like Spencer and Carrol (I.ii) and the two quarrelsome captains at Fayal (II.ii) who stand upon their honor. As the braggart warrior, Roughman, like Falstaff, believes that honor is but a word:

> How many times brave words bear out a man!
> For if he can but make a noise, he's fear'd.
> To talk of frays, although he ne'er had heart
> To face a man in field, that's a brave fellow.
> I have been valiant, I must needs confess,
> In streets and taverns, where there have been men
> Ready to part the fray; but for the fields,
> They are too cold to fight in.
>
> (II.iii.43–50)

The reference here to men "ready to part the fray" reflects the preceding serious action in which Spencer's readiness resulted in a near-fatal wound. The parallel between serious and comic action on the subject of honor is extended when Bess (disguised as a gallant) challenges Roughman in the terms of the formal code of honor that precipitated the fight between Carrol and Spencer.[10] Although Roughman does eventually succeed in becoming a man, he maintains his comic dimension in his inability to find a proper expression for his manhood. Once he finds his courage, he is equally absurd in his eagerness to fight anything that moves. Clem's cowardice, on the other hand, is preserved throughout, although he attempts to mimic the manhood of his companions when he arrives at the court of Mullisheg. Exercising his influence with Bess, Clem becomes increasingly confident as he obtains the release of various Christians held by the king. His desire for recognition and a share in the honors finally leads to a situation that could severely curtail his manhood. When Mullisheg offers to bestow the honor of chief court eunuch upon Spencer, Bess is quick to decline for her lover. Clem, failing to understand the peculiar nature of this honor, steps forward to receive it in Spencer's place. Enlightened moments later, he returns crying, "No more of your honor, if you love me! Is this your Moorish preferment, to rob a man of his best jewels?" With this threat to what he calls his "current commodity" (V.ii.130), Clem acquires a new perspective on "cutting honor."

Perhaps because the theme of honor is so pervasive in the dramatic works of Heywood, the detailed treatment of it in this particular play has never been sufficiently questioned. But we would do well to consider the prominence of this theme within a play that depicts a very recent historical event, the Islands Voyage, and alludes to (even represents in dumb show) famous courtiers of the day. Farfetched as much of the play is, it is, nevertheless, Heywood's most significantly topical dramatic work. The interesting question, then, is how relevant is the quarrel between Essex and Raleigh that erupted over the conquest of Fayal to Heywood's treatment of honor in the play? Norman Council points out that "various accounts of the voyage emphasize the quarrel between Essex and Raleigh which marked it, a quarrel consistently argued in terms of the relative honor due to both."[11] The *Dramatis Personae* lists as one of the "mutes personated" the Earl of Essex, and indeed he is represented in the dumb show at the beginning of act 1, scene iv. The play opens with reference to Essex, his triumph at Cadiz (Cales), and his imminent departure for the Azores. As noted earlier, Spencer comes to Plymouth to follow "The great lord general." A stage direction, *"Enter the two Captains that were before"* (II.ii), informs us that these are the same characters who open the play with a discussion of their general, Essex. With their entrance, the captains continue a quarrel that results in a bloody duel:

> 1 CAPTAIN.   Make good thy words.
> 2 CAPTAIN.   I say thou hast injur'd me.
> 1 CAPTAIN.   Tell me wherein.
> 2 CAPTAIN.   When we assaulted Fayal.
> And I had by the general's command
> The onset, and with danger of my person
> Enforc't the Spaniard to a swift retreat
> And beat them from their fort, thou when thou saw'st
> All fear and danger past, mad'st up with me
> To share that honor which was sole mine own
> And never ventur'd shot for't or e'er came
> Where bullet graz'd.
>   (II.ii.18–27)

Although both men are captains under "the general," Essex, the complaint of the second captain — that he ran all the risks but was obliged to share the honor with one who arrived too late — has a decidedly familiar ring to it when we consider the historical events that are being portrayed. In the Azores adventure Raleigh arrived at Fayal before his commander, Essex, and after four days of waiting, Raleigh decided to

attack the island fortress without the assistance of Essex. When Essex
arrived the following day, he was enraged to discover that the victory,
with all its honor, had been taken from him. Peace was eventually
made between the two proud courtiers on the condition that Raleigh
receive no official recognition or credit for his achievement.[12] The quarrel between the two captains would make perfect sense, historically, if
the second captain had been under the immediate command of Raleigh, while the first captain arrived (too late) with Essex. Perhaps because he conceived of himself as historian as well as poet, Heywood
goes to considerable lengths to give Raleigh recognition for his victory.
When Bess and her crew arrive off the coast of Fayal, a Spaniard from
the island identifies "English Raleigh" as the man who "won and
spoil'd it first" (IV.iv.31).

In his treatment of the Islands Voyage as the great Elizabethan adventure in quest of national and individual honor, Heywood has given
credence to Hamlet's assertion that the players are "abstract and brief
chronicles of the time." The appeal of this play when it was revived for a
performance at Hampton Court before Charles I and Henrietta Maria
in 1630/31[13] derived in large part from the leading character, Bess
Bridges, an image of womanhood that answers even the most strident
antifeminist. But its appeal, then as now, lay also in the fact that it
captured the spirit of the idealized golden age of Queen Bess, Essex,
and Raleigh. In 1 *The Fair Maid* patriotic fervor and a keen desire for
individual honor result in the heroic exploits of this particular period,
but the ideal of honor that Heywood delineates within that historical
context is for all time and all social ranks.

2 *The Fair Maid of the West*.   Both parts of *The Fair Maid* were
published in 1631, but the differences between them cause most critics
to agree that part 2 was written twenty-five to thirty years after part 1.
Although part 2 continues the adventures of Bess, Spencer,
Roughman, Goodlack, and Clem, the emphasis is upon intrigue as
much as adventure. The impediments to the lovers' union results as
much from the perversities of human nature as from the adversities of
fortune. And while Bess is the same ideal combination of beauty and
virtue in part 2, she is now in a somewhat darkened world where her
beauty has greater power to attract but where her virtue does not always
or easily inspire reform. As part 2 presents a greater threat to hero and
heroine, it is closer to tragicomedy than is part 1. Honor is again the
poet's primary thematic concern, but the treatment of the subject con-
tributes to the darkened tone. In part 1 as we have seen, the view of
honor is essentially that of the Christian humanist: it is the reward of
virtue and inseparable from virtue. In part 2 this conception of honor

appears to give way to a personal and essentially courtly code that results in melodramatic situations. Turner, in an effort to define this apparent shift, states that in part 2 "we have a world of Fletcherian absolutes that obviously have different bases from that of Part I."[14] Upon close examination, however, we will see that although Heywood exploits the Fletcherian absolutes of honor for dramatic effect, he does not finally deviate from his conviction in part 1 that true honor is inseparable from wisdom and virtuous love. The following account of the plot will indicate the emphasis in part 2 upon intrigue and the continued exploration of the theme of honor.

With preparations under way for the wedding of Bess and Spencer, part 2 begins where part 1 ends. Suddenly, however, Mullisheg suffers a moral relapse and resolves to enjoy Bess on her wedding night. The pattern of intrigue is set in motion as Mullisheg solicits the help of Goodlack by promising him wealth and honor if he will betray his English friends. Tota, the Queen of Fez, decides to take revenge upon her unfaithful husband by requiting him in kind. While the king enjoys the bride, she intends, with Roughman's assistance, to possess the groom. Goodlack devises a scheme to save English lives and honors: he arranges the bed trick in which king and queen enjoy each other in a mutual misunderstanding of identity. While the king is busy with the woman he believes to be Bess, Goodlack, Roughman, and Bess slip out of the castle to the safety of their ship. Spencer remains behind as a decoy but promises to appear aboard ship at a designated hour. He succeeds in tricking his guard, but is captured by the bashaw, Joffer. Hearing the story of Spencer's love and concern for Bess, Joffer allows Spencer to go free, even though he will have to pay for this generosity with his life. Spencer accepts the kindness but promises to return after a brief farewell to Bess. Finding Spencer resolute in his decision to keep his word to Joffer, Bess pretends jealousy and anger while she devises a scheme to save her husband. She offers her own life in place of her husband's and thus wins the king over to the side of virtue. With the bed trick explained, Mullisheg forgives and offers double joy and wealth to the young bride and groom.

Having thus exhausted the intrigue at the court of Fez, Heywood, in order to fill out the play, was obliged to tack on another plot, this one set in Italy. The two plots are spliced together with a chorus and dumb show, old devices that Heywood had used in *The Four Prentices*. The chorus explains that as Bess's ship sails toward England, it is set upon by French pirates. In the flight Spencer and Bess are separated. When both ships are wrecked by a storm, Bess, Roughman, and Clem are washed ashore "on the coast of Florence," while Spencer floats to the

"Marquis of Ferrara's country," and Goodlack comes to rest with the Duke of Mantua. Soon Spencer and Goodlack become the favorites of their respective dukes and travel to the court of Florence, where Bess is royally entertained by the Duke of Florence, who has hopes of making her his mistress. When Bess sees Spencer on the street, she throws him the rare jewel given her by the Duke. Spencer, who for some reason does not recognize Bess, wears the jewel in the hope that the lady who gave it will later claim it. Instead, the Duke sees the jewel and, assuming that Spencer is his rival, asks Spencer to deliver a letter to his lady. This service is but an excuse to urge Spencer to swear a sacred oath that he will have nothing to do with the lady. When Spencer discovers that he has sworn to shun his own wife, he adheres to his oath despite the pain and bewilderment his aloof behavior causes Bess. Vowing revenge, Bess requests of the Duke the right to dispose of the man who, she claims, has stolen her jewel. As the Duke turns Spencer over to Bess for sentencing, he renounces all rights and resigns all claims over Spencer. Before the entire court Bess then gives Spencer his life and his wife. Her happiness is threatened once more by the vagaries of honor when the bashaw, Joffer, is captured and brought in as a prisoner. When Spencer offers his own life in exchange for that of his barbarian friend, Joffer is so moved by Spencer's virtue that he becomes a Christian and is, of course, released.

This summary makes clear that the essence of Heywood's comedy of intrigue-adventure is calculated deception and manipulation through deception. Mullisheg, attempting to deceive Bess and Spencer, is deceived by Goodlack through the bed trick. Spencer, pretending a spiteful jealousy, dupes his guard, Alcade. He then surprises everyone at court by returning and submitting to Mullisheg in order to save Joffer. Ironically, Joffer feels deceived and deprived by Spencer's noble action because it robs him of his own heroic role and its inherent honor. Bess, in turn, deceives and steals the honor of self-sacrifice from Spencer when she suddenly appears at court to plead for his life. After her experience with Mullisheg, Bess never completely trusts her next host, the Duke of Florence. Because she fears deception, she is not forthright with the Duke when she sees Spencer on the street. The possibility of intrigue requires from her stealth and cunning. Like the bed trick, the oath trick — in which Spencer swears never to love the lady who is his wife — depends upon deception.

The pattern of deception reaches a climax not in devious barbarians or Italianate dukes but in our English heroine, Bess. Not only does she dupe her hosts and her husband, but she also dupes the audience. When Bess experiences the obligatory cold treatment resulting from

Spencer's oath to the Duke, she appear to consider the possibility that he has fallen in love with someone else. She then resolves in an aside:

> But I'll be so reveng'd
> As never woman was. I'll be a precedent
> To all wives hereafter how to pay home
> Their proud, neglectful husbands. 'Tis in my way;
> I've power and I'll do it.
>
> (V.ii.78–82)

We are completely taken in by her assertion here for several reasons. Although in the preceding nine acts of parts 1 and 2 she is shown to be resourceful and occasionally secretive, we have had no reason to doubt her asides and the privileged information they provide. We have also heard this kind of resolve before: "I'll be a precedent / To all wives hereafter" reminds us of the intention in part 1 "To be a pattern to all maids hereafter" (III.iv.94). The plan here to be revenged also recalls her fleeting desire for revenge in part 1 when she believes that Spencer's body was deprived of its resting place. Later, when she sees him on board her ship, she thinks she sees his ghost because she failed to avenge the violation of his grave. As a woman now seeking revenge upon a husband who has abused her, she would also bring the action of part 2 full circle since the play opens with Tota's complaint and desire for revenge. Although a genuine desire for revenge upon Spencer would be out of character, Heywood has manipulated our expectation to give credence to her anger. In the court-scene denouement that she carefully stages (V.iv) we watch her take her revenge by appearing the great, disdainful mistress of the Duke. When Spencer sees her kiss the Duke he cries, " 'Sfoot, I could tear my hair off." We do not understand the trick that Bess is playing until she says to the Duke in reference to Spencer, "If you have any interest in his blood, / His oaths, or vows freely resign them, him / And all at my dispose" (V.iv.92–94). Heywood thus cleverly draws us, the audience, into the pattern of comic intrigue as we realize that we have experienced a deception similar to that of the various characters. As we recognize that Bess now has the means and obviously the intention (eventually) to free Spencer from his oath to the Duke, we enjoy once more our privileged position. Our comic perspective restored, we may even enjoy the momentary discomfort of Spencer, who has so "rashly sworn" (V.iv.118).

The shift in emphasis from adventure in part 1 to sexual intrigue in part 2 necessitated also a shift in the treatment of the theme of honor. From a modern perspective, this shift results in a degree of emasculation. The virtuous male characters are now engaged primarily in an effort to preserve their honors rather than to gain honor through virtuous exploits. This emasculation is figured ironically in the literal castration of Clem, who does not escape Mullisheg's razor as we were led to hope he would at the end of part 1. Clem's mishap results from his failure to understand the nature of true honor, and in his pursuit of a vain honor he is forever disqualified as a lover. Clem is thus a comic, parodic analogue to Spencer, who through his own excessive desire for honor almost loses his jewel, Bess.

In a world of deception and intrigue, honor becomes logically defined by fidelity to one's word. A keen concern for reputation is also an acknowledgment that one lives in a world of deception and intrigue. Spencer, a man of honor, never forgets the requirements of a good name. As he defines the cause of his grief to Joffer, Spencer's emphasis is upon being true to his word:

> When we parted, I swore by the honor of a gentleman
> And as I ever was her constant friend,
> If I surviv'd to visit her abroad
> By such an hour; but if I fail, that she
> Should think me dead. Now if I break one minute,
> She leaps into the sea.
>
> (II.vi.88–93)

Of course, Spencer wishes to prevent Bess's suicide, but in rejecting Joffer's magnanimous sacrifice by swearing to return to Joffer's custody, Spencer makes clear that it is his honor rather than the well-being of his bride that chiefly concerns him. Although Spencer binds himself only with his "hand and word" (II.vi.114), his commitment is ironclad:

> My honor, faith, and country are engag'd,
> The reputation of a Christian's pawn'd,
> And all that wear that sacred livery
> Shall in my breach be scandal'd. Moors will say
> We boast of faith, none does good works but they.
>
> (III,ii.101–5)

When Bess recasts this idealism into the harsh reality of a choice between his love for her and his friendship with Joffer, Spencer chooses friendship because it is based upon mutual love of honor (III.ii.131–36).

The speed and apparent ease with which Spencer makes his choice of

honor over love is disconcerting because we detect in it not only a chau-
vinistic self-righteousness but also a desire at all costs not to be outdone
in this show of honor. There is thus a fine poetic justice in the denouement of this episode. When Spencer keeps his word so that Joffer may
keep his head, Joffer realizes that he has been surpassed in the show:

> I beshew you, sir.
> You come unto your death, and you have ta'en
> Much honor from me and engross'd it all
> To your own fame.
>   (III.iii.39–42)

Then, while Spencer is reveling in his heroism, Bess suddenly appears
with Roughman and Goodlack to offer her life for Spencer's. Mullisheg
is finally overwhelmed by Bess's love for her husband and is convinced
by her resolve to be another Roman Portia or Lucrece rather than lose
her honor. Thus, in the competition for honor, the prize goes to the
one who loves best, the "girl worth gold."

If there is any doubt that Heywood is defining with gentle satire the
excesses of the masculine code of honor, this doubt is laid to rest by the
final scene. Spencer acknowledges the absurdity of his position resulting from his code of honor. To Goodlack's suggestion that he claim Bess
and appeal to the Duke of Florence for justice, Spencer answers,

> But my oath
> Ties me from that; I have quite abjur'd her.
> I have renounce'd her freely, cast her off,
> Disclaim'd her quite.
>   (V.iii.41–44)

Through his own precise adherence to his own honor, he has placed
Bess's honor in jeopardy. She dramatizes this fact as she kisses the Duke
and publicly acknowledges herself as his mistress, while Spencer stands
by tearing his hair. His just punishment is to be publicly accused and
subjected to the wrath of the woman he has injured. Spencer is finally
saved from the disgrace of an oath "rashly sworn" only by the love and
wit of his wife.

In part 2 of *The Fair Maid* intrigue is specifically sexual; perverted
sexuality constitutes the primary threat to individual honor as well as to
civilized societies. The sexual intrigue is appropriately defined by sexual metaphors and wordplay. Through the metaphor of gestation and
birth Goodlack articulates his scheme to contend with the perverted
desires of Mullisheg and Tota. To the impatience and anxiety of Bess

and Spencer, Goodlack protests, "You'll rip it from the womb / Ere it be fully hatch'd now" (II.i.79–80). Pressured by Bess and Spencer to hasten his thoughts, Goodlack complains again: "Still you cross me / And make the birth abortive" (85–86). Then, having successfully conceived his scheme, Goodlack completes the metaphor: "Now is my task in labor and is plung'd / In thousand throes of childbirth" (II.i.144–45). Roughman, in turn, acknowledges he has played "A midwife's part" in bringing this scheme to term (II.iv.3–4). When the scheme for escape is frustrated by Spencer's arrest, the bridegroom laments that on this wedding night Bess has been betrayed "to a black, abortive fate" (II.vi.64).

The metaphoric language of the Mullisheg episode is extended to the Florentine episode and thus serves as a unifying device in the split plot. Spencer, placing Bess under the protection of Roughman and Goodlack, instructs,

> Gentlemen, be chary of this jewel
> That throws herself into the arms of night
> Under your conduct.
>
> (II.iv.49–50)

Heywood's choice of the word *jewel* is made with a consciousness of its richness of connotation and potential for dramatization. "Jewel" is an appropriate epithet for the "girl worth gold," for it is a common term for maidenhead, chastity, and honor. As a cant term, "jewel," like "stone," means testicle. Clem, for example, in part 1 complains of the Moorish preferment that would "rob a man of his best jewels," and acknowledges later that he "sold certain precious stones" for his title of Bashaw of Barbary (V.iv.133–34). The Duke of Ferrara, like Spencer, uses the word as a conventional complimentary metaphor for a beautiful woman (IV.vi.68–69). Although Spencer establishes and reiterates the jewel metaphor, he fails to understand when that metaphor is literalized—when, that is, "this jewel / That throws herself into the arms of night," literally throws him a precious jewel. His failure to recognize, claim, and protect her as his jewel leads to the dramatic denouement in which Bess accuses Spencer of having stolen her jewel. She acknowledges her identity finally by declaring to Spencer, "I give thee back thy life / And in thy arms throw a most constant wife" (V.iv.167). The jewel as a metaphoric stage property here is a refinement upon the same dramaturgical device in 1 *Edward IV* and analogous to Heywood's use of the lute as metaphoric property in *A Woman Killed with Kindness*.

Domestic Comedies

How a Man May Choose a Good Wife from a Bad.   Although Heywood began his dramatic career with adventure comedy, his major contribution to Renaissance drama and to literature of later periods is through domestic drama. This skill is first manifested in *How a Man May Choose a Good Wife from a Bad*, written for Worcester's company, probably in 1601. Although the play was not included in the 1874 Pearson edition of Heywood's dramatic works, Heywood's authorship has been subsequently established by A. E. H. Swaen.[15] Seven anonymous editions, the first in 1602, attest to the popularity of the play during Heywood's lifetime. The first of a series of plays written between 1601 and 1605 that depict the prodigal and the patient wife, *How a Man Man Choose* is thus the forerunner of, if not the model for, *The Fair Maid of Bristol, The London Prodigal*, Marston's *The Dutch Courtesan*, Dekker's *Patient Grissel*, and Shakespeare's *Measure for Measure* and *All's Well that Ends Well*.[16] More important for the purposes of this study, *How a Man May Choose* is the seminal play for all of Heywood's domestic dramas.

Some effort has been made to trace the origin and to define the nature of Renaissance plays of the prodigal son (or husband) and the patient wife, of which *How a Man May Choose* is the prototype. Muriel Bradbrook states that "school plays of the Prodigal Child popularized by Erasmus, were grafted naturally on the tradition of the English moral play and prepared the way for full drama, but they remained themselves allied to declamation and to exemplum."[17] Sylvia Feldman sees *How a Man May Choose* as the clearest example of a Renaissance play patterned on the old morality play.[18] Alan C. Dessen speculates that the Elizabethan dramatic kind referred to frequently in the early seventeenth century and specifically by Heywood in *An Apology for Actors* as "morall" consists of a conflict between virtue and vice, depicted not through allegorical figures but through contemporary, realistic characters. Dessen concludes that one class of plays that fits the term "morall" is the "how to" drama, such as *How a Man May Choose*.[19] Although Heywood refers to "moralls" (along with tragedies, comedies, histories, and pastorals) in the *Apology*, he provides nothing to distinguish "morall" from the other dramatic kinds. Its use or function is didactic and thus essentially the same as the use of tragedy or comedy as defined by Heywood.[20] Despite Heywood's claim for the didactic function of all dramatic kinds, it is obvious that *How a Man May Choose*, more than other plays of his canon, resembles the medieval morality play in its explicit didactic intent and in its pattern of action.

The real threat to the physical and spiritual lives of the characters places the play in a median position between tragedy and comedy. Like the other prodigal son-patient Griselda plays, *How a Man May Choose* is a tragical comedy or tragicomedy, but as such clearly distinguishable from the mature tragicomedy of John Fletcher, Philip Massinger, and James Shirley. As Marvin T. Herrick points out, these prodigal plays "were transitional plays that reflected the theory and practice of the Christian Terence rather than the theory and practice of tragicomedy advanced by Cinthio and Guarini."[21] There is, nevertheless, a significant connection between Cinthio and *How a Man May Choose*. The source of the play's account of this particular cruel husband and patient wife is the sixth novel of Barnabe Riche's *Farewell to Military Profession* (1581), an elaborated translation of Cinthio's *Hecatommithi* III, 5.[22] Cinthio's story provides Heywood and other dramatists the significant pattern of a man's life being saved by the return of the injured woman who is supposed to be dead.[23]

In the essentials of the plot Heywood remains faithful to his Italian-English source. Arthur perversely rejects his beautiful, virtuous wife for the company of Mistress Mary, a prostitute. Despite the advice and urging of friends and family, he refuses to return to his wife. His cruelty gives hope to Arthur's friend, Anselme, who has fallen in love with Mistress Arthur. While Arthur spends his time with Mary, Anselme hopes, with the help of his friend Fuller, to win the rejected wife. However, Anselme's love for Mistress Arthur is as hopeless as Aminadab's love for Mistress Mary. When Aminadab, the Latin teacher, receives Mary's scorn, he resolves to kill himself. Fuller, the scholar-pharmacist and friend of Anselme, overhears this desperate resolve and sells Aminadab a sleeping potion instead of the desired poison. Arthur then steals what he assumes to be poison from Aminadab and gives it to his wife at a dinner party. Like Juliet, Mistress Arthur is buried alive, and her husband proceeds with his plans to marry the prostitute. When be breaks into the tomb of his beloved Mistress Arthur, Anselme discovers that she is still alive. Promising to respect her constancy to her husband, Anselme takes Mistress Arthur to live with his mother.

Meanwhile, Arthur, married to the prostitute, belatedly discovers the good wife from the bad. Hoping to win the love and good will of this second wife (who has become very hateful), Arthur reveals to her that he murdered his first wife in order to make this second marriage possible. When Mary informs the authorities, Arthur flees for his life and is forced to beg for his food. As Heywood's fortune always has it, the protagonist comes upon his true wife but does not recognize her because he thinks she is dead. This loving, generous woman who looks so much like his first wife shows him charity and listens to his sad confession of "the friend" who murdered his wife. When the authorities catch up with him, Arthur's remorse is so great that he does not attempt to escape but goes willingly to his trial. Only the sudden appearance and forgiveness of his wife can and does save his life.

Although this plot is essentially Cinthio's, Heywood fleshes it out with numerous additional characters: the two fathers of the married couple; young Lusam, who offers wise counsel to the erring husband and underscores the virtues of the wife; Pipkin, the stock comic servant who provides satirical commentary on the wayward husband; Mistress Splay and Brobo, bawd and strong-man to the prostitute Mary; Aminabab, Latin teacher to the young boys of the community and suitor to Mistress Mary. Although Anselme, the young man in love with Mistress Arthur, has his counterpart in the source, he has been significantly altered by Heywood. He does not, for example, concoct and provide the "poison" that eventually leads to the arrest of Arthur. Heywood makes Anselme a far more innocent character in order to emphasize the temptation and moral triumph of Mistress Arthur in rejecting him and to show Anselme as yet another victim of love's folly. The spokesman for illicit love and the provider of "poison" is Heywood's own creation, a scholar named Fuller.

These additions and alterations in the characters are essential to Heywood's treatment of love within a realistic, domestic context. It is specifically the domesticity of his theme of love that sets the play apart from its source. In Cinthio's version the failure of the husband to love his wife concerns only the characters directly involved in the sexual relationship: husband, wife, lover, and prostitute. In Heywood's play the failure of the husband threatens the integrity of the family and the entire community. Arthur's contempt for Mistress Arthur extends to his father and father-in-law and thus challenges the patristic authority that arranged the marriage. Arthur is as much the prodigal son as the prodigal husband, and rejection of his virtuous wife seems motivated as much by a desire to define his authority against that of his father as it is by a desire for a new mate. Chided by his father for beating, spurning, and railing at his patient wife, Arthur asserts himself with protestations that display the immaturity he would deny:

> Father I am now past one and twentie yeares,
> I am past my Fathers pampring, I suck not:
> Nor am I dandled on my mothers knee:
> Then if you were my Father twentie times,
> You shall not chuse but let me be my selfe.
>   (476–80)

As in the character of young John Gresham of 2 *If You Know Not Me*, Heywood can be extremely tolerant of the prodigal. The sowing of wild oats (Heywood's favorite expression for the prodigal's behavior) is usually benignly viewed as a rite of passage into manhood. Chartley of *The Wise-Woman of Hogsdon*, for example, is even more of a scoundrel than John Gresham, yet he suffers nothing more painful than public exposure of his lies. Heywood's treatment of the prodigal Arthur is obviously more serious in that Arthur's refusal to love his wife endangers body and soul of husband and wife and threatens the stability of the entire Christian community. His failure to love is, however, but one aspect of the play's serious exploration of the nature of love. Despite its title, the play demonstrates that more important than choosing a good wife is learning to love her. Through the polarized images of the good and the bad woman, Heywood defines constructive and destructive kinds of love. The play defines itself, therefore, as a School of Love by presenting and examining various "schools" of love.

How a Man May Choose is thus closely related to one of Heywood's earliest literary endeavors, his translations of Ovid. In the preface to *The Brazen Age* he tells us of the fate of these translations:

. . . a Pedant about this town, who, when all trades fail'd turn'd Pedagogue, & once insinuating with me, borrowed frome me certaine Translations of Ovid, as his three books *De Arte Amandi*, & two *De Remedio Amoris*, which since, his brazen face hath most impudently challenged as his own, wherefore I must needs proclaime it as far as Ham, where he now keeps schoole, *Hos ego versiculos feci tulit alter honores*, they were things which out of iuniority and want of iudgement, I committed to the view of some priuate friends, but with no purpose of publishing, or further communicating them. Therefore I wold entreate that *Austin*, for so his name is, to acknowledge his wrong to me in shewing them, & his own impudence, & ignorance in challenging them. (Pearson 3:167–68)

The stolen translations first appear, without imprint or date, under the title *de Arte Amandi, or The Art of Love*. Another edition, also undated, was printed in Amsterdam under the title *Love's School*. Clark believes that the translations were not published until shortly before *The Brazen Age* (1613);[24] however, both the *British Museum General Catalogue of Printed Books* and the *Short-Title Catalogue* suggest a date as early as 1600. And even Clark invites a comparison of the title *Love's School* with the following lines from *How a Man May Choose*:

> Never was such a trewant in Loves schoole,
> I am asham'd that ere I was his Tutor.
>
> (570-71)[25]

The parallel between the Ovidian title and the play enhances the possibility that both works appeared at roughly the same time. If the pirated translations began to appear around 1600, their publication might have prompted Heywood to respond with another school of love, *How a Man May Choose*. The cowardly pedant, Aminadab, who inflicts his bad Latin on children, might very well be Heywood's gift of immortality to the infamous pedagogue of Ham.

The opening dialogue between Arthur and young Lusam raises the crucial issues of the nature and foundation of love. In an attempt to understand Arthur's sudden, perverse rejection of his beautiful and virtuous wife, Lusam reminds Arthur that only a short time ago Mistress Arthur was a source of great pleasure to him (21-32). Arthur's initial contentment with his wife serves not only to underscore the irrational nature of his sudden rejection of her, but also to illuminate the superficiality and vanity inherent in his former affection. Now cloyed and glutted, Arthur's appetite demands variety; reason plays no part in the hedonistic pursuit of pleasure that goes by the name of love. Asked for a reason for his sudden loathing of Mistress Arthur, Arthur can only reply:

> My reason is my mind, my ground my wil,
> I will not loue her: If you aske me why
> I cannot loue her, let that answere you.
>
> (35-38)

Arthur's perverted love, a pursuit of pleasure that dissociates affection from virtue and thus from reason, finds definitive expression in his union with the prostitute.

Arthur's dissociation of love from virtue and reason is mirrored in Anselme's illicit love for Mistress Arthur. Anselme tells his friend, Fuller,

> Before I was a Louer I had reason
> To iudge of matters, censure of all sorts,
> Nay I had wit to call a Louer foole,
> And looked into his folly with bright eyes,
> But now intruding Loue dwels in my braine,
> And frantickly hath shouldered reason thence.
>
> (55-60)

Fuller claims to possess a remedy for this love that results in suffering and enslavement. His cure is the simple gratification of desire that results in a general contempt for all women (352–59). When Anselme becomes a pupil in Fuller's Ovidian school of love, Fuller begins his instruction by defining the wrong approach:

> Be not too apish female, do not come
> With foolish Sonets to present her with,
> With legs, with curtesies, congies, and such like:
> Nor with pend speeches, or too far fetcht sighes,
> I hate such antick quaint formalitie.
>
> (377–81)

This "hende Nicholas" draws on his own experience to provide numerous examples of the direct and effective approach to a woman's bed. Despite this expertise, his school of love proves totally ineffective because it denies the fact that in the ideal woman, Mistress Arthur, love and virtue are inseparable. Fuller blames his pupil, but the failure lies in the basic concepts of his school.

The fourth in this series of false lovers is the pedant, Aminadab, who, like Anselme, suffers the pangs of unrequited love. He carries the "antick quaint formalitie" of courtly love to the ultimate extreme when he resolves to die for love. Fuller, in fact, uses Aminadab as a lesson for his pupil, Anselme (1266–69). Aminadab's self-destructive, absurd passion for the prostitute serves also as a comic commentary upon his rival, Arthur, who is passion's greatest victim. The parallel between these fools of passion is developed through the action centering on the alleged poison. Fuller, the spokesman and master of illicit love, gives the "poison" to Aminadab to prevent his suicide. When Arthur steals the potion and gives it to his wife, he too attempts a kind of self-murder, since, as Mistress Arthur explains, husband and wife are one (610). Poison is a metaphor for the base passion of the lovers and for the instruction in the art of illicit love provided, like the potion, by Fuller. The Ovidian banquet of the senses, which is the objective of these lovers, is literalized in the parody of Aminadab's gorging himself at Mistress Arthur's banquet while his lady and his rival sit beside him.

Fuller's school that reduces love to carnal gratification bears resemblance to Mistress Splay's school of love through which the prostitute is educated. The two schools are governed by the same pragmatism and acquisitiveness. Like Fuller, Mistress Splay teaches from her own experience (953–55). The summary of her "lecture" is:

> If thou wilt arme thy selfe against all shifts,
> Regard all men according to their gifts.
>   (975–76)

The sterility and moral disease inherent in this cynical school of love is signified by Mistress Splay's name.

Set in contrast to the schools of illicit love is the love of Christian marriage embodied in Mistress Arthur. Her love first withstands the despair of the two fathers, who urge her to dissolve her marriage by returning to her father's house. As resourceful as she is idealistic, Mistress Arthur resolves to be the better housewife to compensate for her husband's prodigality: "My nedle shall defray my housholds charge" (528). Her love is further tested by Anselme's efforts to drive a wedge between husband and wife by exposing Arthur's villainy. The duty and obedience that are for Mistress Arthur the expression of a wife's love protect her from the natural passions of jealousy and bitter resentment. Her triumph over jealousy is apparent when Arthur brings home the prostitute and places her in Mistress Arthur's seat at the table. Later, feeling gratitude for Anselme's rescue and confronted with the painful reality that she cannot return to the husband who has tried to kill her, Mistress Arthur passes the supreme test of constancy and love by refusing the unchaste love of her suitor. Armed against all rhetoric and circumstance, she is the perfect foil to the morally frail Anne Frankford, soon to make her entrance in *A Woman Killed with Kindness*.

It is Mistress Arthur's school of love, not Fuller's or Mistress Splay's, that ultimately makes converts. Anselme finally repents and even confesses to Arthur his attempts to seduce Mistress Arthur (2705–18). But it is the rehabilitation of the husband that receives full dramatic treatment in a pattern most characteristic of Heywood. In his source, the wife does not see her husband after his attempt upon her life until she appears at the trial and achieves his acquittal. In the play, poetic justice is assured at the expense of probability when Arthur, hiding from the law and impoverished, appeals for charity from a stranger who turns out to be none other than his wife. The remorse and confession of the sinner before the injured spouse who shows compassion is the stock situation of Heywood's scenes of pathos. This situation occurs not only between Arthur and Mistress Arthur, but between Jane and Matthew in *2 Edward IV* and between Anne and Frankford in *A Woman Killed with Kindness*. The potential for the situation and variations upon it are seen in later plays, *The English Traveller* and *The Late Lancashire Witches*.

Although the comic resolution of *How a Man May Choose* allows

Arthur to survive his sin and regain his domestic bliss, he is nevertheless held accountable. When Mary calls for sentencing of Arthur, she
speaks a truth that Arthur cannot deny: "Why stay you then, guie
iudgement on the slaue, / Whose shamelesse life deserues a shamefull
graue" (2570–71). He publicly acknowledges his sin and the justice of
his punishment (2572–79). Mediation of this justice is possible only
through Christian love expressed as mercy. Through Mistress Arthur,
the playwright defines the power of Christian love in marriage. An imitation or mirror of Christ's love for mankind, the love of this ideal wife
transforms the sinner and reunites the family and the Christian community. As a convert to his wife's school of love, Arthur presents the
lesson he has learned to the men in the audience. More than simply a
dramatized manual for marriage, the play defines in concrete terms the
importance of Christian love to the private lives of ordinary men and
women and to the Christian community as a whole.

    Fortune by Land and by Sea.   Apparently neither Heywood nor
those who were fond of pirating his plays thought well enough of *Fortune by Land and by Sea* to publish it during the dramatist's lifetime.
The play comes to us through a 1655 edition, described by Clark as
"the most slovenly quarto of the Heywood canon."[26] It even arranges
much of the blank verse as prose in order to save space. The title page of
the quarto describes the play as a "tragi-comedy" and attributes it to
Heywood and William Rowley. All scholars agree that the entire play is
in the Heywood vein. What part, if any, Rowley had has not been satis-
factorily determined.[27] Despite the title-page description, the drama
bears little resemblance to tragicomedy as defined by the plays of
Fletcher. It does begin on a dark note with the murder of Frank Forrest
in a tavern quarrel and with the subsequent duel in which young Forrest avenges the death of his brother. But after this initial action the
play becomes a moral on the rewards of virtue. Fortune here, as in all of
Heywood's comedies, is another word for the providential scheme that
ensures the triumph of virtue within the temporal world. This thematic concern is dramatized through the intricacies of middle-class
family relationships; thus the play is best classified as domestic comedy.
Clark's description of it as "half adventure play, half domestic tragicomedy"[28] indicates the generic mix or hodgepodge for which Heywood had a distinct predilection.

    The date of composition of *Fortune by Land* is as uncertain as its
generic classification or Rowley's share. The assumption that 1609 is
the most likely date has not been disputed recently, although very little
evidence has been offered to support it.[29] Considerable evidence, on
the other hand, has been offered by Herman Doh to demonstrate the

similarities between the play and *The Fair Maid of the West*. Both plays begin with a tavern brawl and duel from which the hero must flee after killing his politically powerful adversary. Both plays present heroic exploits on the high seas with virtuous characters captured and then rescued by friends or loved ones. Doh concludes that "perhaps no other two plays, as we look at their plots, themes and diction, are so clearly from the hand of the same playwright."[30] Such similarities lead Doh to accept the 1609 date for *Fortune by Land*. If, however, the recent arguments for dating 1 *The Fair Maid* before Elizabeth's death are sound, the similarities between the two plays invites us to consider the possibility that this one also belongs to the reign of Elizabeth. The possibility of an early date, 1601–02, is enhanced by the play's relationship to others belonging to the final years of Elizabeth, specifically *How a Man May Choose*, the revised *Spanish Tragedy, Hamlet*, and 1 and 2 *Henry IV*.[31] Although the similarities between *Fortune by Land* and these late Elizabethan plays cannot constitute a definitive argument for the earlier date, they are, nevertheless, helpful in defining the salient characteristics of Heywood's work.

Fortune by Land has a carefully integrated double plot, one line of action centering on the Harding family, the other on the Forrest family. As such, the plot resembles that of *A Woman Killed with Kindness*, written early in 1603. Problems begin for the Forrest family when Frank Forrest, despite his father's good advice, joins a group of socially prominent acquaintances at a tavern where he is ruthlessly murdered by Rainsforth, a man with many influential friends. Frank's older brother, called simply young Forrest throughout the play, then challenges Rainsforth to a duel, kills him, and is forced to go into hiding. He chooses to hide in the garden of the Harding family, whose problems are less sensational but no less poignant. Old Harding, who has just taken the dowerless but virtuous and lovely Anne as a bride, cruelly threatens to disinherit his oldest son Philip for having taken the equally poor but virtuous Susan Forrest as his bride. The irony of old Harding's hateful response to the newlyweds is compounded by the fact that his lands once belonged to old Forrest before Fortune's wheel reversed the financial status of the two men.

When Anne discovers young Forrest in the Harding garden, she helps him escape to her brother, a merchant in Gravesend. The equally kind merchant then makes possible all of Forrest's good fortune by sea. The merchant is himself less fortunate in that he is captured and his ship plundered by the notorious pirates, Purser and Clinton. When the bad news arrives at the Harding household, old Harding cannot endure the shock of having lost his large investment in his brother-in-law's enterprise. He dies before he can disinherit Philip, who, since his marriage, has been working along with his wife as a menial servant in his father's house. Triumphant over his cruel younger brothers and his fair-weather friends, Philip is charitable to them when their prodigality leaves them at his mercy. Susan and Philip's fortune by land is then augmented by Forrest's fortune by sea as Forrest captures the pirates, frees Anne's brother, and earns a pardon for himself. The play ends with the joyous union of the two families that culminates in the marriage of the widowed Anne Harding to young Forrest. The only flaw in this well-constructed double plot is the digression dramatizing the execution of the pirates, Clinton and Purser, a digression obviously designed to capitalize on the audience's fascination with these notorious contemporary thieves.[32]

No specific source for the Harding story has been found, but any number of works might have suggested it to the playwright since, as Otelia Cromwell notes, it is basically a combination of the stock situation "of true love not running smoothly because of parental opposition" and the Cinderella pattern of the worthy child reduced to servitude in the home until liberated by miraculous good fortune.[33] The story of Forrest, a young man reluctantly involved in a duel and subsequent flight, is also a stock pattern probably deriving in part from the reality of London life. This standard situation, already used or soon to be used in 1 *The Fair Maid*, capitalizes upon contemporary interest in the dueling code and upon the related popularity of revenge plays at the turn of the century.[34]

Of the plays that had significant influence on *Fortune by Land* the most important are the revised version of Kyd's *The Spanish Tragedy* (1601) and Shakespeare's *Hamlet* (1600-01). Although revenge tragedy was not suited to Heywood's sensibility or skill, he could not avoid the obvious dramatic potential of the kind. In *Fortune by Land* he adopts the conventional situation of the murdered son, grieving relation, and a personal pursuit of justice for a crime that cannot be addressed by law. He modifies the revenge situation, however, to suit the domestic and romantic context of comedy, the genre for which his talent was better suited.

Although the opening scene of revenge is patterned upon the revised *Spanish Tragedy*,[35] Heywood transfers the role of avenger from father to brother as Forrest challenges Rainsforth to a duel (751–55). Young Forrest is clearly Heywood's conscious alternative to the tragic revenger. He engages in the duel only because no other course of justice is available; and though the duel is fought "fairly," "valiantly," and "for a good quarrel," Forrest quickly repents the bloody deed:

Had I but known the terrour of this deed,
I would have left it done imperfectly,
Rather then in this guilt of conscience
Labored so far.
                                        (773–65)

Not only does Forrest acknowledge the "terrour of this deed" and feel
the appropriate "guilt of conscience," but he accepts with gratitude the
opportunity of expiation by earning his pardon through the heroic capture of the pirates. Heywood thus exploits the dramatic potential of
revenge, but alters it to suit both his own talents and the requirements
of the comic denouement.

Other plays in Heywood's canon — in addition to 1 *The Fair Maid* —
that bear a close resemblance to *Fortune by Land* are *How a Man May
Choose* and *The Royal King and the Loyal Subject.* The first is the
more important. As noted earlier, *How a Man May Choose* became the
prototype of domestic drama and a chief representative of the ill-
defined Renaissance kind known as the "morall." The principle of how
to choose a good wife is illustrated in the Harding plot of the present
play. Philip's choice, against the will of his father, of the virtuous but
dowerless Susan is the source of adversity. The two Harding women,
Anne and Susan, are very similar to Mistress Arthur in their constancy,
obedience, and patience. Equally important in *Fortune by Land* is the
model of the good husband and the good son. Having chosen his wife
well, Philip accepts with constancy and humility the tyranny of the pa-
triarch. A male patient Griselda, he is the corrective to the prodigal
son/husband of *How a Man May Choose*, as well as to the three prodigal sons of this play, Frank Forrest and the younger Harding brothers.
As a "how to" drama, *Fortune by Land* illustrates how to be a good son.
Perhaps the most important virtues shared by Mistress Arthur and the
ideal characters here are Christian charity and forgiveness. Through
these virtues the family, the microcosm of society, is preserved and
eventually prospers.

As a moral that explores domestic relationships, *Fortune by Land* is
considerably more complex than its Heywood prototypes. Although
the characters are presented with a forthright didacticism that fixes
them as ethical exempla, they find themselves in situations far less
clear-cut than those of, say, Arthur and Mistress Arthur. There is no
ambiguity in how Mistress Arthur, as the ideal wife, must behave. But
in *Fortune by Land* all the central protagonists are caught in a pattern
of relationships in which some degree of violence, disobedience, or
subterfuge is or appears to be necessary for the proper conduct of their
lives and for the comic resolution of the play. The moral complexity

that derives from the need to balance and reconcile multiple obligations gives a depth to the characters here that is not found in the earlier "how to" plays. This achievement calls into question L. C. Knights's assertion that Heywood "was incapable of exploring, modifying, or making effectively his own the morality of the age."[36]

Forrest is caught between the obligations of personal and family honor and the need for justice on the one hand and the obligation to respect social and moral laws that prohibit personal vendetta on the other. Failing to weigh sufficiently these conflicting obligations, he accepts the former and executes revenge upon his brother's murderer. But as soon as he fulfills the obligations to family, he comprehends his violation of the social and moral laws. By capturing the pirates, Forrest both defeats those who would also break societal laws and affirms the social obligations his initial act denied.

Forrest's good fortune comes first in the form of Anne Harding, who is also caught between the dictates of her conscience and her independent moral assessment of Forrest's behavior, and her obedience to her husband and the law. Placing her faith in the dictates of her conscience, she chooses to deceive her husband and the legal authority his position as high constable represents by concealing Forrest and sending him to her brother at Gravesend. This decision is based upon Anne's recognition of a cruel inequity in the law that would take Forrest's life, upon her awareness that atonement for his transgression would be the braver action, and ultimately upon her belief in a divine providence that governs human events (904–33). The principle that finally establishes a priority among her various obligations is simply expressed: " 'Tis charity to succor the distrest" (934).

The same principle governs Anne's behavior within her complex family relations. Her moral integrity, prudence, and wit make Anne the chief source of light and hope in the Harding household. Although her position in the family as old Harding's young and dowerless bride is initially precarious, Anne quickly wins the respect of her spoiled and resentful stepsons. Fully aware that old Harding must never be crossed, Anne carefully attempts to mediate between him and his eldest son, Philip. When this effort fails, she accepts the necessity of covert support for Philip and Susan. Because her assistance is covert, she preserves her position of respect and authority within the household and is able to avert Harding's signing of the will that would wrongly disinherit Philip. The achievement requires of Anne the strength of character to appear cruel in order to be kind (824–32). She treads a fine line between loyalty to her husband and charity to her stepson and his wife, and she does so without moral compromise.

A similar complexity exists in Heywood's treatment of Philip Harding. His most important commitment is to Susan, to whom he is bound by honor and by love. Caught between his engagement to marry Susan and old Harding's insistence that their engagement be broken, Philip places the obligations of love and personal honor over that of obedience to a father who would have him marry for wealth. The consequences of this choice, which is itself a moral triumph, are the hatred and cruelty of the father. Philip proves as humble and patient in submission to his father's hatred as he proves firm in his love of Susan. Reduced by marriage to a menial servant in his father's house, Philip shows that his chief concern is not for himself but for the wife who shares his fate. The ultimate choice between self-interest and love is evident in his forgiveness of and charity toward his younger brothers when, at the end of the play, he rises to a position of judgment and punishment.

The overriding virtue manifest in Forrest, Anne, Philip, and Susan is their belief and trust in a providential ordering of human affairs through what is called fortune, by land and by sea. Their faith that virtue will in the end be rewarded is sufficient to sustain them through all hardships. As Doh observes, this faith and the affirmation of it constitute the thematic substance and unity of the double plot.[37] The benevolence of fortune governs the rise and fall of the Harding and Forrest families; the capture of the pirates and recovery of Anne's brother's wealth; and the falls of the social sycophants, Goodwin and Foster.

For the modern reader the appeal of *Fortune by Land*, like that of most of Heywood's plays, lies not in its philosophical statement but in its valid depiction of domestic life. What makes Heywood's domestic relations true to life is his attention to details that capture the essence of experience. The opening discussion between old Forrest and Frank about the company Frank has been keeping is a good example. Like so many fathers, old Forrest tries to explain to his son that he must live according to his means and social station. Frank's lame defense of his pursuit of pleasure echoes with a familiarity painful to any parent who has tried to prevent a child from wasting time and talent as well as money. Bitter experience then teaches the youth what the father's advice could not.

The price for this experience must be paid not only by Frank, but also by his older brother. This play, better than any other of the period, presents the custom of defending family honor through the private duel as the very real experience of ordinary men. The scene in which Forrest challenges Rainsforth to the duel (I.iv) is another example of Heywood's superb realism through the mastery of detail. The compelling necessity for that duel is expressed in terms that are absolutely convincing:

> You did kill my brother; had it been
> In faire and even encounter, though a child,
> His death I had not questioned.
> But think you though we winck at base revenge,
> A brothers death can be so soon forgot,
> Our Gentry baffel'd and our name disgrac'd?
> No 't must not be, I am a Gentleman
> Well known; and my demeanor hitherto
> Hath promist somewhat: should I swallow this,
> The scandal would out live me: briefly then
> Ile fight with you
>
> (463–80)

The realistic detail of the Harding story is equally important to the sense of verisimilitude of character and situation. Old Harding's cruel treatment of Philip is more than simply the consequence of a pride that will not allow his authority to be questioned, for old Harding takes a perverse pleasure in reducing Susan to servitude because she belongs to a family that was once clearly superior in social rank and wealth to the Hardings. His abuse is a means of retaliating for the superiority of birth. The younger Harding sons, like the father, relish the degradation of Susan through the domestic chores that require her to "sweep a house, serve a hog, grope a hen, feel a duck, wash and wring" (621–22). Heywood carefully documents the shift from flattery and hypocrisy to panic and overt greed as these sons face the prospect that their father will die before disinheriting Philip. In each instance Heywood's depictions ring true to life.

Fortune by Land and by Sea is finally an odd mixture of wish-fulfillment and realism. It is not until Heywood fully commits himself to the latter that he achieves his masterpiece, *A Woman Killed with Kindness*. The importance of Heywood's commitment to and success with domestic realism becomes apparent when we turn to a play without it, such as *The Royal King and the Loyal Subject*. Although it is an early play belonging to the period from 1601–06 when Heywood displayed so well his abilities with domestic realism, the play abandons the problems of domestic life to focus on the courtly concept of courtesy. With central characters who are patient and long-suffering and who are forced to confront the treachery of fair-weather friends, *The Royal King* is thematically related to *How a Man May Choose* and *Fortune by*

Land; but because of its shift from a middle-class to an aristocratic context, it belongs in a subsequent chapter.

Comedies of Intrigue

The Wise-Woman of Hogsdon.   Although *The Wise-Woman of Hogsdon* was not published until 1632, it clearly belongs to the five-year period (1601–06) when the prodigal son-patient wife was a dominant dramatic subject. It is probable that the success of Heywood's own *How a Man May Choose* prompted competitive prodigal plays from other companies and that *The Wise-Woman* was Heywood's effort to meet that competition.[38] The 1604 date generally agreed upon suggests that the play might have been Heywood's attempt to give the final word on prodigal sons and patient wives to the Queen Anne's men at the Curtain and, after 1605, at the Red Bull. Clark finds plausible Fleay's argument that *The Wise-Woman* is identical to *How to Learn of a Woman to Woo*, performed for James I on December 30, 1604.[39] The strongest reason for the 1604 date is an allusion in the play (1205–06) to *A Woman Killed with Kindness*, which was extremely popular by 1603. There are also allusions in *The Wise-Woman* to other plays belonging to the period from 1598 through 1602.[40]

The earlier "how to" play and the prototype for subsequent prodigal plays, *How a Man May Choose* is blatantly didactic and, as noted already, a principal example of the dramatic kind known as "morall." In radical contrast, *The Wise-Woman* presents the prodigal son and patient wife (or, in this case, wives) purely within the context of farce. The moral has given way to lighthearted comedy of intrigue. Clark's assertion that "the comedy of farcical intrigue is, despite its realism in details of style, setting, and episode, a parody of the comic"[41] is particularly applicable to the relation between *The Wise-Woman* and the prodigal-patience plays that precede it. Exaggeration is the key to the humorous treatment of material. The prodigal is virtually compulsive in his deceptions and infidelities; through simultaneous marriage contracts with three women he out-prodigals the worst prodigal of this dramatic kind.

The focus of the play, however, is not so much upon the prodigal as upon the art of one who contends with his deceptions, the master manipulator wise-woman. Using her house as a stage, this counterfeit magus contrives the plot that holds the mirror up to vice. Her ability to expose the deceptions of the prodigal Chartley comes from a long career of confidence games. She has earned her reputation not through the practice of magic, but through an ability to exploit the ignorance of her clients. In addition to the usual talents claimed by those of her trade—diagnosing through urinalysis, casting horoscopes, palm-reading, fortune-telling, and finding lost articles—this wise-woman arranges secret marriages and operates a brothel and home for unwed mothers (850–76). The unwanted babies are delivered by two midwives in her employ and are given a makeshift christening by Sir Boniface. They are then deposited on doorsteps in the middle of the night. The ironic significance of her name is emphasized in the conclusion of her catalogue of trades: "She that is but one, and professeth so many, may well be tearmed a Wise-woman, if there bee any" (1000–1). Like the player who is one but professes to be many, the wise-woman plays upon the imaginations of her clients. By indirection she discovers from them the role they would have her play. Her house, like a theater, is uniquely suited for the creation of the desired illusion. Hidden in a small closet off her main chamber, she eavesdrops on the conversations between her accomplice and each client. Thus she learns the part she must play when she makes her entrance (890–900).

As a farcical comedy of intrigue, the action of *The Wise-Woman* takes precedence over all other elements, and deception is the essence of this action. There is no specific source for the play; instead, Heywood's debts to Plautus, to Plautine farces of the period, and to other prodigal plays suggest a composite rather than a single influence. The significant achievement of the work is the way Heywood is able to weave so much that is conventional and overworked by 1604 into a perfectly patterned whole. Moreover, instead of attempting to conceal his own dramatic contrivances, those well-worn conventions of the trade, he calls attention to them in order to share with his audience an inside perspective on the art of play-making and illusion-making.

The following summary will indicate the exaggerated use of familiar conventions and the perfectly executed structure of the play's triple plot. Young Chartley, the reluctant husband, on the eve of his wedding to the second Luce (Luce-two hereafter), has fled to London, where we find him gambling in a tavern with his friends Sencer, Boyster, and Harington. When Chartley sees Boyster's beloved (referred to throughout as simply Luce to distinguish her from the country Luce-two), he woos her away from Boyster and reluctantly agrees to marry her. In an effort to keep his options open, he insists upon a secret marriage with no witnesses. Luce arranges the marriage at the wise-woman's house, where Luce-two, disguised as a boy, has taken employment while she tries to locate her reluctant husband. Exploiting the wise-woman's dislike for Chartley, Luce-two suggests that the wedding between Chartley and Luce be thwarted. Meanwhile, Boyster comes to the wise-woman to seek her help in preventing the marriage and in securing Luce for himself. The wise-woman achieves her first triumph by instructing Luce and Chartley to appear for their wedding masked and disguised. She then promises to marry Boyster to Luce if he too will arrive masked. At the appropriate hour, Luce-two, whom the wise-woman takes for a boy, is disguised as a masked lady to complete the double wedding. Chartley thus marries Luce-two, assuming she is Luce, while Boyster marries his beloved Luce, who assumes Boyster is Chartley. Each couple is told that the other disguised couple is a lord and lady who are trying to escape the authorities. Through a scare tactic, the wise-woman then arranges for the two brides to exchange their clothes in order to facilitate their escape. Boyster, after the wedding, thinks he discovers that he has not wed Luce but the wise-woman's page. Since he is not at all sure about this confusing situation, he keeps what he thinks is his embarrassing discovery a secret.

Shortly after the double wedding Chartley sees the beautiful Gratiana of Grace Street, whom Sencer seeks to wed. Chartley abandons his new bride, Luce, and arranges a contract with Gratiana by presenting a forged letter of consent supposedly from his father. Sir Harry, Gratiana's father, ironically approves the match with Chartley because he believes Sencer is a prodigal youth. Sir Harry tells Sencer that he must not return or seek Gratiana's hand until Sir Harry invites him to live in the house with wages. Sencer meets this challenge by disguising himself as a pedant and supplanting Sir Boniface, the pedant Sir Harry has hired to instruct his children. Thinking he has been gulled by the wise-woman, Boyster tells Luce of Chartley's imminent marriage to Gratiana. Luce then turns to her gossip, the wise-woman, for help, and together they devise a scheme. On Chartley's wedding day Sencer, again disguised, delivers a letter to Chartley in which Luce offers herself to him if he will meet her the same evening at the wise-woman's. Unable to resist this offer (since he has never managed to consummate the ostensible marriage), Chartley abruptly leaves the wedding feast and his newest bride, Gratiana, by claiming that his old father is ill and that he must ride immediately to take his last farewell.

Meanwhile, letters arrive inviting the fathers of Gratiana and Luce to the wise-woman's at the same time as the liaison between Chartley and Luce. Chartley's father, arriving from the country in search of his son, discovers that the rake has contracted a second marriage (in fact, a third), and old Chartley also turns to the wise-woman for advice. On their arrival at the wise-woman's, Chartley's victims are placed in separate chambers where they may see and hear the events of the main chamber where Chartley enters to find his Luce. The dialogue that ensues between Luce and Chartley reveals that he secretly married Luce, contracted himself to Gratiana for her money, and intends to dispose of Gratiana after he has acquired her wealth. Chartley, confronted by his hidden audiences, compounds his past deceptions with new ones until he is forced to confess all and repent. Sencer then claims Gratiana, whom he has helped to save from Chartley, and receives the blessing of Sir Harry. Boyster and Luce are relieved to discover that in the masked double marriage they were partners. And Chartley is then confronted by Luce-two, who removes her disguise as a youth and claims him as her husband. This final discovery of the sex of Luce-two is equally astounding to the wise-woman, who ends the play with the hope that her secrets are safe.

Although the wise-woman has clever accomplices in Luce, Luce-two, and Sencer, the success of her denouement depends upon her initial invention, the masked marriage of mistaken identities. Like much of the confusion in *The Comedy of Errors*, this device depends upon the duplication of names, and it is surely no accident that the name Heywood duplicates is that of the patient wife in *The London Prodigal*.[42] The marriage trick plays not only on the convention of twins, but also on the convention of the bed trick used by Shakespeare in his own plays of reluctant husbands, *Measure for Measure* and *All's Well*. The final turn of the denouement and the happy resolution for Chartley, however, depend upon yet another conventional form of disguise, the transvestite. Heywood exaggerates and thus calls attention to this dramaturgical device: Luce-two, disguised as a youth, disguises herself as a bride and then shifts her clothes with the other bride, the London Luce. After the wedding the outer layer of the disguise is revealed to Boyster, who is more confused than enlightened. The audience alone enjoys the full knowledge of reality behind this disguise: that a boy actor plays Luce-two, who plays a youth, who plays a bride, who shifts identity to another bride.

In addition to this delightful play upon the convention of disguise, there is a full cast of highly conventional comic characters: the blunt-speaking Boyster, the pedant Sir Boniface, the clever Sencer, the Senex Sir Harry, and, of course, the prodigal. Chartley's stock type derives from both Roman New Comedy and the native English tradition. By addressing Chartley as Lusty Juventus (1467), Taber invites us to see Chartley as a character who descends from Wever's morality play of the same name. But Chartley is also the direct descendant of Heywood's own lusty youths (or "wild-oats" as he prefers to call them), John Gresham of *If You Know Not Me* and Arthur of *How a Man May Choose*. The lighthearted tolerance shown Chartley is very similar to that allowed Gresham and is in sharp contrast to the suffering exacted from Arthur before he can be forgiven. On the other hand, Chartley's abandonment of one wife for another and his intention to dispose of one undesirable wife by poisoning her repeats exactly the scheme that Arthur attempts to execute.

Like the characters for whom the wise-woman contrives the action, the situations are so conventional that the wise-woman observes, "Here were even a plot to make a play on" (987). That she is indeed conscious of making a play of these stock situations is indicated by her instructions to Luce-two: "play but thy part, as Ile act mine" (597). The denouement of the play fashioned by the wise-woman and her accomplices takes place "where these aymes shall be brought to action" (396): the house of the wise-woman. When Chartley's victims gather here, they become an onstage audience as they take their places in the private chambers or boxes off the central playing area. Chartley finally acknowledges the dramatic accomplishment of the wise-woman and her play: "this woman hath lent mee a glasse, in which I see all my imperfections, at which my conscience doth more blush inwardly then my face outwardly, and now I dare confidently undertake my selfe I am honest" (2295–96).

In this final denouement the line of demarcation between actor and audience dissolves as the wise-woman's house becomes the theater and we, the audience, become co-participants in her play by merging with the onstage audience.[43] This line between stage world and real world, between play and life, is also diminished by the fact that the stage world is persistently identified with the real world of the London suburbs where the theaters were located and where actor, playwright, and audience met daily. The white witch, or wise-woman, was a real and familiar phenomenon of London life; her art was as old as the city itself.[44] By providing the audience with a catalog of her sisters in the art and by specifying their London locations, the wise-woman reminds the audience that her house is as real as the playhouse in which they sit. Her catalog of skills may well have held a mirror up to the last time members of the audience sought a horoscope or a palm-reader. Her reference to the "very reverend Matron on Clarkenwell-Green good at many things" seems to be an allusion to the historical wise-woman Heywood refers to in *Gunaikeion*: "a woman of good credit and reputation, whom I have knowne about four and twenty years."[45]

By calling attention to his characters as dramatic types engaging in conventional dramatic situations at the same time that he presents them in a setting so realistic and familiar that it mirrors the world of his audience, Heywood collapses the barrier between art and life, between stage and audience. He thus achieves a literalization of the Renaissance trope of world-as-stage. Characters within the dramatic illusion see their experience as a play. What transpires at the wise-woman's house are "comic acts" (2327), and the characters create, or are caught within, the plot of these acts. Their lives consist of acting, witnessing, discovering, and being discovered in the theater that is the world. The theater audience consequently sees the play as life because it represents life as a play. More than any other play of his canon, *The Wise-Woman of Hogsdon* gives dramatic validity to the poem that prefaces Heywood's *An Apology for Actors*:

> The world's a Theater, the earth a Stage,
> Which God, and nature doth with Actors fill,
> Kings haue their entrance in due equipage,
> And some there parts play well and others ill.
> The best no better are (in this Theater,)
> Where euery humor's fitted in his kind. [A1ʳ]

As a lighthearted farce in which vice is not allowed to become a serious menace and therefore is but gently punished, *The Wise-Woman of Hogsdon* is a refreshing deviation from the usual heavy-handed didacticism of most of Heywood's plays. Although the play discloses the seamy side of the wise-woman, the satirical assessment is primarily an indictment of her clientele whose counterparts in Heywood's audience kept in business the real wise-women of the suburbs. Farcical treatment of a witch, even a white one, is possible only because the character is an absolute fraud, "one who out of her ignorance, can foole so many that thinke themselves wise" (889–90). She is, in effect, spared by her "palpable, grosse foolery" (446). For Heywood's serious judgment on real witchcraft we must turn to the journalistic play, *The Late Lancashire Witches*, a collaborative endeavor with Richard Brome.[46]

A Maidenhead Well Lost. Printed in 1634 and written one or perhaps two years earlier for the Queen's company at the Cockpit, *A Maidenhead Well Lost* is, in style and plot, representative of the Caroline period.[47] With its aristocratic, Italianate characters and its slippery morality, *A Maidenhead Well Lost* is, of all Heywood's plays, the one least suited to the bourgeois audience for which he usually wrote.[48] As a comedy of sexual intrigue, this play demonstrates what women do rather than what they ought to do, and it thus deviates from Heywood's usual insistence upon chastity and charity.

Although the source has not been established, the play seems to have its origin in the Italian novella. With the conspicuous use of the bed trick it bears the direct influence of Shakespeare's *Measure for Measure* and *All's Well*; and with the substitution of a virgin for the deflowered bride on the wedding night it resembles Middleton's and Rowley's *The Changeling*. The play's concern with honor—the noble soldier who has given his all for his country only to be dishonored and the nobleman whose honor is tainted by his kinswoman and who tries to conceal this taint—suggests the play world of Beaumont and Fletcher, specifically *The Maid's Tragedy*. Heywood's Stroza is a Machiavellian master of intrigue whose most conspicuous literary ancestor is Shakespeare's Iago. In *A Maidenhead Well Lost* Heywood has reworked the green-eyed monster, the Italian malcontent, and the theme of honor into "a pleasant comedy."

In his letter to the reader Heywood, as if to meet head-on any Puritan objections to the play, protests that "there is nothing herein contained, which doth deuiate either from Modesty, or good Manners." He goes so far as to defy his old enemy, William Prynne, to find anything objectionable:

Neither can this [play] be drawne within the Criticall censure of that most horrible *Histriomastix*, whose vncharitable doome having damned all such to the flames of Hell, hath it selfe already suffered a most remarkable fire here vpon Earth. (Pearson 4:97)

We detect here a note of satisfaction in the allusion to the recent burning of Prynne's *Histriomastix*. Yet despite Heywood's confidence concerning the play's propriety, there is much here to draw critical censure. Maidenheads are indeed "well lost," but not without raising real moral questions about the manner of losing.[49]

The play's sensational opening line, "That shee should doo't," sounds the bass (or perhaps base) note. Julia, daughter to the Duke of Milan, has just been told by the villainous Stroza that the lady Lauretta is having an affair with Julia's betrothed, the Prince of Parma. This lie is particularly disconcerting since the royal match has been prematurely consummated and Julia is pregnant. Stroza next turns Parma's judgment seamy-side out by convincing him that Julia's jealousy is a ruse for concealing her own infidelity. In a rage, Julia banishes Lauretta and her mother, daughter and wife of Milan's great general, who has given his life for the prince. Parma abandons Julia, who must then face the wrath of her father and comply with his efforts to patch the family honor by making a match for his daughter with the Prince of Florence. Stroza accordingly abandons the newly born infant on a highway where Parma rescues it and begins to realize his error. Before he can make amends, he discovers that the Duke of Milan has engaged Julia to Florence. This engagement, arranged by the royal fathers, disrupts the loving attention that Florence has been paying to Lauretta, who, after her banishment, conceals herself in Florence's forest and is rescued by him. Reluctantly, Florence agrees to the marriage with Julia and informs his true love, Lauretta, who declares that she too will be wed on the same day to a grand prince. Parma then sends an anonymous letter to Florence informing him that Julia is unchaste. Without proof, Florence can protect himself only by declaring that he will renounce Julia and declare war on Milan if on the wedding night he finds she is not a virgin.

To cover Julia's shame, Stroza persuades Lauretta to substitute for the bride on the wedding night. Finding his bed-partner chaste indeed, Florence gives her a diamond ring and a document defining the marriage settlement. Before dawn Julia is substituted for Lauretta by the side of the sleeping prince, and Lauretta returns with her souvenirs to her mother in the Florentine forest. The following morning when Florence hastens to tell Lauretta that his new bride is chaste, Lauretta presents him with the ring and document. Florence then returns to expose his bride, father-in-law, and their accomplice, Stroza. By requesting the diamond and document that he gave his bed-partner, he reveals the deception, rejects his supposed bride, and affirms his love for Lauretta. Parma adds to the discovery by presenting his and Julia's infant (in a covered dish) and by claiming the mother of the child as his wife.

In his treatment of Julia's loss of maidenhead Heywood is, to a point, conventionally moral. Of the premature consummation of the match with Parma Julia says,

> I now repent
> Too late, since I too lauishly haue giuen him
> The vtmost he could aske, and stretcht my honour
> Beyond all lawfull bounds of modesty.
>
> (104)

The triumph of passion over reason in this royal couple is signified not only by their incontinence, but also by their quick suspicion and jealousy of each other. Julia acknowledges that the shame her incontinence brings upon her father deserves the ultimate wrath. Parma's incontinence results not only in injury to Julia's and her father's honor, but also in potential injury to Florence through his marriage to Julia. Discovering his costly mistake, Parma attempts restitution by rescuing his own child and by sending the warning letter to Florence.

Equally moral, to a point, is Heywood's treatment of Julia's father, the Duke of Milan. Confronted with his daughter's pregnancy, Milan rightly rejects the option of killing her to preserve the family honor. He then reveals the deficiency of his moral perspective by attempting to preserve that honor at the expense of Florence's. This attempt makes clear that the honor of father and daughter are equally tainted by the moral choices each makes. Milan's dishonor derives not, as he thinks, from the shame of his daughter, but from his own disregard for the honor of other men. That disregard is blatant in his treatment of Lauretta's father, the great General Sforza. As Heywood makes clear in *The Royal King and the Loyal Subject*, a prince's honor lies in his courtesy and magnanimity toward those who have served him well.

Throughout most of the play the honor of the brave general is mirrored in the integrity of his wife and daughter, who serve as foils to Julia and her father. The integrity of Sforza's wife is, in fact, unqualified; it is manifested in the proper concern for the honor of her husband and of her daughter. To preserve the honor of her dead husband she gives her entire livelihood and all her jewels as back wages for her husband's faithful soldiers. When she and her daughter enjoy the charity and affection of Florence after their banishment from the Milanese court, she uses her strongest influence and authority to protect her daughter's honor. Her refusal is firm when Stroza offers a handsome bribe and the promise of reinstatement at court in exchange for Lauretta's part in the bed trick.

Lauretta's behavior, on the other hand, is considerably more problematic. When she falls in love with Florence, she confesses to her mother her strong physical attraction for the prince and seeks her mother's protection (132). With this touching and frank acknowledgment and with her mother's moral support, Lauretta preserves her chastity through the frequent visits from her prince. Heywood seems, however, to lose control of this character midway through the play. When Florence sadly informs Lauretta that he must be married, she mysteriously assures him that she too will be married on the same day to one "as richly habited as the great / Heire of Florence" (140). This conversation occurs before Stroza offers her the opportunity to be the surrogate bride for a night; therefore, we cannot explain her statement as an allusion to the bed trick. Furthermore, when Stroza does make her the offer, she initially does what any virtuous woman of Heywood's plays would do—she refuses. The grounds for her refusal, however, are not what we might expect:

> If Julia bee disloyall: Let her bee found
> So by the Prince she wedds: Let her be branded

> With the vile name of strumpet: Shee disgrac'd
> Mee, that nere thought her harme; publikely strucke mee,
> Nay in the Court: And after that, procur'd
> My banishment: These Injuries I reap't
> By her alone, then let it light on her.
>
> (151)

Quick to detect that Lauretta's desire for revenge is greater than her concern for her own chastity, Stroza responds,

> Now see your errour,
> What better, safer, or more sweete reuenge,
> Then with the Husband? what more could woman aske?

Lauretta then agrees to the bed trick with a confession that further complicates the question of her motivation and moral perspective:

> My blood rebells against my reason, and
> I no way can withstand it: 'Tis not the Gold
> Mooues mee, but that deere loue I beare the Prince,
> Makes me neglect the credit and the honour
> Of my deare Fathers house.
>
> (151)

Stroza accordingly delights that "Shee yeelds vnto her shame." When, however, the bed trick is discovered, no one seems to feel that Lauretta has yielded to her shame—least of all the Prince of Florence, who has made a substantial issue of chastity throughout. He seems to accept without question, as we apparently are asked to do, Lauretta's explanation:

> Onely the loue I euer bare your honour,
> Made me not prise my owne. No lustfull appetite
> Made me attempt such an ambitious practise,
> As to aspire vnto your bed my Lord.
>
> (156)

We can safely conclude that Lauretta's motivation for surrendering her chastity is none or all of the above. An intricate plot of sexual intrigue, rather than credible character motivation, was obviously the playwright's primary concern.

In our assessment of *A Maidenhead Well Lost* the moral deficiency of the play should not blind us to its felicities. Of all Heywood's plays this is perhaps the most perfectly unified in a single plot; nothing is extraneous. The action involving the two couples is skillfully interwoven, and the auxiliary characters are integrated into the play's concern with masculine and feminine honor. Heywood was obviously well aware of his structural accomplishment, for he calls attention to it in the epilogue:

> Our Play is new, but whether shaped well
> In Act or Seane, Iudge you, you best can tell:
> We hope the best, and 'tis our least of feare,
> That any thing but comely should shew heere.
>   (165)

In his treatment of lost maidenheads Heywood has presented a frank, realistic view of human sexuality—of the power of passion that prevails. That his customary moral censure is missing in this "pleasant comedy" should perhaps be accepted as a dictate of the dramatic kind, the comedy of intrigue. The court setting and the fact that characters narrowly escape the ruin of their reputations and the loss of an infant heir suggest a close relationship between this pleasant play and the tragicomedy that was fashionable in the same Caroline period.

Chapter Four
The Tragedies

Considering the abundance, variety, and (in many cases) the excellence of Heywood's comedies, it is rather surprising that his reputation for most critics rests exclusively with his achievement in tragedy. Equally surprising is the fact that only two of his plays clearly belong to this category: *A Woman Killed with Kindness* and *The Rape of Lucrece*. There are five other plays with pronounced tragic elements: *The English Traveller*, 2 *Edward IV*, *The Brazen Age,* and 1 and 2 *The Iron Age*. Although *The English Traveller* has been classified by some critics as domestic tragedy, it belongs with the tragicomedies because its central protagonist survives his unpleasant experience to become a wiser and richer man. The primary concern of the other four contenders is history or pseudohistory, although a strong case could be made for 2 *The Iron Age* as a revenge tragedy. We might call these four plays tragical histories. Of course, the line between them and *The Rape of Lucrece* is fine. Although *The Rape* is a history of the reign of Tarquin Superbus, it follows the conventional patterns of *de casibus* and revenge tragedy. It is, therefore, historical tragedy as opposed to tragical history.

As different as Heywood's historical and domestic tragedies are, they have a common origin in the playwright's earliest endeavor in the tragic vein, the Jane Shore story of 1 and 2 *Edward IV*. The temptation, fall, expiation, and death of Jane provide the pattern for *A Woman Killed with Kindness*. At the same time, the story of Mistress Shore is part of the larger history of the reign of Edward IV, just as the story of Lucrece is part of the larger pattern of Roman history. Despite the obvious difference between historical and domestic tragedy, *The Rape of Lucrece* and *A Woman Killed* are companion studies in tragic retribution.

A Woman Killed with Kindness

Virtually every anthology of Renaissance drama includes *A Woman Killed with Kindness* as the best example of the dramatic kind known as domestic tragedy. This term designates plays in which the central protagonists are ordinary people engaged in events associated with domestic life (particularly with the relationship between husband and wife) that lead to suffering and death.[1] Other earlier examples of the kind are *Arden of Faversham, A Yorkshire Tragedy, Two Lamentable Tragedies,* and *A Warning for Fair Women*. Produced in the final month of Elizabeth's reign (March, 1603) for Worcester's men, *A Woman Killed* was the first play to bear Heywood's name on the title page when it was published in 1607.[2] Although we have only one other edition (1617) during his lifetime, the play was an instant and enduring success.

To define the nature of its perpetual attraction and to assess its literary worth have been the objectives of many modern critics since Professor Clark's definitive study and T. S. Eliot's pronouncement that Heywood was a "facile and sometimes felicitous purveyor of goods to the popular taste."[3] Negative evaluations of *A Woman Killed* have been collected by Freda L. Townsend and more recently by R. W. Van Fossen[4] and can therefore be summarized here as (1) a failure to achieve unity in the double plot, (2) a failure to provide adequate motivation and development in the characters, and (3) a failure to present either a moral or a tragic treatment of material worthy of a serious reader or audience. As they are listed here, these charges present ascending levels of difficulty for the Heywood apologist. In fact, much has been done over the last fifty years to demonstrate and affirm the thematic and structural unity of the play. Attempts to deal with characterization, moral vision, and genre have been equally numerous but far less definitive. Eliot's particular charge, "that the interest is always sentimental, and never ethical," that "Heywood's is a drama of common life, not, in the highest sense, tragedy at all,"[5] has never been adequately answered. This charge is well worth our attention because it obliges us to confront the generic label, domestic tragedy, that tends to justify and at the same time reduce the play.

Theme and Structure.   Before we venture on the difficult subjects of characterization and moral vision, let us examine the play's impressive thematic and structural unity. One of seven Heywood plays with a double plot, *A Woman Killed* consists of a main plot that is tragic and a subplot that is tragicomic. At first glance, the two appear to have only a tenuous or superficial connection. The main plot begins with the marriage of Anne Acton to John Frankford. Shortly after the wedding Frankford manifests his generosity and trust by inviting a poor but attractive young gentleman, Wendoll, to share his home and wealth. The friendship between Wendoll and Frankford is so complete that Wendoll becomes virtually a second master of the household. Wendoll repays this kindness by falling in love with Anne, seducing her, and continuing to live in the Frankford home until the faithful servant Nicholas reveals the treachery to his master. Returning home unexpectedly, Frankford discovers his wife and his best friend *flagrante delicto* and proceeds to kills his wife with kindness. He abstains from the expected violence of revenge and instead banishes her with full provisions to one of his country estates. Surcharged with such kindness and overcome by remorse, Anne starves herself to death. In her dying hour she sends for her alienated husband, begs and receives his pardon, and is spiritually reunited with him on her deathbed.

Like the main plot, the subplot begins with the match of Anne and Frankford, for at the wedding "a match" or wager is made between Anne's brother Sir Francis Acton and Sir Charles Mountford. The two knights meet the following morning in a contest of hawks and hounds. The sporting occasion degenerates suddenly into a quarrel, then into a brawl, and Mountford kills two of Acton's men. Punished with his own remorse and a prison sentence, Mountford is reduced to poverty and physical labor in order to maintain himself and his virtuous sister Susan on the land that is all that remains of their inheritance. In his impoverished state Mountford naively accepts a sum of money from Shafton, who then demands repayment with interest. Refusing to forfeit his land and unable to pay his debt, Mountford returns to prison. Overcome by Susan's beauty and honor, Acton attempts to win her by paying her brother's debt. When Mountford discovers that he is indebted to his enemy, he offers Susan to Acton as precious payment demanded by honor. Acton then matches Mountford's concern for honor by marrying Susan.[6]

In addition to the obvious connections — the filial relationship of Anne and Acton, the presence of characters from both plots in the opening and closing scenes, the presence of Wendoll in the hunting episode of the subplot and his narrative of it to the Frankfords — the two plots are unified thematically. Both plots present an act of passion that endangers or destroys an ideal state of contentment. Mountford's murderous rage and Anne's adultery represent the violation or loss of honor. Both plots depict an intricate relationship between masculine and feminine honor: Anne's forfeiture of her honor brings shame upon Frankford; Susan's adherence to her honor becomes the means by which Mountford redeems his.[7] In both plots honor (developed as a masculine code in the subplot and as chastity in the main plot) is the context in which the theme of Christian charity and forgiveness is defined.[8]

Susan's charity is expressed as a willingness to lay down her life (though not her chastity) for her brother. Such charity finally makes friends and family of the enemies through the marriage of Acton and

Susan. In the main plot charity is most obvious in Frankford's relationship with Wendoll. So complete is this love that Wendoll is invited to
be "a present Frankford in his absence" (vi.79). Frankford's kindness
toward the souls of Wendoll and Anne dictates his restraint when he
discovers their transgression. Although it is indeed impossible "To
undo things done, to call back yesterday" (xiii.53), Frankford's restraint makes possible the expiatory suffering and final reconciliation
in death. Consenting to visit Anne in her dying hour, Frankford not
only forgives her but reinstates her as his wife and the mother of his
children.

Although the charity and forgiveness shown Anne by her injured
husband are obviously honorable alternatives to the revenge that such
a sin conventionally evoked, Frankford's conscious resolve to kill his
wife with kindness and his final acknowledgment of having accomplished this morally questionable goal underscore the limitations of
kindness or human charity in both plots. The recurrence of the word
kindness in the main plot and subplot plays upon "the sinister equivo-
cation that the word allows."[9] The kindness of Acton in paying Mountford's debt and Frankford's kindness in providing for his fallen wife
generate in the recipients an insufferable sense of obligation to repay;
they feel what Mountford calls the "surcharge" of kindness (xiv.63).[10]
Each responds in a drastic and spiritually dangerous way to this exact-
ing demand: Mountford pays with his beloved sister, and Anne pays
with her life. The response for each sinner is thus a form of unkindness
that reveals the inadequacy of the kindness shown to them.

Mountford's responses to his imprisonment and release remind us
that the words *kind* and *kin* are etymologically and connotatively related.[11] Mountford naturally expects his kin to prove kind when his
survival and the family name are at stake. Suddenly released from
prison, he assumes his "faithful kinsmen" are to thank until Susan tells
him, "our kindred with our plenty died" (x.70). Later he perceives that
his own resolve to repay his enemy's "strange kindness" by offering
Acton his sister is contrary to both kind and kinship. He tells Susan
accordingly, "Call me not brother but imagine me / Some barbarous
outlaw or uncivil kern, . . . not thy brother Charles" (xiv.4–8). When
Susan offers to give her life for Charles, his response acknowledges that
acceptance of this offer is again contrary to kind/kin: "I challenge it
and kindred set apart" (xiv.35). Even if we give Charles every benefit of
the doubt in the bizarre final scene of the subplot, we cannot deny that
Mountford has accurately defined his desperate ploy as anything but
kind and, in light of what we have seen of Acton, hardly probable.
Acton has, after all, shown himself to be less than honorable on virtu-

ally every occasion. It is thus highly ironic as well as improbable that through submission of self and sister to the will of his enemy Mountford experiences release and reconciliation or that he evokes true kindness and kin-ness in Acton.

Anne's first words to her husband after he has discovered her sin are an acknowledgment that the bond of kind implied in the names of husband and wife has been broken: "O by what word, what title, or what name / Shall I entreat your pardon?" In her remorse and despair she perceives herself severed even from human kind: "When do you spurn me like a dog?" Then, recollecting her kind, she makes her single appeal:

> For womanhood — to which I am a shame,
> Though once an ornament — even for His sake
> That hath redeem'd our souls, mark not my face
> Nor hack me with thy sword, but let me go
> Perfect and undeformed to my tomb.
> (xiii.94–100)

The kindness she requests comes with her assurance of requital, "This granted I am ready for my grave" (105), and sharply contrasts with the charity "That hath redeem'd our souls." Frankford responds to her request by emphasizing his former kindness — "Did I not lodge thee in my bosom? / Wear thee in my heart?" — and by defining for Anne the full extent of her unkindness: her act against her kind, her own children. In light of this injury to her children, the expiatory death with which Anne would requite Frankford's kindness now seems to her totally inadequate. She therefore offers a greater treasure than her life: "Nay, to whip but this scandal out, I would hazard / The rich and dear redemption of my soul." Her conclusion that "He cannot be so base as to forgive me, / Nor I so shameless to accept his pardon" (139–40) is a renunciation of hope that does, in fact, hazard the soul.

This despair finds full expression in Anne's self-inflicted starvation. Through mortification of her flesh, an act unkind in the sense of being contrary to nature or to kind, Anne discovers that forgiveness is not base nor acceptance of it shameless. Anne's triumph over despair makes possible the final affirmation of both kind and kindness. In her final hour she tells Frankford, "My prostrate soul lies thrown down at your feet / To beg your gracious pardon. Pardon, O pardon me!" The terms in which Frankford finally grants this pardon make clear that his own soul, as well as Anne's, was hazarded in the kindness that sought to kill:

> As freely from the low depth of my soul
> As my Redeemer hath forgiven His death,
> I pardon thee. I will shed tears for thee,
> Pray with thee, and in mere pity
> Of thy weak state, I'll wish to die with thee.
>   (xvii.93–97)

As proof of this sincere and complete forgiveness, he reaffirms the bonds of kind in words and actions of true kindness:

> My wife, the mother to my pretty babes,
> Both those lost names I do restore thee back,
> And with this kiss I wed thee once again.
>   (115–17)

Whether Frankford's final line regarding Anne's epitaph — "Here lies she whom her husband's kindness killed" — is an acknowledgment of his failure to show sufficient kindness has been much debated and will be discussed later. Beyond debate, however, is the fact that the complex theme of kindness is carefully conceived and skillfully dramatized in this play.

Parallel action in both plots is signified by key words and image patterns. The sin of blood in each plot is appropriately defined by the prominent image of the bleeding heart. Charles acknowledges his sin by telling Susan that he is "wounded through the heart" — that "The sin of murder it hath pierc'd my heart" (iii.61, 67). When Nicholas informs his master of Anne's and Wendoll's adultery, Frankford responds, "Thou hast kill'd me with a weapon whose sharp'ned point / Hath prick'd quite through and through my shivering heart" (viii.56–57). Later, Frankford tells Anne, "It was thy hand cut two hearts of one" (xiii.185). The sin that metaphorically pierces Charles's heart results in a "thrall'd heart" (x.94) and the potential of a more literal piercing. He is confident Susan will "bring me out of debt, her rigorous hand / Will pierce her heart" (xiv.90–91). The hand that wounds the heart also defines the false friend. Wendoll, contemplating his treachery to Frankford, asks himself, "Hast thou the power straight with thy gory hands / To rip thy image from his bleeding heart?" (vi.45–46). As variations upon or responses to these bleeding hearts, there are besieged hearts, cold hearts, relenting hearts, drowning hearts, madly beating hearts, and even a card game in which hearts are trump — all of which point toward Frankford's final assessment of Anne as "honest in heart" (xvii.120).

Reiteration of the word *match* calls attention to the fact that both plots begin and end with a match. The opening scene celebrates the match between Anne and Frankford. Charles defines the perfection of this union when he tells the bridal couple, "You both adorn each other, and your hands / Methinks are matches" (i.65–66). At the celebration of this match, another match is made, the wager between Mountford and Acton (i.93–103). The sport that proves fatal in the subplot anticipates the illicit match between Anne and Wendoll. The card game that Frankford perceives as a metaphor for their "playing false" (viii.135) begins with Wendoll's insistence that Anne be his partner, "else it is no match" (127), to which Frankford responds, "I do not like that match." The hostility that begins with matching of hawks and hounds is finally resolved by the match made between Susan and Sir Francis. The broken match between Anne and Frankford is remade as their well-matched hands are joined again in the final scene.

Subplot and main plot are also connected through plays on the word *angel*. The hawking wager requires a pawn or pledge: Acton produces "ten angels" (i.96), and the sum of Wendoll's wager is "ten angels" (103). At the opening of scene iii Wendoll laments the loss of his ten angels but is soon compensated in the household of Frankford where Anne becomes his "fair angel, chaste and wise" (vi.106). Wendoll becomes for Anne the embodiment of "This sin that with an angel's face / Courted mine honour till he sought my wrack" (xvi.109–10). Wendoll and Anne, as "two seeming angels" (xi.2) that but "play at saint" (viii.150), are sharply contrasted with Susan, whom Acton describes as "an angel in a mortal's shape" (vii.100). Frankford, in his suspicion of the guilt of his two angels, brings to completion the dramatic plays on the word. He first compares Nicholas's "base report" of Anne's and Wendoll's treachery to "the double gilt, the well-hatch'd ore of their two hearts" (viii.106–7). The contrast between base metal and double gilt is, of course, highly ironic because of the obvious pun, double guilt. Frankford's metallurigical metaphor continues as he resolves to "play the touch" or serve as a touchstone "to try two seeming angels" (xi.1–2). The only true angel Frankford finds is the maid who saves him from killing Wendoll (xiii.68–69).

Unity of subplot and main plot is achieved not only through theme and wordplay, but also through the balanced, progressive structure of the scenes. Both plots present a triadic division: a movement from happiness, to grief, to reconciliation. In the main plot the initial state of bliss, the marriage of Anne and Frankford, is destroyed by the illicit union of Anne and Wendoll, and reinstated to some degree by the second marriage in death at the end of the play. In the subplot the

happiness of Mountford and Susan is shattered by the deadly quarrel
between Mountford and Acton and then reestablished by the perfect
union of Mountford, Susan, and Acton in the betrothal at the conclusion. The action in both plots that begins with the marriage of Anne
and Frankford is resolved in a second marriage, but with the significant
difference that through the perfect chastity of Susan life is possible,
whereas the inconstancy of Anne makes death inevitable and the final
reconciliation painfully incomplete. The triadic division of the action
in each plot is executed through a trio of characters in each.

Heywood's skill with double-plot structure is further evident in the
dramatic juxtaposition and reiteration of material. The foundation for
both plots is laid so smoothly and in such an integrated fashion in scene
i that it is not until scene iii that we realize a double plot rises from this
one foundation.[12] In scene iii of the subplot and in scene iv of the main
plot, felicity and the threat to it are defined in terms of the home and
the relationships within the home. The violent resolve to "strike
home," to send another to his "long home" (iii.37), results in Mountford's banishment from home to prison. Mountford's loss contrasts
sharply with the opening of scene iv and the emblematic image of
Frankford as the *beatus vir*[13] whose chief source of bliss is "a fair, a
chaste, and loving wife" (11). By taking Wendoll into his home and his
heart, Frankford shares the good fortune with which he has been
blessed. That this world of domestic felicity can be shattered as suddenly as Mountford's is intimated first by Nicholas's emblematic description of Wendoll as he arrives with the news of Mountford's ruin. In
this description horse and rider are fused into an emblem of passion:

> his horse is booted
> Up to the flank in mire, himself all spotted
> And stain'd with plashing. Sure he rid in fear
> Or for a wager: horse and man both sweat;
> I ne'er saw two in such smoking heat.
>   (22–25)

Wendoll has indeed ridden "for a wager," that is, as a result of the
match between Mountford and Acton. He will ride in fear, "spotted
and stain'd," at the close of the play as the result of his match with
Anne.

The turning points of both plots are carefully juxtaposed; that of the
main plot occurs in scene vi, that of the subplot in scene vii.[14] Each
consists of a submission to love or lust. In the main plot the turning
point is the fall, first of Wendoll and then of Anne, which leads to the

tragic resolution in death. In scene vii the tragic action is reiterated as Mountford is again thrown into prison. The turning point that leads to the happy ending is Acton's submission to the "violent humour / Of passion and of love" (vii.108–9) that he feels for Susan. In the turning point of the main plot Wendoll at first asserts his freedom of will only to conclude that it is his fate to play the villain:

> If I say
> I will not do it, what thing can enforce me?
> Who can compel me? What sad destiny
> Hath such command upon my yielding thoughts?
> I will not. Ha! some fury pricks me on;
> The swift Fates drag me at their chariot wheel
> And hurry me to mischief. Speak I must —
> Injure myself, wrong her, deceive his trust.
>
> (vi.96–103)

He reinforces this conclusion: "Such is my fate; to this suit I was born, / To wear rich Pleasure's crown, or Fortune's scorn" (vi.112–13). As Wendoll defines himself as the victim of fortune, so the action of scene vii defines Mountford in these terms. Having repented and paid for his sin of rage and become "a plain countryman / Reform'd in all things" (v.8–9), Mountford appears in scene vii a humbler and wiser man. He tells Susan, "All things on earth thus change, some up, some down; / Content's a kingdom, and I wear that crown" (vii.7–8). No sooner has he invoked the image of Fortune's wheel, "some up, some down," than Shafton enters with the Sergeant of Arms and Mountford is forced to wear the irons of a prisoner (60, 71) rather than the crown of contentment. Fortune's wheel spins once more as Mountford is freed through the "strange kindness" (x.119) of his enemy — only to feel a greater thralldom (x.92–95).

Fortune's wheel spins as quickly for Acton as for Mountford in scene vii, and Acton's response mirrors Wendoll's psychological struggle in scene vi. As Acton enters the scene, his will is set against his enemy, and his firm resolve is to do all he can against the name of Mountford. However, with one glance from Susan, Acton is overcome by a passion that completely defeats his cruel will. Like Wendoll, Acton responds to this passion by asserting the sovereignty of his wit and will only to acknowledge and submit to the passion and to the altered course of behavior that it dictates. By juxtaposing in scenes vi and vii the "violent humour / Of passion and love" Heywood achieves a fine dramatic irony: in one plot this passion leads to joy; in the other, to deepest sorrow.

The preliminary stage of the resolution of main and subplot is achieved through a similar concern for dramatic juxtaposition and balance. In scene viii Nicholas discovers to Frankford the betrayal of wife and best friend, a betrayal then metaphorically dramatized in the card game of double entendres. At the close of the scene Frankford decides upon a course of entrapment that will lead to the tragic denouement. In this longest scene of the play Frankford is forced to surrender his finest illusions about his life. His golden world is shattered by the loss of what was dearest in it, the fidelity of wife and friend. Although ocular confirmation of guilt through the entrapment is yet to come, Frankford has already looked into the abyss. This long scene depicting his shock and grief is balanced by two short scenes of the subplot (ix and x) in which first Susan and then Mountford are similarly stripped of their illusions as they face betrayal. Scene x ends with Mountford's plan, also a form of entrapment, that will bring about the happy resolution of the subplot.

The next three scenes constitute the enactment of Frankford's plan "to try two seeming angels." To try here means not only to test and to trap, but to place on trial and to sentence. Frankford's trying of Anne and Wendoll in scenes xi, xii, and xiii is balanced by Charles's testing of Susan's love and Acton's honor in scene xiv, the denouement of the subplot. Scenes xiii and xiv emphasize the tremendous value of a woman's chastity: in forfeiting hers, Anne has forfeited everything; by preserving hers, Susan possesses "that rich jewel" with which she may pay her brother's debt, reconcile enemies, and gain a noble husband. Whereas Frankford's test in scene xiii makes clear the double guilt of Anne and Wendoll, Mountford's test in scene xiv confirms the honor not only of his sister but also of his enemy. Mountford offers Acton his sister trusting that Acton's honor will not allow him to accept "such honourable wrested courtesy" (121) without exceeding it with an offer of marriage. It is with this understanding that Mountford dresses his sister as a bride. Although he gambles with her life as well as his own, Mountford never intends to prostitute his sister.[15] His desperate plan to redeem his honor brings the subplot full circle. In this second wager one angel rather than ten is the pawn, but the stakes are still honor, life, and death.

The denouement of the subplot illustrates the reforming power of love in the "metamorphos'd foe" (xiv.141). Scene xiv ends with Susan, Acton, and Mountford as the perfect triad of love and friendship that calls to mind all that Frankford, Anne, and Wendoll have lost. The final scenes of the play, devoted to the tragic denouement of the main plot, are thus set off by sharp contrasts and by ironic analogies.

Whereas in the denouement of the subplot the erstwhile foe is perceived in his new form as friend and lover, in the main plot Wendoll, the erstwhile friend and lover, is perceived as a Judas and as "the Devil . . . ugly black" (xvi.108–11). The final scene brings together the characters of both plots in what Van Fossen calls "the triumphant justification of the dramatic structure which Heywood has worked out."[16] The deathbed reunion of Anne and Frankford is analogous to the union of Susan and Acton but with the difference made poignant by comparison. All of the principal characters of the first scene are again on stage in the final one, except for the fact that Wendoll has been replaced by Susan, the figure of perfect honor and reforming love. There is another wedding between Anne and Frankford in which the bride will dance the shaking of the sheets. Yet the contrast between the Frankfords' first and second weddings, like the contrast between the marriages of the two plots, heightens the sense of tragic loss expressed by Frankford: "New marry'd and new widowed; O, she's dead, / And a cold grave must be our nuptial bed."

Characterization. As we pointed out earlier, questions concerning the play's thematic and structural unity are relatively simple compared to questions concerning characterization. Controversy centers on whether the characters are essentially conventional homiletic types and embodiments of Renaissance faculty psychology, or whether they are "strikingly modern" and thus require a newer "instinctive" or even depth-psychology approach.[17] The disparity in critical approaches and thus in the perceptions of the characters calls to mind the wry warning of the epilogue: "The wine was new, old, flat, sharp, sweet, and sour. . . . good wine may be disgrac'd / When every several mouth hath sundry taste."

The major obstacle to understanding the characterization in *A Woman Killed* is the motivation of central characters, particularly of Anne. Some critics have managed to avoid the issue altogether as irrelevant to what they perceive as the simple, didactic, and highly conventionalized treatment of characters in a play of the "popular school."[18] For others, specific questions of motivation and character development do not arise because of an assumption "that Heywood could not develop great character or sustain vigorous action from initial motivation through the complexities of situation to the climaxes of success or failure."[19]

Among the critics that have enhanced our appreciation of Heywood's characters are those who remind us that characterization is often governed by the full design of the play — by its structure and diverse thematic concerns. The material of the main plot, after the opening-

scene prologue, is carefully divided into three blocks depicting the seduction, the discovery and judgment, and the reconciliation and
death.[20] These divisions can also be defined according to the characters
who are the focal points in each: the seduction focuses on Wendoll, the
judgment upon Frankford, and the expiation upon Anne.[21] The question of the motivation for Anne's fall is thus related to the decision to
give priority in scene vi to the motivation for Wendoll's fall rather than
hers. The reason for this decision is in part the importance of the theme
of friendship, the fact that Wendoll's betrayal of Frankford is as painful
and profound as Anne's.[22] When, for example, Nicholas tells
Frankford of the adultery, Frankford responds first to Wendoll's transgression rather than Anne's.

Priority is given to Wendoll's motivation for yet another reason. Hardin G. Craig suggests that a detailed delineation of the motivation for
Anne's fall would not be necessary for the Renaissance audience because of conventional assumptions which the play consistently articulates. *A Woman Killed with Kindness* "is consciously written within
the lines of Elizabethan formal thought in matters of ethical and psychological import."[23] Heywood's treatment of Anne's fall exemplifies
the Renaissance assumption that women, however virtuous, are more
susceptible to passion than are men. Anne's later reflection that she
submitted to Wendoll "for want of wit" (xi.112) — assuming wit here
means reason — confirms this perspective. If the transgressions of Wendoll and Anne are of equal moral and emotional significance and if
conventional conceptions of women in part explain Anne's fall, then
obviously the playwright was obliged to give more attention to the motivation of the male character.

The question of motivation and development of the tragic heroine
begins with the image of Anne provided in the play's exposition. She is
feminine perfection,

> Both of mind and body. First, her birth
> Is noble, and her education such
> As might become the daughter of a prince.
> Her tongue speaks all tongues, and her own hand
> Can teach all strings to speak in their best grace,
> From the shrill treble, to the hoarsest bass.
> To end her many praises, in one word,
> She's beauty and perfection's eldest daughter.
>
>   (i.16–23)

Given, then, the perfection of this wife and her marriage, how do we
account for the ease and speed with which she is seduced? The question

is compounded by the fact that Anne never shows any sign of being in love with Wendoll or, for that matter, less in love with Frankford. Her sin, unlike Wendoll's, seems devoid of pleasure and an immediate source of shame. How, then, do we understand it in contemporary human terms?

First of all, Anne's innocence and perfection preclude any former experience of temptation and thus preclude the strength and self-knowledge that comes with experience. She is conditioned to trust and please this young man who shares a place beside her in her husband's heart and who is encouraged by the master of the house to "be a present Frankford in his absence." Having received no prior intimations of Wendoll's passion for her, she is unprepared mentally and emotionally for his sudden, adamant appeal. Her initial shock quickly gives way to appropriate moral indignation:

> O with what face of brass, what brows of steel
> Can you unblushing speak this to the face
> Of the espous'd wife of so dear a friend?
> (vi.119–21)

She is disarmed of her indignation, however, first by Wendoll's desperation and, second, by the sense that she is responsible for his great suffering. The gentle, affectionate disposition that is her asset becomes at this moment her grand liability. The kind pity that diffuses her anger underscores again the ambiguity and paradox of kind and kindness. Perceiving that she is moved to pity (140), Wendoll then disarms her of her fear of injury to her husband. By assuring her that he too loves her husband, that his love for her will not diminish his love for Frankford, Wendoll encourages Anne's trust and delusion that the harmony of her domestic world will not be altered by the transgression.

The next stage in the process of her fall reveals a nature that is malleable and submissive, one predisposed to accept the authority of others, even to elicit it with a pitiful expression of helplessness:

> What shall I say?
> My soul is wand'ring and hath lost her way.
> O Master Wendoll, O.
> (vi.150–52)

This sense of helplessness is accompanied by a full awareness of transgression and of the innocence she forfeits. Her imagination offers a safeguard:

> My fault, I fear, will in my brow be writ:
> Women that fall not quite bereft of grace
> Have their offences noted in their face.
> I blush and am ashamed.
>
> (155–58)

Her will too weak to accept this safeguard, she shifts responsibility for her submission to Wendoll and to fate: "Pray God I be not born to curse your tongue, / That hath enchanted me." Compressed though this characterization may be, it is perfectly comprehensible in timeless human terms. Anne's fall is not only consistent or compatible with the image of the ideal woman that she initially presents, but is ironically connected to the very qualities her society defines as most admirable in women.

"Want of wit" — the inability to think about and assume responsibility for her actions — is the key not only to Anne's fall but also to her subsequent behavior. Her painful awareness of transgression continues to be coupled with a sense of helplessness (xi.103–14). At the moment of her fall, Anne conceives of sin as the maze or labyrinth in which she wanders and has lost her way. Later, it is the lake or pool into which one wades to the shoe-tops only to be suddenly drawn under (xi.114). Frankford's judgment upon Anne makes clear, however, the responsibility that at the time of her fall she attempted to deny. At no point in the long and painful "debate" with Frankford does Anne attempt to shift responsibility to Wendoll or to offer any defense for her sin. Her full acceptance of guilt and responsibility at this point is necessitated by her evasion earlier. Likewise, the form of her expiation derives coherently from the form of her temptation and fall. The sin of the flesh is punished in the flesh.

Still more important, Anne's slow death of self-imposed starvation is the ultimate validation of her will. On her deathbed Anne is haunted by the image of her sin recorded in her face:

> Blush I not, brother Acton? Blush I not, Sir Charles?
> Can you not read my fault writ in my cheek?
> Is not my crime there? tell me, gentlemen.
>
> (xvii.55–57)

Having made complete expiation for her sin through a metaphoric and a literal purging of blood, Anne becomes the antithesis of Wendoll, who flees punishment and bears forever in his face the mark of his sin. Anne is finally able to see and to assess:

> This sin that with an angel's face
> Courted mine honour till he sought my wrack
> In my repentant eyes seems ugly black.
>
> (xvi.109–11)

After her soul's wandering, Anne has found her "long home" and regained her place in Frankford's heart, whereas Wendoll "must now go wander like a Cain" (xvi.126).

Combining the temptation and fall of Wendoll and Anne into one scene, Heywood gives the greater treatment to Wendoll; but he does so in a way that serves as a key to the more abbreviated treatment of Anne. Wendoll, like Anne, perceives the "stigmatic" (vi.86) quality of the sin, knows that it should be resisted, but clearly lacks the will to do so. Wendoll attributes this weakness of will to a power beyond his control: "The swift Fates drag me at their chariot wheel" (vi.101). Though Wendoll and Anne both become victims of a passion that leaves the will impotent, Anne's subsequent acceptance of guilt and her atonement lead to the regeneration of her infected will and to her moral triumph. Despite her husband's explicit instructions to the contrary, she dares to send for him and to ask his true and complete forgiveness. By this affirmation of her will she and Frankford are reunited and set free from the sin that resulted from a failure of will.

As we focus on the shared experience of Anne and Wendoll — specifically their aversion to sin but weak-willed submission to it and their different ways of contending with that sin — we perceive Wendoll in realistic, human terms. After the discovery, his suffering again attests to his humanity (xvi.32–40). His punishment is perpetual because his repentance, unlike Anne's, is qualified by a continued inclination to deny responsibility for his actions: "O my stars / What have my parents in their lives deserved / That you should lay this penance on their son?" He vacillates between self-pitying lament — "O my sad fate!" — and forthright confession — "O god, I have divorc'd the truest turtles / That ever liv'd together" (45–48).

Although Wendoll appears in all his wretched humanness as one who might well run mad (xvi.74–74), Anne, with her "repentent eyes," sees him quite differently when he approaches her to offer kindness: "O for God's sake fly! / The Devil doth come to tempt me ere I die" (xv.108–9). Anne's new perception reminds us that Wendoll has been defined in a diabolical as well as human context throughout the play. Even before he is taken into the Frankford household, he is for Nicholas the harbinger of bloodshed and the emblem of unrestrained sexual passion (iv.21–25). Through his illicit union with Anne, Wendoll will transform Frankford's gate into a hellgate, his bedchamber into "earth's hell" (xiii.15).[24] As Nicholas says of him, "The Devil and he are all one in my eye" (iv.88).

The dual perspective of Wendoll as human and as devil is reinforced by the fact that Wendoll's perception of himself shifts from individual to type or archetype. Conceiving of himself as fated to play the villain, he accepts his role as it is defined in the revenge play:

> So call me, call me so! Print in my face
> The most stigmatic title of a villain
> For hatching treason to so true a friend.
>   (vi.85–87)

Nicholas later does call him so as he tells Frankford, "I know a villain when I see him act / Deeds of a villain" (viii.53–54). Wendoll's sense of altered identity is also emphasized by the fact that with his transgression his name will be scratched out of the "holy book" of Frankford's remembrance (vi.47–48). With Frankford's discovery of the truth, Wendoll is renamed; he becomes in Frankford's mind "that Judas that hath borne my purse, / And sold me for a sin" (viii.102–3). The new name, however, is but an ironic confirmation of the old one, for the name Wendoll is scarcely distinguishable in pronunciation from the Latin infinitive, *vendo*, meaning to sell, specifically to betray for money. Because of the Judas-like nature of his sin, Wendoll sees himself as "damn'd without redemption" (vi.2). In his judgment of Wendoll Frankford emphasizes this archetype:

> Go, to thy friend
> A Judas; pray, pray, lest I live to see
> Thee Judas-like, hang'd on an elder tree.
>   (xiii.75–77)

Wendoll exits the play with a full awareness that as he has been a Judas to Frankford, so he has also been a Cain to Anne:

> She's gone to death, I live to want and woe,
> Her life, her sins, and all upon my head,
> And I must wander like a Cain
> In foreign countries and remoter climes.
>   (xvi.124–27)

Heywood maintains consistently throughout the play the dual perspective of Wendoll as well-intentioned, frail human being and as Devil-

Judas-Cain, thus showing clearly that the character functions on both a literal, realistic level and on a typological, mythic level. His character, in short, is drawn according to both the new and the old modes.

We might expect the same to be true for Frankford, since critical response to him is equally varied. Although Frankford's situation is ancient, his reaction to it is novel. *A Woman Killed with Kindness* is thus a radical departure from, and a significant innovation upon, the Elizabethan revenge play.[25] Frankford's kindness is manifested not only in his refraining from violence, but also in his provision for and protection of his fallen wife. The custom of dealing with adultery through a violent response is reflected in Anne's expectation of physical punishment and in the response of Nicholas and Acton to Frankford's injury. Acton emphasizes the unusual kindness of his treatment of Anne:

> My brother Frankford show'd too mild a spirit
> In the revenge of such a loathed crime.
> Less than he did, no man of spirit could do.
> I am so far from blaming his revenge
> That I commend it; had it been my case,
> Their souls at once had from their breasts been freed;
> Death to such deeds of shame is the due meed.
>
> (xvii.16–22)

To assess the nature and degree of Frankford's kindness, which is the crucial issue of his character, we must first be certain about the terms in which the play defines transgressions. Wendoll sees himself as "damn'd without redemption," doomed to "wander like Cain." Anne likewise argues, "I am as far from hoping such sweet grace / As Lucifer from Heaven" (xiii.79–80). She has lost the name of wife, acquired the name of strumpet, and left a legacy of shame to her children. Both Anne and Frankford are acutely aware that her transgression constitutes an irrevocable loss. They can, to some extent, through repentance and forgiveness, repair the ruin, but the Edenic domestic world is forever gone. Anne's transgression alters temporal reality as permanently as the original Fall that it mirrors.

Given the gravity of Anne's sin, we may still object to what appears to be Frankford's God-like, judgmental response. The Renaissance audience, however, would have seen the situation quite differently. From its perspective the husband is the head of his wife even as Christ is the head of His Church. The husband's authority derives from his superior reason and from the hierarchical relationship established between Adam and Eve at the time of their judgment in the garden. According to Protestant tradition, the submission of the wife was safeguarded by the loving protection of the husband so that the ideal marriage was a domestic partnership.[26] With Anne's transgression, she loses her identity as wife and thus the right to claim the protection of her husband; at the same time, the authority and moral responsibility that Frankford bears as the Christian husband is intensified. His stern words, "Woman, hear thy judgment" (xiii.157), are an honest acknowledgment of the gulf that suddenly exists between them as result of her transgression. As H. H. Adams notes, "his punishment of her is designed to bring home the implications of her sin and to prepare her mind and soul for repentance."[27] Anne's flood of penitential tears attests to the effectiveness of this sentence. In his forgiveness that follows her penance Frankford completes the typological scheme of the play. On the typological level of the action, that is, Frankford is the Christ figure who loves, is betrayed, judges, and forgives; Anne is the Eve figure, the penitential woman taken in adultery; Wendoll is the Satan-Judas-Cain figure.

But what of Frankford on the purely human, realistic level? In the confrontation and judgment of Anne, Frankford manifests empathy and suffering as well as righteous indignation. Her sincere acknowledgment of shame and sorrow elicits from him an affirmation of their shared identity: "Spare thou thy tears, for I will weep for thee; / And keep thy countenance, for I'll blush for thee" (xiii.84–85). He then shows his gentle nature by allowing her to speak first. The detached tone that prevails in his sentence only temporarily masks the pain which Frankford later reveals in his effort to rid the house of all reminders of his former life with Anne. The lute that Anne leaves behind, "Now mute and dumb for her disastrous chance," recalls her singular power to move him. His emptiness is acknowledged: "Now nothing's left; / Of her and hers I am at once bereft" (xv.23–24). Because he fears that his emotion could undermine his reason and resolve, he tells her,

> But as thou hop'st for Heaven, as thou believ'st
> Thy name's recorded in the Book of Life
> I charge thee never after this sad day
> To see me, or to meet me, or to send
> To move me, by thyself or friends,
> Nor challenge any part in my two children.
> (xiii.172–77)

Frankford abandons this resolve never to see his wife again only after her repentance is made manifest in her approaching death. That his forgiveness must be evoked by Anne's expiation defines the nature of human kindness as it contrasts with divine forgiveness through grace. The reconciliation and second marriage of Frankford and Anne are possible only through the ultimate mortification of the flesh. This tragic reality derives not only from the human and thus limited capacity to forgive, but from the nature of the sin itself. By refusing to deny the irrevocable consequences of Anne's sin and by refusing to invest Frankford with the power of divine forgiveness, the playwright preserves the human dimension of his characters and the tragic vision of his play. To have done otherwise would have resulted in a sentimentality at odds with moral truth.

Our final assessment of Frankford should not rest in his resolve to kill his wife with kindness, but in his response to her in the final scene. His defensive coldness gives way as Anne appeals to the goodness she has always known in him. The qualities she ascribes to him—grace and humanity (77)—are confirmed as he takes her hand, acknowledges his past love for her, and invokes God's pardon on "them / That made us first break hold." Thus encouraged, Anne indicates the terms in which true pardon, the ultimate affirmation of grace and humanity, must be made: "O good man, / *And father to my children*, pardon me" (italics mine). Frankford's response acknowledges the humanity or bond of kind that he shares with Anne as one equally in need of God's forgiveness; her direct allusion to their bond of kind thus occasions the final lesson of kind:

> As freely from the low depth of my soul
> As my redeemer hath forgiven His death,
> I pardon thee . . .
>
> (93–95)

> Even as I hope for pardon at that day
> When the Great Judge of Heaven in scarlet sits,
> So be thou pardoned . . .
>
> (105–7)

His affirmation of their bond of kind and of the correspondence between God's pardon and man's pardon sets Frankford free so that he may restore, in part, what has been lost:

> My wife, the mother to my pretty babes,
> Both these lost names I do restore thee back,
> And with this kiss I wed thee once again.
>
> (115–17)

Moral Vision and Domestic Tragedy.   Having examined Heywood's characters as they function on both the typological and realistic levels, we have already gained some insight into the question of the play's moral vision, a question crucial to assessment of the play as tragedy or as mere sentimentality. Eliot poses the question succinctly enough:

The capital distinction is that between representation of human actions which have moral reality and representation of such as have only sentimental reality.[28]

Concerning Heywood, Eliot insists, "the interest is always sentimental, and never ethical."[29] Hallett D. Smith has responded to this judgment by arguing first that Anne, not Frankford, is the tragic protagonist; and second, that "sentimental validity is substituted for moral validity in drama [only] when the character's will is made irrelevant or impotent."[30] We have noted that however impotent the will may appear to the characters at the time of crisis, they are never relieved of responsibility for their actions. Anne's will to atone for her sin and to achieve Frankford's forgiveness and Frankford's will to forgive affirm the moral validity of the play's central protagonists. Furthermore, the reconciliation of Frankford and Anne does not discount the tragic consequences of her fall or the limitations of his kindness. Heywood's achievement in the main plot is illuminated by the apparent inadequacy of the subplot, for it is here, if anywhere, that the moral reality is wrenched to accommodate sentimentality.

In contrast to Eliot, Robert B. Heilman asserts that Heywood "has the most consistent tragic sense of character outside of Shakespeare"; nevertheless, his dramatic achievement is qualified by "a strong homiletic intention" that causes him "to construe characters with reference to concepts that he wanted to illustrate." The result is a "generic malformation" known as "allegoric tragedy."[31] Heilman's view of the homiletic intent is a modification of Henry H. Adams's earlier statement:

The subordination of the action of the main plot to the demonstration of religious teaching spoils any effect of tragedy which might arise from the situation. Because Heywood is eager to present his thesis, he makes the characters act in a way which will best serve his ends, not in a manner best calculated to create the illusion of reality.[32]

Certainly, Heilman and Adams are justified in stressing the homiletic, allegorical element of the play; Heywood, after all, acknowledges the wine is old. The homiletic intent is nowhere more obvious than in Anne's direct address to the audience:

> O women, women, you that have yet kept
> Your holy matrimonial vow unstain'd,
> Make me your instance: when you tread awry,
> Your sins like mine will on your conscience lie.
>
> (xiii.141–44)

The didactic value of drama is the cornerstone of Heywood's defense in *An Apology for Actors*. Here he states that "Women . . . that are chaste, are by us extolled, and encouraged in their vertues. . . . The unchaste are by us shewed their errors."[33] The assumption, however, that the homiletic or allegorical diminishes the tragic must be scanned.

Domestic tragedy is by definition a marriage of the old and the new in English drama. In the pattern of temptation, sin, discovery, repentence, and forgiveness, its action and didactic intent are obviously related to the old morality play and to the entire homiletic tradition. Characterization is thus to some extent governed by conventional theological and social assumptions. The genre is new in its psychological realism — in the temporal context of the specific lives of individuals — and in its violation of the literary conventions that traditionally separated tragedy from comedy. The penitential pattern historically associated with the Christian comedy of the morality play is adapted to the tragic pattern that focuses upon human suffering and loss. The central protagonists are not royal, but ordinary men and women involved in ordinary human experience. They are designed to meet the moral concerns of a common audience.

Given the precarious combination essential to domestic tragedy, it is not surprising that in many plays of this kind the tragic dimension is not achieved. Most critics agree that such failure is not the case of *A Woman Killed*, and that the final challenge the play presents is to understand how and to what extent the tragic dimension is achieved. David Cook raises the crucial question: "how is action of an unexceptional nature to be raised to tragic intensity," but his argument that it is through various methods of "concentration" does not fully answer.[34] What we need to see is that elements that are usually called "allegorical," rather than diminishing, actually serve to heighten the ordinary to the tragic level. But the more appropriate terms for the nonrealistic dimension of *A Woman Killed* are typological and emblematic, not allegorical.

In Heywood's dramatization the actions of ordinary people emerge as an archetypal pattern or myth of experience that constitutes our deepest tragic awareness: the myth of the Fall. The analogy between Anne's fall and Original Sin is the key to the tragic import of this play about ordinary people. It was Heywood's unique vision that allowed him to define common domesticity in terms of Original Sin and the loss of our first home. The analogy is achieved not through concentration, but through typological and emblematic amplification.

The play begins with the condition of bliss and with the covert threat to it. Two of the finest of their kind are joined together in an ideal marriage designed to perpetuate perfection. Mountford's description of Anne, "She's beauty and perfection's eldest daughter," constitutes an emblematic image of prelapsarian Eve. Music and dancing dominate as metaphors of harmony and perfection on earth. But the emblematic dance conveys *in malo* as well as *in bono* connotations, for the reference to the dance known as "The Shaking of the Sheets" associates the sexual act with the dance of death. The condition of bliss is further underscored by Frankford's magnanimity toward Wendoll and by the emblematic portrait in scene iv of Frankford as the *beatus vir*. Juxtaposed immediately is the emblematic portrait of Wendoll as centaur — a personification of unbridled lust[35] — and thus the threat to the Edenic world of marital bliss. Nicholas, the rough-and-ready guardian angel of this domestic paradise, sounds the warning note against the intruder: "The Devil and he are all one in my eye."

Anne's fall brings an alteration that is also defined in a typological and emblematic context. She is no longer "beauty and perfection's eldest daughter," but Eve's youngest daughter. Previously secure in the enclosure of Frankford's heart and home, she now wanders into the "labyrinth of sin." This maze is glossed by Wendoll in traditional iconographic terms as "the path of pleasure" and "the gate of bliss." As a result of Anne's fall, the former symbols of blessed domesticity — the house, the bed, and the board — undergo a terrible transformation. Frankford's housegate becomes a hellgate when it, like his wife, becomes Wendoll's gate of bliss. As Frankford returns home to apprehend the lovers, he enters his "polluted bedchamber, / Once my terrestial heaven, now my earth's hell." Frankford's table, once the center of hospitality and communion, becomes a symbol of carnal appetite. Nicholas tells Frankford of Anne and Wendoll's adultery when Frankford enters "*brushing the crumbs from his clothes with a napkin.*" Left to themselves by the sudden departure of Frankford, Anne and Wendoll take their supper in her private chamber. Jenkin emphasizes the obvious: "and if they do sup together, pray God they do not lie together." Anne's self-inflicted starvation is the appropriate symbolic punishment for this sin of sexual appetite that has transformed bed and board, symbols of domestic solace, into symbols of lust and gluttony.

Frankford sees the tragic alteration of his world in terms of Original Sin:

> O God, O God, that it were possible
> To undo things done, to call back yesterday;
> That Time could turn up his swift sandy glass,
> To untell the days, and to redeem these hours;
> Or that the Sun
> Could, rising from the West, draw his coach backward,
> Take from the account of time so many minutes,
> Till he had these seasons call'd again,
> Those minutes and those actions done in them,
> Even from her first offense; that I might take her
> As spotless as an angel in my arms.
> But O! I talk of things impossible,
> And cast beyond the moon . . .
>
> (xiii. 52–64)

Anne's "first offense" brings into his Edenic world an awareness of the tyranny of time and death, expressed here in the verbal emblem of the running hourglass.[36] The reference to the sun that cannot "draw his coach backward" prepares us for the coach that will carry Anne out of the garden into banishment. The transgression of the woman who was once "spotless as an angel" anchors Frankford in the sublunary world of mutability and death.

Just as the transgression is projected into amplified tragic context by typological association and emblem, so too are Frankford's judgment and Anne's acknowledgment of guilt. Frankford's sending for the children as part of his judgment has struck some modern critics as a rather histrionic low blow, but it is in fact a crucial aspect of Heywood's emphasis upon the analogy between Anne and Eve and thus part of the heightening of the tragic action. Anne is told to look on the white brows of her children where her shame "is character'd / And grows in greatness as they wax in years." Frankford fears that "her spotted body / Hath stain'd their names with strips of bastardy" and that "her adult'rous breath may blast their spirits / With her infectious thoughts." The legacy Anne leaves her children is thus analogous to that left to all mankind by Eve.

The ramifications of Anne's sin extend beyond the immediate family to all those who gather at the wedding in the first scene and who gather again at the deathbed in the final scene. Frankford's household, as a microcosm of society, appears according to the stage directions "*as newly come out of bed*" to witness Frankford's judgment and to mourn Anne's fall. The visual image of the entire household standing in nightgowns "as newly come out of bed" establishes for the Renaissance audience a typological association with the Last Judgment, when all mankind will be awakened for the final reckoning.[37]

The play's last scene of reconciliation, reunion, and tragedy is also heightened by emblematic amplification. The scene opens with Anne, in the company of a coachman and carters, on a road. Jenkin's attempt to comfort her only reinforces Anne's awareness that although there may be many manors belonging to her husband, there is but one home, the one from which she has now been banished. What lies beyond is the wasteland, the land where she must waste away. But if the road is the path to the "long home" of Anne's final resting place, it is also the penitent pilgrim's way to restoration and forgiveness.

Nicholas meets Anne on the road to give her the lute that was left behind, "flung in the corner" (x.12). This instrument is an emblem of Anne herself, and as such it carries the *in bono* and *in malo* significations relevant to her former state of harmony, to her present state of discord, and to her future death. Frankford first defines its emblematic significance in relation to past pleasure and perfection and to the present change:

> Her lute! O God, upon this instrument
> Her fingers have run quick division,
> Sweeter than that which now divides our hearts.
> These frets have made me pleasant, that have now
> Frets of my heartstrings made. O Master Cranwell,
> Oft hath she made this melancholy wood,
> Now mute and dumb for her disastrous chance,
> Speak sweetly many a note, sound many a strain
> To her own ravishing voice, which being well strung
> What pleasant, strange airs have they jointly sung.
>
> (xv.13–22)

Anne sees in the lute a reflection of her present state: "We both are out of tune, both out of time." For Nicholas, the lute affords an association with her transgression: "Would that had been the only instrument that e're you had played on." Anne takes the lute from Nicholas, tunes it, and tells her audience of attendants:

> Gird me about, and help me with your tears
> To wash my spotted sins. My lute shall groan;
> It cannot weep, but shall lament my moan.

Tuned, the lute becomes once more the symbol of "marital concord and the well-ordered being,"[38] or of what Anne defines as "all earth's joy." As an acknowledgment that this Edenic state of innocence is lost forever, she commands her servant, "Go break this lute upon my coach's wheel." The lute broken upon the wheel is a perfect image of Anne's tragic experience and imminent death. It calls to mind Frankford's image of the sun's coach that cannot be drawn backward and Wendoll's image of Fate's chariot wheel that drags him on to sin. That "all earth's joy" is wrecked upon the wheel of time and fortune is the consequence of Anne's sin. Her sin, however, is a consequence of kind, of Original Sin that establishes kind and dictates the tragic limitations of human kindness.

Whatever the critical approach to *A Woman Killed with Kindness*, the common conclusion is that Heywood's sensibility and talent are uniquely suited to domestic tragedy. He is, in the positive sense, a homely poet whose best heroes and heroines are husbands and wives. His verse is graceful and natural and thus a perfect vehicle for defining the experience of ordinary people without calling attention to itself.[39] The imagery of the best set speech, Frankford's wish "To undo things done," is commonplace but emotionally and morally charged by the typological associations it evokes. The only classical allusion that the playwright allows himself is in the comparison of Anne's skill on the lute to that of Orpheus (xv.13–22, xvi.51–57). This mythological allusion perfectly reinforces the play's pattern of spiritual descent, ascent, death, and transcendence. Itself a kind of domestic tragedy, the myth of Orpheus provides an analogy to the Fall and is frequently glossed in Christian terms.[40]

There is no doubt that we do not find in Heywood's best play the great poetry of Shakespeare. In fact, we do not find such poetry in any of Heywood's works, dramatic or nondramatic. But for our understanding of *A Woman Killed with Kindness* it is important to recognize that, at least once, Heywood found a dramatic subject and thus a dramatic form for which his poetic deficiency was not a liability — a dramatic form that allowed him to capitalize upon the vision and the significant dramatic skill he did possess.

The Rape of Lucrece

In his letter to the reader of the 1638 edition of *The Rape of Lucrece* Heywood again complains of the unauthorized, inaccurate printing of his plays and offers for contrast this complete and accurate edition. Despite its title, the play is not chiefly concerned with the rape of Lucrece; instead, it depicts the rise and fall of Tarquin Superbus — Tarquin the Proud. The primary source, therefore, is not Shakespeare's poem, but Livy's *Early History of Rome*.[41] Taking his cue from Livy, Heywood presents the rape as the turning point in Tarquin's reign. The title page, defining the play as "a true Roman tragedy," calls attention to the fidelity with which Heywood handled his Roman source. The play is tragic in that it follows both the *de casibus* and the revenge patterns that shaped the Elizabethan understanding of the genre.

The next lines of the title page, however, advise us of what appears to be a significant departure: this tragedy is accompanied by "the several Songs in their apt places, by Valerius the merry Lord among the Roman Peeres." Such a combination leads us to wonder how we shall find the concord of this discord. Critics of the play, however much they may differ on questions of date and influence, are unanimous in their opinion that no such concord exists. All agree that Valerius's songs in the midst of the tragedy violate every principle of artistic decorum and good taste. Nevertheless, the fact remains that this was an extremely popular play during Heywood's lifetime. Written in 1607, it went through five quarto editions from 1608 to 1638, with the number of songs increasing from thirteen in the 1608, 1609, and 1614 editions, to seventeen in the 1630 edition, to twenty-two in the 1638 edition.[42] After gaining considerable popularity at the Red Bull, the play was performed in 1612 before Queen Anne and the young Prince, with a combined cast of the Queen's and the King's companies. In 1628 it was played at the Cockpit before the Duke of Buckingham. Even at the end of the 1630s the play was still popular enough to be among those transferred from Queen Henrietta's men to Beeston's boys.[43] In short, it was extremely popular for at least three decades, with bourgeois and aristocratic audiences alike. Moreover, since the number of songs grew with the play's popularity, we are obliged to acknowledge that what the modern critic most objects to in the play was one source of its appeal for the seventeenth century.

The odd intrusion of the character of Valerius and his too many merry songs is only one aspect of the play that has puzzled critics. Professor Alan Holaday calls attention to what he sees as an inordinate number of rhymed lines and "the curious violence of the dialogue." He accounts for these characteristics, along with the many songs, by supposing that Heywood wrote *The Rape* not in 1606 or 1607, as Clark argues, but in 1594, shortly after Shakespeare's poem appeared. According to Holaday, Heywood then revised the play by expanding the character of Valerius with his songs to suit the particular talents of his actor friend, Robert Browne. The excessive number of rhymes and the inflated language of the play thus reflect its early date, whereas the role of Valerius indicates the 1606–07 revision.[44] Holaday's hypothesis is not convincing for a number of reasons. Ascribing dates on the basis of an evolutionary theory of style is hazardous in the case of any dramatist, but particularly Heywood. We need only recall that 1 *The Fair Maid of the West*, a play manifesting what is perhaps his best style, was probably written as early as 1600. And, as Clark points out, Heywood was quite capable of that "curious violence of dialogue" long after 1606.[45]

When all the details pertinent to the question of the date of composition are explored, we confront the fact that the antic disposition of the revengers is an integral part of the revenge pattern of the play. The role Brutus plays as the harmless half-wit is, in fact, alluded to by Heywood's source, Livy. If we assume that the play was conceived from the beginning with Brutus and Valerius engaging to some degree in their antic dispositions and thus with some songs for Valerius, then it seems more probable that the date of composition is 1606–07 than 1594. At this later date Heywood had precedents for his experiment in tragedy mixed with song in such works as John Marston's *Antonio's Revenge* and *The Malcontent*, both written for the private theater. If the Queen's company of the Red Bull had an actor with considerable musical talent, it is likely that Heywood attempted to capitalize on the appeal of this mixture of tragic and lyric. Success in such an endeavor would have broadened his audience to include the more refined patrons of the private theaters and the Globe. The appeal of the "matter" of Lucrece with the intelligentsia had already been established by Shakespeare's poem, which was reprinted in 1607. Thus, in his subject matter and stylistic innovation the experienced playwright in 1606–07 made his bid. It is perhaps this aspiration toward a more refined audience that drew the satirical attack of the aristocratic Francis Beaumont in 1607–08—precisely when the popularity of Heywood's play was at its peak. *The Knight of the Burning Pestle* is perhaps Beaumont's effort to put Heywood in his professional place as a writer for the unrefined audiences or, more specifically, as the writer of the very primitive *Four Prentices of London*.[46]

The Rape of Lucrece is for Heywood an experiment on yet another level; it is his first attempt, as far as we know, at revenge tragedy. The conflation of the conventional *de casibus* and revenge patterns is Heywood's chief concern in the play, a concern that becomes apparent in the following summary of the play's action. Inspired by the ruthless ambition of his wife, Tullia, Tarquin Superbus asserts his genealogical claim to the throne of Rome, kills his father-in-law, the virtuous King Servius, and takes the crown. Manifesting her monstrous pride and impiety, Tullia treads on the body of the old king and then drives her chariot over it. Together Tullia and Tarquin establish a reign of terror, drawing their strength not from their Roman peers but from foreign allies. All who resist are executed or banished. The Roman peers who survive this rape of justice divert the wrath of the tyrant by acquiescing to his power and placing their faith in divine justice as it operates through the passage of time. In so doing, they assume various antic dispositions. Brutus conceals his indignation behind the role of the half-witted fool, Valerius becomes the merry balladeer, Collatine and Lucretius retire into their domestic worlds. Horatius Cocles and Mutius Scevola appear to be the disinterested professional soldiers who support the military exploits of the Tarquins.

This strategy of waiting upon divine justice culminates in two significant events: Brutus's comprehension of the oracle and Sextus's rape of Lucrece. Brutus is taken along for amusement when Tarquin's sons Aruns and Sextus consult the oracle to learn of the fate of the Tarquin dynasty. When the oracle states that power shall reside ultimately with the Tarquin who first kisses his mother, Brutus (Tarquin's nephew) falls to kiss mother earth while Aruns and Sextus, failing to interpret the riddle, rush to Tullia in an attempt to gain the first kiss. When Aruns receives the kiss, Sextus leaves the court in anger to join the enemy forces. Later, Sextus regains Tarquin's confidence by betraying Tarquin's enemies, the Gabines. As part of their disguise as carefree, indifferent courtiers, Brutus and his faction share the tent and the wine of Sextus during the siege of Ardea. Late one evening when conversation turns to the virtues of women, each husband defends his wife against the antifeminist sentiments of Sextus Tarquinius. Confident of the perfection of his Lucrece, Collatine proposes that they ride immediately to Rome and, entering unannounced, discover which wife is most virtuously employed. When the other wives are found at a feast and Lucrece is found supervising the work of her servants, Collatine easily wins the wager. Halfway back to camp that evening, Sextus Tarquinius suddenly claims to have urgent business in Rome. When he offers to deliver a message to Lucrece, her husband fondly gives Tarquin a ring as a token of his love. The ring assures Lucrece of her husband's trust in Tarquin and thus gains for him Lucrece's hospitality, even though it is very late at night.

The cruel rape accomplished, Sextus returns to camp and Lucrece sends for her father, husband, and friends. Eliciting a promise of revenge, she tells her story and stabs herself. Collatine and Lucretius carry Lucrece's body to the Forum where the entire city rises in anger against the Tarquins. Tullia and Tarquin are forced to take refuge with their Tuscan ally, Porsenna, and with his help attempt to regain the city. In the final battle, Tarquin is wounded, Tullia refuses to leave him, and both are killed. When Sextus appears to defend his father, he is surrounded and outnumbered, but he succeeds in challenging Brutus to a duel in the grand Homeric style. Both men are killed in the duel, and Collatine is named Consul of Rome.

The rise of the Tarquins and their downfall through the revenge of Brutus and his faction are clearly defined as part of a providential pattern of justice. At the outset, the revengers submit to the rise of Tarquin: "Since Fortune lifts thee, we submit to Fate" (325). But their trust is placed in a divine justice that will not allow the gross violation of moral law to go unpunished (361–87). Although Brutus complains of the slowness of this justice, he recalls that "Jove often delayes his vengeance, / That when it haps t'may proove more terrible" (453–54). His right reading of the oracle is but one form of divine reassurance. He takes hope also in the knowledge that time is the agency of providence:

> Dispaire not *Brutus* then, but let thy countrey
> And thee take this last comfort after all,
> Pride when thy fruit is ripe t'must rot, and fall.
> (455–57)

The embodiment of Tarquin and Tullia's pride is the fruit of their union, Sextus Tarquinius. Although Tullia and Tarquin gain the throne by the unnatural crime of patricide, their strength resides ironically in their offspring. Tullia acknowledges:

> We are secure, and yet our greatest strength
> Is in our children, how dare treason looke
> Vs in the face, having issue? barren Princes
> Breed danger in their singularitie,
> Having none to succeed, their claime dies in them.
> But when in topping on three Tarquins more
> Like Hidraes heads grow to revenge his death;
> It terrifies blacke treason.
> (834–38)[47]

The comparison here of the fruit of her womb to the monster Hydra recalls the imagery through which her lust for power is defined in the opening scene of the play. In her second extended speech she tells Tarquin,

> To be a queen I long, long and am sicke
> With ardency my hot appetite's a fire,
> Till my swolne ferver be delivered
> Of that great title Queene . . .
> (85–88)

Collatine uses the same image of pregnancy in defining Tullia's ambition: "The wife of Tarquin would be a Queen, nay on my life she is with childe till she be so" (158–59). The ultimate expression of poetic and divine justice is evident in the ardency and hot appetite of Sextus that compels him even against his will to commit the rape that will bring death to his parents. Heywood, in contrast to Shakespeare, diminishes the will of Sextus to underscore the providential pattern of retribution. Sextus goes to perform the fatal deed by acknowledging: "Oh fate! thou hast usurpt such power o're man, / That where thou pleadst thy will no mortal can" (1936–37). The rape is a sacrilege committed upon the "divin'st Lucrece," but it is also a crime against his kinsman Collatine. The breach of the familial bond by Tullia and Tarquin in their murder of King Servius is concluded by the revenge of Brutus, nephew to Tarquin, and by the death of this revenger who, in the noblest of causes, sheds the blood of his cousin, Sextus Tarquinius.

To achieve this neat pattern of poetic justice, Heywood was obliged to deviate from his source in his dramatization of the deaths of Tullia, Tarquin, Sextus, and Brutus. In Livy's account Tullia is simply driven from the city for having broken the sacred ties of blood. Sextus seeks refuge with the Gabines, who assassinate him, while Tarquin Superbus goes into exile with the two remaining sons. Lucius Junius Brutus and Lucius Tarquinius Collatinus are elected Consuls of Rome. Later Collatine is forced to surrender his position as consul simply because he bears the hated name of Tarquin. On the other hand, where Livy's narrative fits the *de casibus*-revenge patterns, with their strict poetic justice, Heywood adheres closely to the source. Such is the case, for example, in his delineation of the characters of Tullia and Lucrece.

The modern reader, looking at Heywood's depiction of Tullia's ambition to be queen and her goading of her husband to take the crown by killing the good old king, inevitably assumes the influence of Shakespeare's Lady Macbeth. In fact, there is little in Heywood's portrait that does not have its origin in Livy's graphic description of Tullia.

The character of Tullia is only slightly less developed than that of Lucrece, and each stands as a foil to the other. As Lucretius witnesses the cruelty of Tullia to her father, he emphasizes the contrasting natures of the two women: "I have a Daughter, but I hope of mettle, / Subject to better temperature" (293–94). In general, Heywood subordinates his treatment of Lucrece and her suffering to the larger political issues of the *de casibus*-revenge drama. His dramatic design does not call for a psychologically complex tragic heroine, but for absolute innocence of a sacrificial victim. What concerns Heywood is the way in which the rape serves as the culminating symbol of the violations of family and state. He faced a difficult task in defining with economy the chastity and familial loyalty that Lucrece must represent. Providing a standard of chastity, she disciplines her servants for their promiscuous behavior. While her husband is away, she maintains an austere household by guarding against all shows of luxury through a rigorous domestic industry. For the modern reader, the character Heywood thus creates manifests a certain self-righteous primness rather than the heroic dignity normally associated with Lucrece.

Heywood does considerably better in defining Lucrece's suffering and the relationship between victim and revengers. Left alone the morning after the rape, Lucrece poignantly questions the divine scheme that allows the sacrifice of innocents. She cannot understand why she, of all women, should be the victim of Tarquinius's lust (2356–69). Her indignation and bewilderment over the apparent injustice of her fate is directed also at Collatine, who sent the ring that assured Sextus's welcome: "This Ring, oh *Collatine*! this Ring you sent / Is cause of all my woe, your discontent" (2446–47). The detail of the fatal ring reminds the audience that it was Collatine who originally proposed the wager and who is thus responsible for bringing the wolf into the sheepfold. Painful as Lucrece's narrative is, it has an immediate cathartic effect upon her onstage audience; Brutus and his allies are restored to their true identities. As they swear revenge, Brutus instructs them:

> all humorous toyes set off.
> Of madding, singing, smiling, and what else,
> Receive your native valours, be your selves,
> And joyne with *Brutus* in the just revenge
> Of this chaste ravisht Lady, sweare.
>
> (2464–68)

Lucrece's rape is the fateful event that ensures the fall of the Tarquins and the liberation of Rome. The emergence of the nobles from their antic dispositions to affirm their native valor consoles and transforms in turn the tearful Lucrece. She puts aside her grief, as they put aside their disguises:

> Then with your humours heere my grief ends too,
> My staine I thus wipe off, call in my sighes,
> And in the hope of this revenge, forbeare
> Even to my death to fall one passionate teare.
>
> (2480–84)

She stabs herself not out of a sense of irrevocable shame, but in order, as she explains to the revengers, "that you may henceforth know / We are the same in heart we seem in show" (2485–86). The tragic irony of the play is Lucrece's perception that the dissimulation essential to the survival of her loved ones under Tarquin's reign now necessitates for her the ultimate gesture of verification—suicide. She is not so much afraid of becoming a precedent for incontinence as she is eager to become a positive example: "Let all the world learne of a Roman dame / To prise her life lesse than her honor'd fame" (2489–90).

By establishing a causal connection between Lucrece's suicide and her need to prove "We are the same in heart we seem in show," Heywood emphasizes the importance of the revengers' "show." As the play's action prior to the rape manifests the disguise of these revengers, so the action after the rape is a show of their natural valor. The theatricality of their respective shows is comparable to that of Lucrece in her suicide. Collatine and Lucretius carry the body of Lucrece to the Forum where their pitiful show moves the city to revolt. Horatius stages his performance of heroic valor at the bridge across the Tiber. Here Romans and Tuscans alike marvel especially at the denouement of his show as he leaps fully armed into the river. The final show of valor is performed by Sextus and Brutus as they recast the "monomachie" (2924) of Hector and Achilles. Like Lucrece, Brutus goes to his death confident that his show will be remembered: "that the times / Succeeding may of *Brutus* thus much tell, / By him Pride, Lust, and all the *Tarquins* fell" (2940–42).

This conscious self-fashioning to achieve revenge is relevant to the most difficult problem of the play, the songs of Valerius. With the rise of Tarquin, all instruments of order, justice, and social harmony are cast aside. As a tyrant who governs by fear, Tarquin cuts himself off from the council of his peers. This abolition of the established moral and political order is expressed through the metaphor of music. Lucretius observes, "we are but mutes / and fellows of no parts, violes unstrung, / Our notes too harsh to strike in Princes eares" (500–502). As one of these unstrung viols, Valerius is "transhaped to a meere Ballater" (541). The harmony he fashions serves to heighten the discord of his world. Singing for sorrow, he moves his onstage audience: Horatius states, "This musicke mads me, I all mirth despise," and Lucretius concurs, "To heare him sing drawes rivers from mine eyes" (599–600). Surely the response of the onstage audience indicates the response expected from the theater audience. Valerius's marking time through song is also a way to "laugh at time; till it will change our fate" (627) and is thus a symbol of patience and trust in the providence that governs fate.

The merry tune, in contrast to the song of sorrow, serves as an ironic contrast or counterpoint to the tragic political context in which it occurs. Perhaps because of the problems inherent in trying to define Lucrece's chastity, Heywood prefaces her first appearance (1078) with two bawdy songs that serve as foils to her chastity. The antifeminist bias of Sextus culminates in a vision of woman's sexual willingness that is but a darkened version of the bawdy catch. Valerius's disguise as the balladeer singing obscene songs is thus a dramatically efficient commentary upon a world of appetite and perversion.

Clearly, the most beautiful and most effective song in the play is the one immediately following the rape scene, "Packe cloudes away, and welcome day" (2119). The juxtaposition of Lucrece's tragic night and following morning with this joyous aubade achieves a fine pathos and a poignant irony. The disparity between Lucrece's reality and the idealized world of the song underscore the tragic alteration in the private life of the heroine. But with the news of her suffering will come the liberation of bondaged Rome. Thus the song signals the turning point for the restoration of harmony and order in Rome, the dawning of a politically bright day.

"The fourth new Song entitled In the praise of *Lucrece*" (2153) is also dramatically effective in its juxtaposition with Collatine's inexplicable sadness. The song's metaphor, which delineates Lucrece as an architectural masterpiece, reinforces the association of her with Rome itself, and her rape with the violation of temple, home, and city.

In defense of Heywood's experimental union of lyric and tragedy, we must conclude that the songs are often extremely effective as they reinforce or provide contrast to a dramatic situation. The degree of failure in the experiment lies not in the idea but in the carelessness of its execution. There are simply too many songs, too many that are irrelevant, and at least one ("Did he take faire *Lucrece* by the toe man?") that is an astonishing example of crudeness and bad taste. Perhaps Heywood allowed the popular demand for these songs to overrule his own aesthetic judgment. Perhaps, then, he had his own *Rape of Lucrece* in mind when his playwright-persona of *Love's Mistress* explains that "Art some-times must give way to Ignorance" (v.119).

If we can get beyond the issue of the songs—and there is virtue in "if "—we realize that this play is a powerful dramatization of familial relationships, of the family as a microcosm, of revenge and justice, of private and public virtues and vices, and finally of appearance, reality, and self-fashioning. In short, much of what we take to be at the very heart of Renaissance drama can be found in this play. Furthermore, as a true history of private and public lives, *The Rape of Lucrece* looks back to Heywood's own earlier history plays. As a study in familial relations and revenge, it prepares us for 1 and 2 *The Iron Age*. As an experiment in mixed form and in the union of song and play, it anticipates Heywood's masque-play, *Love's Mistress*.

Chapter Five
The Tragicomedies

The term tragicomedy was used loosely in the sixteenth and seventeenth centuries, as it is often used now, simply to designate the coupling of the tragic and the comic in a single play. With Guarini's *Il Pastor Fido* (published in 1589) and with John Fletcher's *The Faithful Shepherdess* (published in 1609 or 1610), tragicomedy acquires a more precise definition for designating a dramatic kind distinct from tragedy and comedy and not simply an amorphous mixture of the two.[1] Tragicomedy, as defined and exemplified by Fletcher (under the influence of Guarini) and by those who imitated Beaumont and Fletcher, has been conveniently labeled Fletcherian tragicomedy. According to Madelein Doran, such tragicomedy consists of

(1) a mixture of tragic and comic episodes, and of the feelings appropriate to these; (2) a mixture of social classes, or a violation of the distinguishing class lines of tragedy and comedy; (3) a combination of the serious action of tragedy with the happy ending of comedy.[2]

The third and most important of these characteristics, the averted catastrophe, applies to two different types of plays, both on occasion referred to as tragicomedy:

plays in the religious tradition having a serious theme of temptation to vice and ending with repentance and reformation of character; and . . . plays of love and peril in which tragedy is narrowly averted by some fortunate discovery.[3]

If we take the averted catastrophe in religious and romantic dramas as the chief delineating characteristic of tragicomedy, we confront the problem that most of Heywood's plays fall under this rubric and the generic term thus becomes relatively useless. Acknowledging, therefore, that "tragicomedy" might well apply to many Heywood plays, we have, with one noted exception, rather arbitrarily restricted the classification to those plays of the Caroline period written after Fletcherian tragicomedy had effected a shift in theatrical taste. The attitudes and values, if not the social rank, of the characters in these plays are, in general, courtly rather than domestic and thus reflect the playwright's

113

effort to appeal to a more genteel audience. All of the plays discussed in this chapter reveal significant concern with courtly codes of love, honor, and friendship.

The Royal King and the Loyal Subject

With little evidence to go on, most editors and scholars believe that *The Royal King and the Loyal Subject* was written around 1600.[4] Although it is not a domestic drama, it nevertheless constitutes a kind of trilogy with Heywood's earlier plays, *How a Man May Choose* and *Fortune by Land*. Together, the three plays present the loyal wife, the loyal son, and the loyal subject. They thus affirm the patristic authority of husband, father, and king so essential to the Renaissance concept of degree. Like the two domestic comedies, *The Royal King* demonstrates the virtues of patience and faith within a scheme of prolonged testing. The Lord Marshal's loyalty withstands the intrigues of jealous courtiers as well as the deliberate and rather ruthless ordeals orchestrated by his sovereign. At the same time, the contest of courtesy and the clever contrivances of king and noble subject establish in *The Royal King* a rarefied world of aristocracy quite distinct from the ordinary experience of the middle-class domestic plays. It is this quality that justifies our discussion of the play as a tragicomedy, despite its early date and its resemblance to the domestic plays.

The close similarity between *Fortune by Land* and *The Royal King* is evident not only in the main plot of king and patient subject, but also in the subplot of the soldier-noble Bonvile and his obsession with the ugly fact that money is more prized than virtue—that it will buy friendship and love. Philip Harding's painful discovery of the avarice that governs family and friends is similar to Bonvile's discovery of his "Summer-friend" and "silken Unkle" (Pearson 6:60–61). The subplot of *The Royal King* is Heywood's patching together of stock characters and situations. Bonvile is both the prodigal and the soldier newly returned from war who appears to be penniless and is therefore shunned by friends and relatives. His poverty, however, is merely an appearance to test the affection and the loyalty of those who should care for him. Only Lady Mary, his betrothed, loves him for his virtue and accepts his poverty without hesitation. After going to great lengths to show the world its hypocrisy and greed, this Diogenes figure finally puts aside his pretense of poverty and takes his place as a secondary courtier in the main plot.

The story of the royal king and loyal subject derives from a novella by Matteo Bandello, translated by William Painter in *The Palace of Plea-*

sure.[5] Bandello's tale about the complex relationship between the Persian King Artaxerxes and his steward Ariobarzanes begins with the question, "whether commendable deede, or curteous and gentle act done by the Gentleman or Courtier towardes his soueraine Lord, ought to be called Liberalitie and Curtesie, or rather Bond and Dutie" (176). The story demonstrates that when such commendable deeds are viewed as courtesy and liberality, the subject not only imitates his sovereign but also runs the risk of competing with him and undermining his sovereignty. To check this competition, Artaxerxes cautions Ariobarzanes, "Do you not know that it appertaineth vnto me in all myne affaires and deedes to be liberal, curtious, magnificent, and bounteous? Be not those the virtues that make the fame of a Prince to glister among his subiectes, as the Sunne beames doe vpon the circuit of the world?" (186). He then makes clear that courtesy and liberality are princely virtues: "They be the comly ensignes of a kynge" (186–87). Anyone who attempts to surpass his king in these virtues attempts "to vsurpe the Kinglye qualitie which belongeth only vnto him" (187). The deed performed as courtesy also creates an obligation that can endanger the king's freedom: "Shall I be tyed by your desertes, or bound by curteous deedes, or els be forced to rendre recompence?" Although Ariobarzanes defends himself against his king's charges by insisting that all his noble deeds were done out of a sense of duty and love for the king, the conflict between king and servant remains because the intent behind these deeds is subject to interpretation.

In his dramatic adaptation of this story Heywood changes the setting from Persia to medieval England, but keeps the identity of his English monarch deliberately vague. The loyal subject is the Lord Marshal (called simply Martial throughout), who has saved his sovereign's life in the recent crusade. The tension that Bandello describes as inherent in the relationship between king and courteous servant Heywood redefines as simply the malice of envious courtiers. What in the source is a delicate matter of intent and interpretation becomes in Heywood's play the villainy of characters Heywood was obliged to add. The play thus simplifies the issues and the personalities of the story in much the same way that Ariobarzanes, after his trial, simplifies the conflict by attributing it solely to the envy of his enemies. What in the Bandello story is a real problem articulated by the king is, in the play, reduced to a malicious lie spoken by Clinton to the king:

> Doth he not strive
> In all things to exceed your courtesie,

Of purpose to out-shine your Royale deeds,
And dazell your brightnesse, that himselfe may shine?
(15–16)

To what extent the king believes that the marshal's courtesy is a reflection of ambition rather than love is never made clear. Certainly the
king intends to test the patience and loyalty of his subject and does so
first by stripping the marshal of all honors, bestowing these on his enemies, and banishing him from the court. When the king demands the
fairer of the marshal's two daughters, the audience is asked to believe
somehow that her honor or life is in jeopardy and, at the same time,
that the king's intentions are honorable. At one moment the king im-
plies that the virtues of Isabella (the daughter sent to him) have overcome him and taken "the threatning edge / Of our intended hate"
(42). Hate apparently quickly replaces love when the pregnant queen
admits that she has a fairer sister whom the king has been denied.
When both sisters are given to the king and both are honored by him,
the king assures his queen, "I never meant thee lesse" (66). In short,
the reader is finally so confused by this character that he cannot tell
what is a genuinely angry response and what is merely a calculated test
of the marshal's patience and loyalty; or, for that matter, to what extent
the king is indeed deceived by the marshal's jealous enemies, Chester
and Clinton.

We must acknowledge that what Heywood did with the Bandello
story is disappointing in light of the dramatic potential that was there.
The struggle between courtesy and slander, the problem of perception
or interpretation that accompanies courtesy, the delicate balance essential to the relationship between sovereign and courtier—these are the
themes or problems inherent in the Bandello story, but quite beyond
the art of Thomas Heywood. The material here was rich enough to en-
tice Fletcher to try his hand at it in his tragicomedy, *The Loyal Subject*
(1618). Although Fletcher clarifies the characters, he too grossly over-
simplifies or avoids altogether the thematic potentials of the source.

The Captives; or, The Lost Recovered

Although the Office-Book of Sir Henry Herbert, Master of Revels,
indicates that "a new Play, called The Captive, or the Lost recovered:
Written by Hayward" was licensed for production in 1624, the play was
not discovered until 1885, when A. H. Bullen found it in manuscript
form in the British Museum.[6] A. C. Judson notes that in versification
and plot structure the play closely resembles *The English Traveller*.[7]

Both tragicomedies have a double plot in which a story by Plautus is coupled with one told in Heywood's own *Gunaikeion*. The main plot of *The Captives* is a fine adaptation of Plautus's *Rudens*; the subplot, told in *Gunaikeion* as the true story of "The Fair Ladie of Norwich" (Book V, 253–56), closely resembles its original source, Masuccio's first of fifty narratives published under the title, *Novellino*, a work that perhaps reached Heywood through a 1555 French translation.[8]

The following plot summary of the play will serve for a comparison with Heywood's sources and facilitate a discussion of the relationship between the play's two plots. As the main plot begins, a young merchant, Raphael, has discovered that two innocent young girls, Palestra and Scribonia, are being kept in a brothel by a villainous bawd, Mildew. Raphael declares to his skeptical friend Treadway his love for Palestra and his intention to free her. Mildew agrees to a price for Palestra and promises to deliver her to Raphael at the nearby monastery. He instead attempts to flee with the money and the girls but is shipwrecked by a storm in the harbor. In search of his beloved, Raphael enlists the help of an old English merchant, John Ashburne, whose daughter was stolen from him years before. Eventually the casket with Palestra's tokens of identity is fished out of the sea and Ashburne discovers that she is his long-lost daughter, Mirable. This reunion is crowned by the engagement of Raphael to Palestra-Mirable and of Treadway to Scribonia. In the midst of the happy denouement Thomas Ashburne, brother of John, arrives to bring the good news of John's reinstated fortune and to learn that Scribonia is his own lost daughter, Winefryde.

The monastery that provides sanctuary to the two virtuous girls is also the setting of the subplot. Here dwell two friars, John and Richard, whose enmity not even the wise abbot can resolve. The monastery is separated only by a wall from the residence of its benefactors, the Lord and Lady of Averne. Friar John's hatred for Richard is matched by his lust for the Lady Averne, and he deludes himself into thinking that she will accept his courtship. Enraged by this hypocrisy and presumption, Averne murders Friar John and places the corpse within the monastery walls where Friar Richard will be the prime suspect. Late at night Richard sees the body of his enemy propped in what he conceives to be a contemptuous attitude, strikes the corpse, and then concludes that he has murdered Friar John. Knowing of John's attempt to seduce the Lady Averne, Richard attempts to incriminate the jealous husband by placing the corpse on Averne's porch. Horrified to discover that the corpse has returned, Averne attempts once more to get rid of it by dressing it in full armor, strapping it onto an old stallion, and turning this macabre knight errant out of the gate. At this moment, Richard rides by on a mare in season and is pursued by the stallion and its deadly knight. As the stallion attempts to mount the mare, Richard, in terror, confesses to the entire village the murder he did not in fact commit. The guilt-ridden friar is saved from the gallows by an even more guilt-ridden lord, who also confesses the murder. Lord Averne is then saved by a pardon from the king obtained by his provident and loving wife.

Although the setting of both plots is the Renaissance port of Marseille and its surroundings, the characters of the Plautine plot are decidedly English and thus provide the playwright with the opportunity once more of a patriotic tribute and an enrichment upon his source in the treatment of chattel bondage. Carolyn Prager argues that Heywood's modification of the Plautine story shows his "conscious artistic effort to lift the matter of the Roman play into the context of recent history."[9] In choosing Marseille as his setting, Heywood was aware that chattel slavery was a reality of contemporary life, sanctioned by the laws of Christian nations. The Christian Englishmen of his play clearly perceive that such slavery is antithetical to Christianity and to the constitutional liberty of all free-born Englishmen (III.ii.93–97). Although Heywood "argues not the inalienable right to freedom of mankind under natural law but the constitutional liberty of free-born Englishmen heralded by the Tudor propagandists,"[10] he nevertheless provides significant moral commentary on a social institution that was antithetical to his convictions about the dignity of man.

It is, moreover, the dignity of women in particular that is Heywood's chief concern in this play written most likely immediately after his full history and defense of women, *Gunaikeion*. The opening dialogue of *The Captives* is a debate on the controversial subject of the nature of women and an affirmation, through Raphael, of their basic goodness. Heywood is once again challenging the antifeminist assumption that the entire sex deserves condemnation because of the misconduct of a few bad women:

> Say perhapps
> Some frend of yours miscarried in his choyse;
> Will you condeme all women for that one?
> Bycause wee reade one Lais was vnchast,
> Are all Corinthian ladyes cortesans?
>   (I.i.15–19)

Schooled by Raphael's charity and reverence for women, Treadway, in the final scene, decides to save Scribonia from Mildew and to take her as his wife. The doctrine of charity taught here (as it is throughout the Heywood canon) is not so readily embraced by other characters in the play. Palestra asks, "Oh, charity, where art thou fledd, / And nowe how long hast thou been dead?" The echoing voice of Friar John coming from within the monastery responds to the girls' song requesting charity: "Yet even there, there you scarce, scarce can find her" (II.i.106). Friar John in his hour of need will also be denied charity by the Lord Averne. The absence of charity causes Mrs. Ashburne to drive her own long-lost daughter from her doors and thus to undermine the charitable efforts of her husband.

Besides the theme of charity, *The Captives*, like *The English Traveller*, illustrates Heywood's treatment of the disparity between appearance and reality. Purest chastity is found, paradoxically, within the walls of "a house of prostitution." Fierce enmity and lust, on the other hand, are found within the walls of the monastery. Friar John, in his lust for Lady Averne and in his hatred for Friar Richard, fails to uphold the values of his religious order; his social-religious identity belies his spiritual reality. In the ruthless and anti-chivalric murder of a helpless cleric Lord Averne violates his noble station in life and his honored reputation as an heroic knight. The corpse within the rusty armor of a knight, tied upon the back of an old stallion, is an appropriate metaphor for the reality to which the lord's ignominious crime has reduced him. The disparity between being and seeming results here as elsewhere in faulty perception. The Lord Averne seems reasonable and charitable as he promises his wife not to harm the deluded friar. The violent reality behind this deceptive, gentle appearance results in his own inability to perceive accurately. He feels haunted by the corpse that will not remain where he places it. Richard's concealed hatred for Friar John likewise results in the false perception that he has killed his old enemy and in the equally false perception that forces him to confess the crime he has committed only in his heart.

The inadequacy of human charity and perception necessitates a benevolent providence to ensure a happy resolution of events. Mildew is prevented from escaping with the girls only by a providential storm and shipwreck. Ashburne's charity is rewarded by the miraculous retrieval of the casket containing the evidence that restores to him his lost child. The least probable of these fortuitous events is the arrival of Thomas Ashburne with news of the miraculous recovery of his brother's fortune and the restoration of yet another lost daughter to her father. As in *Fortune by Land and by Sea*, all probability gives way to a demonstration that virtuous men and women are rewarded in this world by a benevolent providence. The sequence of improbable events in which fathers are separated from and then miraculously reunited with their daughters in strange lands after storm and shipwreck and ominous threats to life and chastity — all within the ostensible scheme of divine providence — defines the play as a romance and calls to mind the late plays of Shakespeare, especially *Pericles*.

In assessing the literary worth of *The Captives* we must admit that it does not exhibit the structurally unifying metaphors and analogies found in *The English Traveller*. Despite its inadequacies, however, the play does reveal Heywood's ability to entertain and amuse. The plots are perfectly paced as the playwright shifts at precisely the right point from one to the other.[11] The macabre events involving the corpse of Friar John constitute one of the finest examples of gallows humor in all of Renaissance drama and provide a superb satirical commentary upon the hollow concept of honor that necessitates blood revenge. In the tragicomedies that follow *The Captives* Heywood develops this satirical skill as his concern turns away from charity and toward a more courtly and fashionable kind of love.

The English Traveller

Published in 1633 as a play "Publicly acted at the Cockpit in Drury Lane: By Her Majesty's Servants," *The English Traveller* was written most likely in 1627, shortly after *The Captives*.[12] Like *The Captives*, the play presents one plot based upon Plautus (*Mostellaria*) and another based upon a tale in Heywood's *Gunaikeion*.[13] The 1633 edition is dedicated to Sir Henry Appleton, a nobleman close to Heywood's family. Heywood's high opinion of *The English Traveller* is apparent in his dedication, where he twice refers to the play as "Poem" and draws an analogy between Appleton's patronage and that by "many other mighty Princes . . . even by Augustus Caesar himselfe" (Pearson IV, 3). The famous epistle "To the Reader," in which Heywood refers to the 220 plays in which he has had "either an entire hand, or at the least a main finger," also reveals considerable pride in "this Tragi-Comedy." The Prologue likewise announces "A strange play," one of originality in which the playwright forsakes the conventions of drum, trumpet, dumb show, combat, marriage, song, dance, and masque so frequently used "to bumbaste out a Play." Here, instead, the playwright "tries if once bare Lines will beare it."

The prefatory matter thus invites us to consider this play as a conspicuous departure from Heywood's earlier dramatic works, yet many readers have dismissed it as a facile repetition of and attempt to capitalize on the popularity of *A Woman Killed with Kindness*. Henry Hitch Adams, for example, insists that

The English Traveller is a far weaker play than *A Woman Killed with Kindness*. Heywood has begun to repeat himself. The play fails to hang together; the subplot vies for attention with the main story. In general, the characters are lightly sketched, and the dialogue lacks color and brilliancy. [14]

To the extent that *The English Traveller* is a departure from Heywood's earlier work, it is, according to Clark,

his domestic variety of Fletcherian tragicomedy. . . . Young Geraldine is the Fletcherian prig, sickled o'er with the unhealthy complexion of the age of decadence. . . . on the Fletcherian stage the situations are themselves unreal; something more piquant was required and the ethical standards were strained, perverted, loosened, stretched to suit. Many of the situations in *The English Traveller* are normal and presented with considerable skill. It is the core of the play that is rotten; it is not the husband of the woman who is wronged, not even the lover of a widow, but the lover of another's wife; and this hero has exchanged with the woman oaths of constancy to be effective after her aged husband's death. [15]

To make matters more unpleasant and absurd for Clark, Geraldine has free access to Mrs. Wincott's bedroom all hours of the night, and it is here that their sacred vows of love and fidelity are exchanged. To note, as Grivelet does, that Heywood is drawing on the conventions of courtly love in which the knight is granted the "noble courtesy" of attending his lady in her chamber, [16] does not answer Clark's objections to this morally ambivalent situation. It is indeed difficult to reconcile the definition of Geraldine as the epitome of honor and virtue with his clandestine love for a married woman. How we are supposed to perceive this central character is one of the major questions of the play.

Let us begin, however, with Adams's argument that *The English Traveller* is a repetition of *A Woman Killed* and that the main and subplots fail to hang together. A summary of the action will indicate the similarities between the two plays and show the relations between main plot and subplot.

As the main plot begins, young Geraldine, returned from his grand tour, is taken in as a son and constant companion of old Wincott and Mrs. Wincott. Mrs. Wincott and Geraldine were childhood friends whose intended marriage was prevented by Geraldine's travels and by her arranged marriage to Wincott. Their childhood affection rekindled, Geraldine and Mrs. Wincott pledge to marry as soon as old Wincott dies. In the interim they will live in perfect honor as brother and sister. To the Wincott household Geraldine has brought his best friend Dalavill, who appears to court Mrs. Wincott's sister, Prudentilla. In

fact, Dalavill prefers Mrs. Wincott and thus tells old Geraldine that his
son's reputation is compromised by an apparent affair with Mrs. Wincott. Old Geraldine confronts his son and forces him to avoid the Wincott household. Hurt by the sudden and unexplained absence of
Geraldine, Wincott sends for him, and Geraldine comes secretly, late
at night, to make his explanations to his surrogate father. Before leaving the house, Geraldine decides to pay an unexpected visit to his beloved's bedchamber, where he has spent many pleasant (and perfectly
chaste) hours. Outside her door he overhears her voice and that of his
best friend and realizes that they have become lovers. Totally disillu-
sioned, Geraldine resolves to leave England forever, but is coerced into
a farewell feast given by Wincott. At the feast Mrs. Wincott's hypocrisy
becomes more than Geraldine can bear, and he privately denounces
her. She is overcome with shame, writes a confession to her husband,
and then conveniently dies. Freed of his vow to this corrupt woman,
Geraldine abandons his plan to travel and becomes, instead, Wincott's
heir.

Next door to the Wincott house is the Lionell house, the setting for
the subplot. While old Lionell is at sea making his fortune, young
Lionell and the family servant Reignald have turned the house into a
brothel. Through drunken feasts and riot they have not only spent
their generous allowance, but also gone into debt and destroyed most
of Lionell's valuables. After a particularly destructive evening of debauchery—during which young Lionell and his friends in a drunken
fantasy conceive of the house as a storm-tossed ship and throw all the
furniture "overboard"—the old father returns unexpectedly. To keep
his old master out of the house, Reignald concocts a story that the
house is possessed by the ghost of a man murdered by the previous
owner, whom old Lionell then attempts to take to court. When the
moneylender arrives to collect on young Lionell's debt, Reignald persuades old Lionell to pay the debt by claiming that the money was
borrowed to purchase neighbor Ricott's house. The embarrassing misunderstanding between Ricott and old Lionell over this house eventually leads to old Lionell's realization that he has been duped. Despite
great expense and shame, old Lionell forgives his suddenly repentant
son and even the tricky servant, and agrees to attend the farewell feast
given by Wincott for Geraldine.

As this summary indicates, the main plot repeats the situation of the
main plot of *A Woman Killed*: again the elements are the betrayal by a
woman and a best friend, the subsequent discovery of betrayal, the
flight of the friend, and the repentance and death of the woman.
The primary victim of this betrayal, however, is not the husband but

the idealistic young lover, Geraldine. Mrs. Wincott's sin is compounded by her betrayal of both a present and a future husband. The playwright makes no effort to depict this betrayal in psychologically realistic terms. Mrs. Wincott's death is a mere convenience for freeing Geraldine and old Wincott from their commitments to an unworthy woman and elicits no more sympathy from them than it does from us. Because the death of one of the main characters is the cause of relief rather than suffering and sorrow, the play is in no sense tragic.[17] We remain emotionally detached from all of the characters, even from Geraldine, because the playwright's attitude toward his courtly love for Mrs. Wincott is consistently, if gently, satirical. Geraldine's discovery of Mrs. Wincott's true nature is but the final state in the education of a young gentleman who has recently completed his "travels" and must now take his place in the world. The similarity of plot between *A Woman Killed* and *The English Traveller* is finally of little significance because the themes, characterizations, and overall tones of the two plays are radically different. This difference becomes apparent as we understand the relationship between the main plot and the subplot of *The English Traveller*.

Norman Rabkin has shown that both plots depict the confusion and final discovery of appearance and reality.[18] Geraldine announces this popular theme:

> I should be loath
> Professe in outward shew to be one Man,
> And proove my selfe another.
>
> (12)

Dalavill and Mrs. Wincott prove to be precisely such dissemblers, and their counterpart in the subplot is the fox-like Reignald. All three characters are defined by "smooth Dissembling meet with Impudence" (37). In each plot an English traveler returns to England to become the victim of domestic intrigue and deception. In each plot the action consists first of preserving the deception, then of unmasking the dissemblers, and finally of reordering the household.

The theme of deception is also conveyed through the manipulation of dramatic conventions to frustrate the audience's expectations.[19] Our surprise at the truth of a situation is thus analogous to that of the various characters, and our understanding of motivation is deliberately curtailed. First we are led to believe that the main plot will be a farcical version of old January and young May. With the tribute to the Wincott marriage and to Mrs. Wincott's virtue, and with the scene in which

Geraldine and Mrs. Wincott declare their chaste love and respect for old Wincott, we are suddenly forced to see these characters in an idealized context. As soon as we accept the virtue of Mrs. Wincott, we discover her betrayal not only of her husband but also of Geraldine. Reignald, in the subplot, is equally protean as he appears initially to be totally self-serving but is, in fact, loyal to the interests of his young master and is finally reconciled even to old Lionell.

The two plots are also obviously related through the father-son relationship that is paramount in each. Although Lionell remains at home while his old father seeks a fortune in foreign lands, Lionell is the archetypal spendthrift prodigal. The ultimate threat to his relationship with his father is his match with the prostitute, Blanda. Having compared himself to a stately building constructed by his loving father (18), Lionell admits that Blanda is the "Haile, Shower, Tempest, Storme, and Gust" (19) that threaten destruction. Despite this acknowledgment, Lionell attempts to elevate his relationship with her through a constancy more appropriate to marriage. But he finds himself incapable even of this misplaced constancy (23). Reconciliation with his father is later contingent upon his renunciation of Blanda. Geraldine, in contrast to Lionell, is the obedient, dutiful son. The relationship between father and son is again, however, threatened by an untenable commitment—here to Mrs. Wincott. Through his submission to the commandment of his father not to visit the Wincott home, Geraldine eventually discovers the truth that Mrs. Wincott is closer to Blanda than anyone thought. Disillusionment and shame now threaten to separate Geraldine forever from his father and fatherland until the death of Mrs. Wincott allows the reunion with both natural and adoptive fathers.

The overriding theme of both plots, which incorporates problems of appearance and reality with those of sexual and filial relationships, is the education and maturation of the young man: *The English Traveller* is a play on coming of age. The proper fashioning of the young man in both plots is defined through the metaphor of a house or vessel that will survive the storms and the seas of life.

Still, it must be confessed that the two plots, for all their thematic and imagistic echoing, are not integrated in the manner characteristic of Heywood's other double plots. Freda Townsend speculates that the separation of the two plots facilitates the relief of the "heavy atmosphere" of the main plot by farcical subplot.[20] But as we look more closely at the analogies between the two plots, it is clear that the subplot does not simply relieve but provides satirical commentary upon the action and the characters of the main plot. Through the analogies the serious main plot also forces us to see the action of the subplot as something more substantial than mere farce. The distinct separation of the two plots, in fact, enables the characters of the main plot to view those of the subplot as though they were an audience watching a play. As the characters of the Wincott household witness and narrate the events next door, they are amused and entertained by the farce. But they also provide moral commentary upon it (27–28).

If it is true that the subplot offers a satirical perspective upon the main plot, then we should expect to find within the main plot itself a degree of irony and ambivalence, and such is, indeed, the case. The opening lines of the play, which initiate the main plot, announce the theme of the education of youth: notion and theory are contrasted to practice and experience. Geraldine, the perfect gentleman, having just completed the final stage of his formal education by extensive travels, is credited with experience, whereas his friend, Dalavill, claims only theory and notion. Geraldine's acknowledgment of this disparity between being and seeming appears to confirm old Wincott's conviction that Geraldine is "much older than I in his experience" (11). Where experience is concerned, however, Geraldine and Dalavill will both ironically "Professe in outward shew to be one Man, / And prooue another" (12). We learn shortly that Geraldine is actually governed by a theory—the platonic or courtly "school of love"—as he foolishly pledges himself to another man's wife. Dalavill, on the other hand, is all experienced practice as he devises the scheme to exclude Geraldine and achieve Mrs. Wincott's bed.

There is, moreover, an important disparity between Geraldine's idealized notion of his love for Mrs. Wincott and our at best ambivalent response to it. Before we learn of Geraldine's love for her, we learn of old Wincott's love for Geraldine. We are reminded constantly that Wincott thinks of Geraldine not simply as a friend but as a son. In the private conversation designed to make explicit the innocence of Geraldine and Mrs. Wincott (30–33) the two young people acknowledge a chaste sexual love and the intention to marry as soon as old Wincott dies. The love scene concludes with Mrs. Wincott's statement, "Y'are now my Brother, / But then, my second Husband" (33). By this point the relationship has assumed a certain incestuous flavor; it is a supreme example of a young man's misplaced passion. Our reservations about the relationship are reinforced by the fact that this love scene follows immediately upon the salacious conversation between Prudentilla and Dalavill on the delights of the marriage bed (30). The innocence of the pseudosiblings is called into question, in short, by the naive inclination to invite temptation, to play with fire. Mrs. Wincott tells Geraldine,

Mid-night hath beene as Mid-day, and my Bed chamber,
As free to you, as your owne Fathers house
And you as welcome too't.

(30)

Although Geraldine sees his access to his lady's chamber as her "Noble Courtesie" (30) and thus as a manifestation of their ideal courtly love, we see, in the play's climax, the full significance of these midnight visitations. Violating his promise to his father, Geraldine sneaks into the Wincott household and falls back upon an old habit:

The way vnto her chamber frequently
Trodden by me at mid-night, and all houres:
How ioyfull to her would a meeting be,
So strange and vnexpectd; Shadowed too
Beneath the vaile of night; I am resolu'd
To give her visitation, in that place
Where we haue past deepe vowes, her bed-chamber:
My fiery loue this darknesse makes seeme bright,
And this the path that leades to my delight.

(69)

The language of the speech undercuts Geraldine's presumptions of innocence, and it is perfectly appropriate that this anticipated delight should turn out to be his own dark surrogate, Dalavill.

Geraldine's response to the treachery of Mrs. Wincott and Dalavill is a testament to the extent to which his idealized notions of love and self have deluded him. He is saved from an act of bloody revenge only by the fact that he has forgotten his sword. In one breath he declares, "Although I pardon, / Heauen will find time to punish," only to reveal how incapable of pardon he is:

Damne on, reuenge too great; And to suppresse
Your Soules yet lower, without hope to rise,
Heape Offa vpon Pelion . . .

(70)

His later denunciation of Mrs. Wincott is inspired as much by his wounded pride as it is by any moral indignation, and his primary concern is not with her repentance but with his own freedom, to be obtained by the death that he urges upon her. His responsibility for a relationship that was at best questionable escapes him entirely. Old Geraldine makes the point his son fails to perceive:

> shew me reason
> Why you desire to steale out of your Countrey
> Like some Malefactor that had forfeited
> His life and freedome.
>
> (86)

Mrs. Wincott's death is all that prevents Geraldine from imitating the flight of the literal malefactor, Dalavill. Geraldine's response to that death is another commentary upon his fallacious notions of love, for it is totally self-centered and void of all compassion (94). In the final moments of the play Geraldine is schooled in a truer love by old Wincott, who tells him,

> This Meeting that was made
> Onely to take of you a parting leaue,
> Shall now be made a Marriage of our Loue,
> Which none saue onely Death shall separate.
>
> (94)

In the subplot the relationship between Lionell and the prostitute prefigures and parodies that between Geraldine and Mrs. Wincott. Although Lionell knows that his match with Blanda is detrimental, he still tries to idealize it through a religion of love. He professes his constancy to Blanda and elicits a similar commitment from her. His religion of love is countered by "the damn'd / Erroneous Doctrine" taught by the bawd Scapha (20–21). In response to the bawd's school of love, Lionell promises Blanda,

> a new Indenture Sealed,
> Of an affection fixt, and Permanent,
> Ile loue thee still, bee't but to giue the lye,
> To this old Cancker'd Worme.
>
> (21)

Because the "Cancker'd Worme," and "old damnation," is a heretic to his idealistic amatory doctrine, Lionell castigates and sentences her (22). In response, she swoons and must be carried away (23). This action at the close of act 1 prepares for the delineation in act 2 of the idealized relationship between Mrs. Wincott and Geraldine. Lionell's sentencing of Scapha and her fainting is also a parodic foreshadowing of Geraldine's final judgment upon Mrs. Wincott when she too faints. Mrs. Wincott merits Geraldine's judgment because she has fallen under the influence of another "Cancker'd Worme" or "old damnation," Dalavill, whose name is an obvious form of "devil" (92).

The unity of main and subplots, therefore, is achieved not through the direct integration of events and characters but through analogy. The analogy itself is emphasized by the imagery in both plots that conveys the theme of youth's education. The first two scenes which initiate the two plots are set in the Wincott and Lionell houses. As the central protagonists, Geraldine and Lionell, come of age and become heirs to these houses, setting becomes metaphor. Both houses must be put in order: each young man must become the proper son. The subplot begins with Lionell's awareness that he has violated the house his father built. The riot and abuse within the literal house metaphorically represents the condition of the young man. This house suffers chaos and neglect when "That lasie Tenant, Loue steps in" (18). Through the drunken fantasies of Lionell and his debauched companions his home becomes not "a house well built," but a ship caught in a high sea. Old Lionell returns from the real dangers of a literal sea to the "shipwreck" of the night's brawl. It is significant that we receive the account of Lionell's fantastic sea adventure from Geraldine as he tells it to the Wincotts. Later, when old Geraldine confronts his son about his behavior in the Wincott house, he describes Geraldine as a ship:

> You are growne perfect man, and now you float
> Like to a well built Vessell; 'Tweene two Currents,
> Vertue and Vice; Take this, you steere to harbour;
> Take that, to eminent shipwracke.
>
> (46)

This warning is validated by the fact that Geraldine's relationship with Mrs. Wincott comes close to obliging him to forfeit forever the safe harbor of his home and homeland. Through repentance and reform young Lionell is reinstated as his father's heir and as eventual landlord, as opposed to the endangered sea-voyager. This reform does not occur, however, until old Lionell lays siege to his own house and threatens to burn it down. Geraldine, who presumed himself the landlord of the Wincott estate, learns from Bess that "another / Inioyes the rent" (57). Geraldine will eventually become the legitimate landlord, not as the husband of Mrs. Wincott but as the son "well built" by Mr. Wincott.

Of all the Heywood plays discussed so far *The English Traveller* is the most sophisticated in its use of metaphor. Perhaps this achievement is what Heywood had in mind when he referred to the play as "this Poem." The metaphorical-allegorical sensibility of the characters in the subplot serves to enrich the Plautine farce by adding to it both the morality of the English prodigal play and the delight of a mock epic.

Lionell, as the "Prince of Prodigality" and the emblematic house, is
endangered by an invasion of multiple personifications: Pride, Wan-
toning, Wasting, Rioting, Reveling, Spoiling, Spending, Gluttony,
and Gourmondizing (20). In his ingenious and brazen schemes to conceal his young master from an angry father, Reignald is Mercury (36),
Hercules (49), Alexander, Agathocles, Caesar (61), Charlemaine (73),
and finally the brave Orlando, blowing his horn when the pretense is
over (73). The clown-servant of the Wincott household also captures
the mock-heroic madness of the subplot by describing the feasting and
revelry within the Lionell household as an epic combat (25–27).

Whereas the action of the subplot literally concerns money, debts,
purchases, and usury, such terms are used in the main plot to define
metaphorically the love between Geraldine and the Wincotts.
Geraldine tells Mrs. Wincott:

> Of all the Treasure of my Hopes and Loue
> You were th'Exchequer, they were Stor'd in you;
> And had not my vnfortunate Trauell crost them,
> They had bin heere reserued still.
>
> (31)

She reiterates the metaphor:

> Troth they had,
> I should haue beene your trusty Treasurer.

Old Wincott, expressing his gratitude to old Geraldine for sharing his
son with the Wincotts, falls to the same figure:

> By trusting him to me, of whom your selfe
> May haue both vse and pleasure, y'are as kind
> As money'd men, that might make benefit
> Of what they are possest, yet to their friends
> In need, will lend it gratis.
>
> (41–42)

So pleased are Mrs. Wincott, Prudentilla, and old Geraldine with this
metaphor that Dalavill remarks,

> What strange felicitie these Rich men take,
> To talke of borrowing, lending, and vse;
> The vsurers language right.
>
> (42)

With Geraldine's enlightenment, he acknowledges that he is, ironically, the debtor bound by a cruel contract. Hearing of the sudden death of Mrs. Wincott, Geraldine completes the money metaphor:

> She hath made me then a free release,
> Of all the debts I owed her.   (94)

In conclusion, we should acknowledge that in *The English Traveller* the characters do not have the human appeal of those in *A Woman Killed with Kindness*—nor is the theme of commensurate profundity. But *The English Traveller* is an extremely clever combination of energized Plautine farce and satirical tragicomedy, perfectly integrated through metaphor and analogy. The achievement here more than fulfills the playwright's modest promise in the Prologue of "Some Mirth, some Matter, and perhaps some wit."

A Challenge for Beauty

Published in 1636 as a play "Svndry Times Acted, By the King's Majesties Servants: At the Blacke-friers, and at the Globe on the Bankeside," *A Challenge for Beauty* represents, along with the masque-play *Love's Mistress*, the best of Heywood's late dramatic production. The allusion to the punishment of William Prynne (Pearson V, 41), in addition to the courtly fashion of platonic love explored throughout the play, make clear that it was written sometime between February 1634 (the date of Prynne's trial) and the 1636 publication. Clark observes that *A Challenge for Beauty* "is the most polished and fashionable of his dramas and shows him adapting himself with great success to the standard that the King's men demanded."[21] The precise source of the two plots of the play is not known, although Grivelet has noted similarities between the subplot and *Two Gentlemen of Verona* and between the main plot and *Cymbeline*. He has also suggested that the model for Hellena is Angelica in Robert Greene's *Orlando Furioso*.[22] As a showcase of dramaturgical contrivances, *A Challenge for Beauty* invites comparison with many others plays as well. In the sensational trial scene at the end Hellena, for example, is the direct descendant of Shakespeare's Portia (*Merchant of Venice*), Isabella (*Measure for Measure*), and Helena (*All's Well*). Clark notes "the likelihood that Heywood derived some features of the tragicomedy from Massinger's *Picture*, licensed for the stage on June 8, 1629."[23]

Although Swinburne called *A Challenge for Beauty* "the best of

Heywood's romantic plays . . . the most graceful and beautiful, in detached scenes and passages, of all his extant works,"[24] few critics have shared this opinion. Clark sees it as "only a passible imitation of the Fletcherian model" and concludes that Heywood

> had served too long an apprenticeship to the popular stage, and had too little experience of the fashionable world to furnish the Caroline theatre-goers with the caricature of life which they were pleased to imagine a reflection of their own. He was too plebeian and home-loving to provide them with the heroic inanities and slippery ethics of tragicomedy. . . . He has taken over the Fletcherian dramatis personae, a uxorious king, a dictatorial queen, Italian dukes, scheming courtiers, an outspoken noble, controversial heroes and heroines, a wronged but not squeamish princess, unpaid soldiers, and the rest. But they are rather like Heywood's earlier characters masquerading than genuine creations of the Fletcherians. There are the usual villains exposed, honour tested, chastity vindicated, moral paradoxes, questionable situations, bold solutions, and the end justifying the means. But however well Heywood managed these surprise plots, he never could force the note to the required shrill pitch, for he had little command over passion.[25]

This assessment is worth quoting at length because it perfectly defines the characteristics of Fletcherian tragicomedy pertinent to this play. But the conclusion that Heywood has failed to capture the essence of the Fletcherian mode because he had "little command over passion" hardly accords with the genuine emotional intensity we have seen in *A Woman Killed with Kindness* or with the successful achievement of the "shrill pitch" in *2 The Fair Maid of the West*. Clearly Heywood is presenting in *A Challenge for Beauty* the courtly world of Fletcherian tragicomedy, but his intention in doing so invites closer consideration. The emotional tone of the play is appropriately high-pitched, but at the same time it is essentially playful. There is a fine line between an inept imitation of a high style (Clark's view of the play) and a parody of it. As Clark points out, all the dramaturgical contrivances of Fletcherian tragicomedy are present here, yet the end product is decidedly Heywood's. What we should entertain is that *A Challenge for Beauty* is Heywood's satire upon the Platonizing fashion at the court of Henrietta Maria and a playful parody of the heroic, courtly mode established by his more fashionable rivals, Beaumont, Fletcher, Massinger, Davenant, and Shirley.[26] Since Heywood himself contributed to this mode in *2 The Fair Maid* and influenced it with *The Royal King*, the parody is also self-reflexive.

The parodic intention becomes somewhat evident even in a plot summary, which suggests that the play is a deliberately exaggerated

form of the "heroical but *precieuse* tragicomedy of *anagnorisis*" — the
Cavalier play as Alfred Harbage defines it.[27] The main plot begins with
the vain Spanish queen's assertion that there is nowhere in the world
her match for beauty and virtue. The outspoken hero, Lord Bonavida,
is banished from court and homeland until he finds her equal in the
English lady, Hellena, and succeeds in winning her hand. The lovers
exchange a ring and carkanet (containing her picture and name), swear
never to part with these tokens, and the lord returns to court to prepare
for the instatement of his bride. Naively announcing to the court his
discovery of Hellena, their exchange of tokens, and the oath upon her
honor never to part with the ring, Bonavida is thrown into prison and
his lady's carkanet is confiscated by the queen. In the exposition of the
subplot another vain Spanish lady, Petrocella, is the inspiration for the
heroic feats of a Spanish lord, Valladaura. Instead of being pleased
with his service, Petrocella defines Valladaura's heroism as a tribute to
the superiority of his English vanquisher, Ferrers. Subsequently, Ferrers
and his friend Manhurst are captured by Turks and sold upon the slave
block to Valladaura. Manhurst is allowed to return to England where,
in disguise, he enters the service of Hellena, who just happens to be the
sister of Ferrers. Hellena learns that her maid has stolen Bonavida's ring
and given it to the queen's henchman, Pineda. This conspiracy to foil
her marriage and the news of her brother's imprisonment give Hellena
a double motive for sailing to Spain.

Meanwhile, Ferrers, indebted to Valladaura for his kind treatment,
is obliged to help his enemy-now-turned-friend in the courtship of Petrocella. Although the lady falls in love with Ferrers and he with her,
Ferrers is bound by his honor to serve the interests of Valladaura. Ferrers thus obliges Petrocella to consent to marry Valladaura. Aware of
the love between Ferrers and Petrocella and of the honor of his friend,
Valladaura puts Ferrers to the supreme test by obliging him first to
serve, in disguise, as the priest in the marriage and then, under the
disguise of darkness, as bridegroom on the wedding night — with, of
course, the stipulation that the bride must not be touched. Valladaura
then attempts to spring his surprise — that the testing of his friend is a
prerequisite for his surrender of Petrocella to Ferrers — by claiming on
his wedding night that his wife has cuckolded him. When the household arrives at the bridal chamber to witness Petrocella's dishonor, she
surprises everyone by appearing with a bloody knife and claiming to
have killed her husband, Valladaura, because the marriage was forced.
Valladaura steps forward to bemoan the presumed loss of the surrogate
bridegroom, Ferrers, and to explain his intention to test Ferrers before
surrendering Petrocella. Her deception successful, Petrocella bursts

into laughter and, with Ferrers's entrance, reveals that her revenge was counterfeit.

This comic resolution of the subplot occurs on the day set for Bonavida's execution. Convinced by the evidence of the ring that his lady is false, Bonavida makes his peace with his queen and kneels before the executioner. Hellena suddenly interrupts the execution with a cry for justice. She claims to have been seduced by one who has stolen the mate of a priceless slipper and identifies Pineda as the thief. To clear himself, Pineda swears, quite truthfully, that he has never before seen Hellena. Since Pineda's earlier false testimony that he had obtained the ring by seducing Hellena was the grounds for executing Bonavida, his admission now clears Hellena's reputation and saves the courtier. Hellena's carkanet on the queen's person proves Hellena's identity as Pineda's oath attests to her innocence. When all seems thus ingeniously resolved, Ferrers suddenly denounces his sister on the basis of her earlier claim to have been seduced by Pineda. Valladaura and Manhurst come to the defense of Hellena by threatening to duel with Ferrers if he cannot think better of his own sister. Bloodshed is averted when Valladaura and Manhurst finally convince Ferrers that the sister of so honorable a man must also be honorable. This flattering argument for the nobility of blood resolves the final obstacle to the happy ending.

Before considering the more difficult issue of parody, let us examine the various ways in which the play, at first glance, might appear to be simply an example of the Cavalier mode. The characters are restricted to types—"all silhouettes in black, white, and gilt—animate but unalive."[28] The fashionable Platonism and Petrarchism are designed to appeal to the court of Henrietta Maria. As it emphasizes heroic deeds and masculine honor, *A Challenge for Beauty* also focuses upon the sovereignty of women and thus exhibits the "marked Feminism" that is another characteristic of Cavalier drama.[29] Deluded by what appears to be the evidence of his beloved's dishonor, Bonavida falls into the slough of antifeminist despond from which he must be extricated by the virtuous Hellena. And even the noble Ferrers shows in the final moments of the play the male gullibility in his inclination to think the worst of his sister after she has cleverly demonstrated her innocence and saved the life of Bonavida. The compulsive preoccupation with honor—with chastity, friendship, courtesy, and morally absurd oaths—also places this play within the context of a Cavalier mode that eventually culminates in the heroic plays of the Restoration. The heroic but helpless victims of fate and honor flounder from one impossible and sensational situation to another in the classic Fletcherian manner.

But the humorous, satirical treatment of these characters and of their values is very different from what we find in the conventional Fletcherian tragicomedy. Satire does sometimes occur in a true Fletcherian play, but we are also encouraged to take seriously the characters' limitations. The satire here is more broadly parodic, and the limitations exposed are so exaggerated that the characters themselves are rendered ridiculous. In *A Challenge for Beauty* the characters of both plots are presented through a challenge or contest: in the main plot the test is feminine beauty and virtue; in the subplot it is masculine courtesy and honor. The contest in both cases illuminates the absurdity rather than the nobility of the action and reveals the self-love that sickens rather than enlightens the court. This sickness, like the Platonizing fashion that masks it, descends from its purest form in the queen down to the noblest of the courtiers who dares to challenge her, Bonavida. The symptom of the sickness is the vanity evident in the inclination to sing one's own praises.

Bonavida prides himself on his perception of the true essence of Beauty, "Beautie match'd with Vertue." He is confident of his choice of Hellena as rival to the queen because, as he explains to the Clown,

> of her chastity
> Some proofes I have made, and found it like the Diamond,
> Save by a Diamond never to be wrought.
>
> (17)

Nevertheless, his pride in his perception of beauty matched with virtue is easily shattered by Pineda's possession of the ring that Bonavida naively equates with his lady's chastity. Bonavida's pride in his ability to perceive shadowed truths is undercut by his willingness to accept surface appearances. He has failed to learn the most basic principle of his ostensible Platonism — the illusory nature of man's temporal existence. As he accepts Pineda's deception as the truth, Bonavida ironically reverses himself and abandons his Petrarchan idealism of women for an antifeminist condemnation of the entire sex.

Initially, Hellena's motives for accepting Bonavida's love seem to define her as the feminine ideal. She tells her suitor,

> And should I not in unseene Vertue strive
> To equall that seene beautie you so prayse,
> I should then much wrong that great character
> You have bestow'd upon mee.
>
> (21)

Her professed concern with unseen virtue and the modesty that allows others to bestow great character establish Hellena as a foil to the queen and Petrocella. Yet in her acceptance of Bonavida, we see no aversion to his more dubious promise, "To fixe you in that spheare a splendant starre" (21). The Clown is somewhat less Petrarchan as he explains what Hellena stands to gain:

[Bonavida] means to make her a great Lady, to possesse her of all his fortunes, to put downe all the prime ladies of *Spaine*: and for Beautie and Virtue, to bee preferr'd before the great Princesse herselfe.

(20–21)

That Hellena should object to this intention is clear, for to present at court one who will be preferred to the princess herself smacks of the same folly as the attempt to surpass a king in the contest of courtesy and thus to diminish the king's magnificence. The maid Rosella's expectation to gain "a Ladyship at least" by her match with Pineda serves as a satiric analogue to Hellena's own great expectations. The consequences of the attempt to "winne [her] selfe a name throughout the world, / And purchase admiration" is the loss of her reputation and the necessity of a desperate ploy to regain it. Hellena finds herself in the absurdly ironic situation of denying her chastity before the entire Spanish court in order to affirm it. She then finds herself in the more humiliating position of having vindicated her honor to all except her own brother.

We find a similarly humorous and satirical perspective in the subplot. The contest of courtesy is not treated as the manifestation of noble character (as it is in the earlier *Royal King and Loyal Subject*), but as a source of delusion, absurdity, and comedy. Indebted to Valladaura for his kindness, Ferrers shows a transcending courtesy by consenting to woo Petrocella for his erstwhile enemy. The code of honor that dictates such courtesy also requires the sacrifice of Ferrers's own interest in Petrocella and even justifies, at least for Ferrers, the cruel entrapment of her in a marriage she does not want. After Ferrers has once acquiesced to the tyranny of this code, he can find no way to extricate himself: "I am in, / Past halfe already, why not up to th' chinne?" (51). He thus becomes the victim-beneficiary of Valladaura's absurd scheme to test his friend's courtesy and to reward him with Petrocella.

Heywood's own wry commentary on this entire plot may be heard in the punctuating laughter of Petrocella herself. Her suddenly humourous perspective overturns the whole contest when Valladaura, demanding to know if Ferrers fulfilled the promise of sexual abstinence during the wedding night, evokes from her a mocking ridicule:

Do but name the word, abuse my love, and Ile kill him indeed; what should he
doe? He came to bed, and for his eyes sake, slept with mee, yet ne're so much
as kist me, but I confesse, I gave him twenty.

(62–63)

The parodic dimension of this subplot is underscored by the conscious theatricality of the characters and by their growing sense of their
own absurdity as they play out the roles that their commitment to the
code of honor dictates. The roles Ferrers plays in securing the marriage
between Petrocella and Valladaura, in performing the marriage ceremony, and in abstaining from the natural (even desired) performance
as the bridegroom, create in him a sense of living in an illusion: "I
would 'twere but a dream, then there were hope / I might once awake,
and so see day" (50). Ferrers surrenders to the roles Valladaura devises
for him with a self-mocking helplessness:

> I will do 't; sleepe with your wife? Ile do 't.
> No Eunuke like me.
>
> (58)

With the mock marriage performed by a layman disguised as a
priest, with his improvisation upon the bed trick, and with his performance as the husband cuckolded on his wedding night, we sense that
Valladaura has seen too many plays. His tendency to manipulate reality
on the model of those old plays is magnificently requited in kind when
Petrocella greets him at the door of the bridal chamber playing her own
role as the feminine avenger. To Valladaura's horror, Petrocella has recast the play he thought he had written, and has become instead another Evadne of *The Maid's Tragedy*. Her performance and jest
complete, Petrocella gives away one of the secrets of the players' stage
effects when she explains that the dagger was dipped in the blood of a
turtle dove (62).

These are not the only characters with a keen talent for the theatrical
and with a sense that life is but a dream or a play. Bonavida, entering
the place of execution, articulates his perception of the world as a stage:

> The Queene playes with my death
> And bids me act a bold Tragedians part
> To which, such moving action I will give,
> That it shall glaze this Theater round with teares,
> And all that shall behold me on this stage,
> Pittying my fate: shall taxe her cruelty.
>
> (66–67)

As he makes his eloquent farewell speech to the queen and kneels before the grim executioner, he is suddenly upstaged by another player who will reverse this final action from tragedy to comedy. Recognizing Hellena, Bonavida, like Ferrers, wonders, "is this a vision? / Or else some waking dreame?"

Hellena comes equipped for her performance with an unusual property, a single "pantofle" or slipper, the mate to which she claims was stolen by the man who seduced her. The slipper, she explains, was "Valewed at no lesse than a Thousand Crownes" (70). Granted Hellena cannot accuse Pineda of stealing the ring without implicating the queen, we nevertheless wonder why she devises the tale of the stolen slipper. Perhaps the answer depends upon our perception of the major characters as conscious amateur actors and playwrights in the theater of life. As the characters conceive of life as a play, *A Challenge for Beauty* becomes, to some extent, a play about plays. The lie about the slipper is Heywood's improvisation upon an old dramaturgical device, the bed trick. The slipper itself is a metaphor of the theatrical fashion that such devices serve. The metaphoric dimension of the slipper is corroborated by one of Heywood's self-reflexive epilogues. In 1637, the year following the publication of *A Challenge for Beauty*, Heywood published an old play, *The Royal King and the Loyal Subject* (ca. 1600), which had been instrumental in the development of the theme of masculine honor through the fashionable contest of courtesy. To this edition, he appended a new epilogue commenting upon the changed taste of the theater audience. The metaphor of the epilogue compares the changing fashion in plays to that in clothes:

> We know (and not long since) there was a time,
> Strong lines were lookt after, but if rime,
> O then 'twas excellent: who but beleeves,
> But Doublets with stuft bellies and bigge sleeves
> And those Trunke-hose, which now the age doth scorn,
> Were all in fashion, and with frequence worn;
> And what's not out of date, who is't can tell,
> But it may come in fashion, and sute well?
>
> (83)

Certainly by the time he wrote *A Challenge for Beauty*, Heywood had witnessed a refashioning of the old material of *The Royal King and the Loyal Subject*, for this play became the primary source for Fletcher's *The Loyal Subject*.[30] *A Challenge for Beauty* is a good-humored acknowledgment of the new fashion and, with the detail of the stolen slipper, a gentle reminder of the revisionist's debt. If *A Challenge for*

Beauty, a play about rivalries, is a contribution to and a gentle parody of the new theatrical fashion established by Beaumont and Fletcher, Heywood at last succeeded in requiting his young rivals for *The Knight of the Burning Pestle*, a parody of the old fashion typified by Heywood's *Four Prentices of London*. It is most likely no accident that *A Challenge for Beauty* appeared in print in 1636 and was perhaps performed in 1635, the same year of the popular revival of *The Knight of the Burning Pestle* at the Cockpit in Drury Lane.

Chapter Six
The Mythological Plays
The Ages

The plays we have looked at so far in this study clearly illustrate that Heywood took seriously the didactic obligation and potential of his profession. Toward this objective to enlighten the relatively uneducated audiences of the Curtain, the Rose, the Red Bull, and the Cockpit at Drury Lane, there was no subject too humble or, as the plays of this chapter will show, too grand for his pen. With the publication in 1609 of his verse history, *Troia Britannica*, he had already given his readers a full account of the deification of the Greek gods, of the major myths defining their identities, of the Trojan war, and of the establishment of the new Troy, London. But a verse narrative of the gods and heroes did not, according to Heywood, have the same didactic power as a dramatization of the same matter. In *An Apology for Actors* he explains:

Description is only a shadow receiued by the eare but not perceiued by the eye: so liuely portrature is meerely a forme seene by the eye, but can neither shew action, passion, motion, or any other gesture, to mooue the spirits of the beholder to admiration: but to see a souldier shap'd like a souldier, walke, speake, act like a souldier: to see a *Hector* all besmered in blood, trampling vpon the bulkes of Kinges. A *Troylus* returning from the field in the sight of his father *Priam* . . . To see as I haue seene, *Hercules* in his own shape hunting the Boare, knocking downe the Bull . . . and lastly, on his high Pyramides writing *Nil vltra*, Oh there were sights to make an *Alexander*.

[B4–B5]

Thus he began, shortly after finishing *Troia Britannica*, to adapt this material for the stage. The result is a five-part sequence known as *The Ages: The Golden Age, The Silver Age, The Brazen Age,* and 1 and 2 *The Iron Age*. The first play of the series was published in 1611, the second and third in 1613; the two parts of *The Iron Age* did not appear until 1632.[1] In 2 *The Iron Age* Heywood writes of his intention to publish all five plays in a handsome volume "with an Explanation of all the difficulties, and an Historicall Comment of euery hard name, which may appeare obscure or intricate to such as are not frequent in Poetry"

(Pearson 3:352). Although Heywood was not able to produce this glossed edition, his plan for it makes clear the didactic impetus behind these works.

The five plays were a tremendous success on the popular stage as well as at court. The address to the reader of 1 *The Iron Age* tells us with considerable pride, "I desire thee to take notice, that these were the Playes often (and not with the least applause,) Publickely Acted by two Companies, uppon one Stage at once, and haue sundry times thronged three seuerall Theaters, with numerous and mighty Auditories (Pearson 3:264). J. Q. Adams and Clark agree that the two companies were the King's and the Queen's men and that the houses were the Red Bull, the Curtain, and the Globe or Blackfriars.[2] The combined companies performed *The Silver Age*, along with Heywood's *Rape of Lucrece*, before the Queen and Prince Henry in 1611/12. Clark's assessment of *The Ages* corroborates the author's pride:

They were written with evident gusto and unflagging energy. The matter of Caxton and Ovid, Plautus, Virgil and Lucian—his delight throughout his life—he fashioned with amazing vigour and skill into gay comedies, rollicking farces, beautiful pastorals and masques, and blood-and-thunder tragedies, with a superabundance of dumb shows, spectacles, and machines. These popular parallels to the graceful court-dramas of Lyly and Peele are the best specimens of Heywood's versatility, and contain, though most critics . . . have failed to recognize it, some of his truest poetry.[3]

Heywood's objective—to present in dramatic form the major Greek myths and the full story of the Trojan war—dictated the highly episodic structure of the work. The first three *Ages* depend upon the choric figure Homer for narrative links and commentary. The episodic nature of these three plays is compounded by the fact that *The Silver Age* is three one-act plays and *The Brazen Age* is five one-act plays. The selection and the ordering of the material are governed by the playwright's resolve "to vnlocke the Casket longe time shut, / Of which none but the learned keepe the key, / Where the rich Iewell (*Poesie*) was put" (Pearson 3:85).

Clearly, the selection of material from *Troia Britannica* to be staged in *The Ages* was not made with the ease of staging as the primary consideration. As George F. Reynolds observes, these plays "demand some of the most spectacular staging ever suggested for the Elizabethan public stage"[4] and surely strained to the limit the technical ingenuity of both the King's and the Queen's men. At the beginning of act 2 of *The Silver Age* choric Homer acknowledges the problem of staging as he appeals to the imagination of the audience to assist in the depiction of the supernatural: "Your suppositions now must lend vs ayd, / That [Jupiter] can all things (as a God indeed)" (97). The stage directions "Iupiter appeares in his glory vnder a Raine-bow" (122), "Enter Juno and Iris aboue in a cloud" (130), "Enter Pluto his Chariot drawne in by Diuels" (135), "Earth riseth from vnder the stage" (139), and "The riuer Arethusa riseth from the stage" (140) indicate the elaborate use of properties and machinery. The onstage incineration of the pregnant Semele and Jupiter's rescue of the "abortive infant" Bacchus (154–55) provide perhaps the ultimate challenge to the companies' art of *trompe-l'oeil*. The stage directions make clear that the importance of spectacle to these plays cannot be overestimated. The challenge of staging presented in *The Ages* invites our reconsideration of the sophistication of staging in the Renaissance public theaters.

   The Golden Age.   Subtitled "The liues of *Jupiter* and *Saturne*, with the deifying of the Heathen Gods," *The Golden Age* affords an excellent example of Renaissance euhemerism. The principal action is the struggle for power, first between Saturne and Tytan, then between Jupiter and Saturne, to which are added, as digressions, the amorous conquests of Calisto and Danae. The deification of Jupiter, Neptune, and Pluto provides Heywood with the opportunity to pay tribute to the creative power of the poet. Homer tells us,

> I am he
> That by my pen gaue heauen to *Iupiter*,
> Made *Neptunes* Trident calme, the curled waues,
> Gaue *Aeolus* Lordship ore the warring winds;
> Created blacke hair'd *Pluto* King of Ghosts,
> And regent ore the Kingdomes fixt below.
> By mee *Mars* warres, and fluent *Mercury*
> Speakes from my tongue. I plac'd diuine *Apollo*
> Within the Sunnes bright Chariot. I made *Venus*
> Goddesse of Loue, and to her winged sonne
> Gaue seuerall arrowes, tipt with Gold and lead.
> What hath not *Homer* done, to make his name
> Liue to eternity?
>   (Pearson 3:5)

   In his presentation of Jupiter as a human who accomplishes his martial and amorous feats without the aid of supernatural power, Heywood has ironically reversed the Homeric achievement of creating the deities. This reversal is particularly problematic in the love scenes between Jupiter and Calisto and between Jupiter and Danae. The result of Jupiter's human identity is that the scenes are among the most explicitly erotic in all of Renaissance drama and must have fueled the puritanical fire of Heywood's adversary, William Prynne. In both episodes Jupiter's sexual desire is not to be defeated by chastity. Like a self-preening gallant, he tells Calisto:

> Women, fair Queene, are nothing without men:
> You are but cyphers, empty roomes to fill,
> And till mens figures come, vncounted still.
>
> (25)

When Calisto tricks Jupiter into granting her wish to preserve her chastity, he offers her a seductive argument worthy of the best sonneteer or Cavalier rake:

> To liue a maid, what ist? 'tis to liue nothing:
> 'Tis like a couetous man to hoord vp treasure,
> Bar'd from your owne vse, and from others pleasure.
> Oh thinke faire creature, that you had a mother,
> One that bore you, that you might beare another:
> Be you as she was, of an Infant glad,
> Since you from her, haue all things that she had.
> Should all affect the strict life you desire,
> The world it selfe should end when we expire.
>
> (25–26)

The Golden Age is dramatically effective in its individual scenes — specifically in Sybilla's heroic and clever protection of her male children and in the amorous conquests of Jupiter. The disregard for unity, the pastoral interlude with a masque-like dance, and the elaborate special effects suggest that *The Golden Age* is not so much play as dazzling spectacle. The same may be said, to some extent, of all the plays except the last in the series.

   The Silver Age.   The diverse matter of *The Silver Age* is specified on the title page as "The loue of *Jupiter* for *Alcmena:* The birth of *Hercules.* AND The Rape of PROSERPINE. CONCLUDING, With the Arraignment of the Moone." Although this description gives little hope that the play will be more unified than its "older brother," *The Golden Age*, the address to the reader assures us that these plays "shall encrease in substance, weight, and estimation." Indeed, we can detect a degree of thematic substance and unity as the action of the various episodes reveals a divine ordering of events within a framework of justice. Old Acrisius is punished for the cruel imprisonment of his daughter, Danae, and learns to submit to his inevitable fate. Pretus, who is "Joues rod" (Pearson 3:87) in the punishment of Acrisius, is punished in turn for his cruelty to Bellerophon and Acrisius (92–94). Jupiter's will is equally apparent in his comic manipulation of mortals that results in his enjoyment of Alcmena and in the birth of Hercules. Jupiter's pursuit of Alcmena, the matter of the second act, is defined by Ganimede and Jupiter himself as a play within the play (99, 122). Amphitrio comes through this divinely contrived comedy with a sense of contentment in Jove's will and omnipotence. Jove's sovereignty is fully tested in the third act by the vengeful schemes of Juno. Despite her efforts, Hercules is born and triumphs over the various monstrous adversaries contrived by his goddess stepmother. Semele is not so fortunate, but her death is the just consequence of her vanity. Jupiter's justice and the order he establishes in the cosmos is the subject of the final episode, the story of Proserpine's abduction by Pluto and Jove's settlement of the dispute in the "Arraignement of the Moone."

The Brazen Age. With *The Brazen Age* the cosmic order and harmony deriving from Jove's justice is superseded by violence, treachery, entrapment, and death. The title page sounds the warning that the playwright has shifted from comedy to tragedy: "The first Act containing, The Death of the Centaure Nessus, The Second, The Tragedy of Meleager: The Third The Tragedy of Iason and Medea The Fovrth. VULCANS NET. The Fifth, The Labours and death of HERCVLES." Of the five plays in the cycle, this one is in all respects the least satisfying, particularly as it presents the greatest challenge to unity and coherence. The first and fifth acts depicting the deaths of Nessus and Hercules obviously cohere and frame the other three acts. In the stories of Meleager, Jason and Medea, and Hercules we have a fallen world defined by a prevailing pattern in which tragedy results from within the family unit. Even the fourth-act comic interlude of Mars and Venus caught in Vulcan's net reflects the violation of the family, the symbol of order. Sexual love and jealousy are disruptive forces among the gods as well as men. This pattern culminates in the death of the greatest hero, Hercules, who survives his labors only to be destroyed by his well-intentioned wife.

1 The Iron Age. 1 *The Iron Age*, "Contayning the Rape of Hellen: The siege of Troy: the Combate betwixt Hector and Aiax: Hector and Troilus slayne by Achilles: Achilles slaine by Paris: Aiax and Vlisses contend for the Armour of Achilles: the Death of Aiax, &c," was dedicated to Heywood's friend, Thomas Hammon of Gray's Inn. As the title-page description suggests, it is an attempt to provide a full history of the events leading up to the sack of Troy, the subject reserved for 2

The Iron Age. These events are thematically related through Heywood's treatment of the motivating force behind them—familial and sexual bonds.

In his account of the cause of the war Heywood repeatedly underscores not only the importance but the irony of familial and sexual relationships. The Trojans seek revenge upon the Greeks because Hesione, sister of Priam, was taken by the Greeks in a previous war. News that she has been shamefully treated causes Hector, who initially supports the Greeks' right to Hesione, to commit himself to the plan for requital, the abduction of Menelaus's queen, Helen. By dramatizing the seduction and abduction of Helen, the playwright focuses upon her willing betrayal of husband and homeland and thus underscores the irony of the war initiated by her rape. Once in Troy, where she is warmly adopted by the royal family of Priam, she becomes the recipient of familial commitment. The familial bond is again crucial in the single combat between Hector and Ajax, son of Hesione and Telamon and thus the cousin of Hector. Respect for the family bond between Ajax and Hector forces a truce, a feast, and Polyxena's amorous conquest of Achilles. Regard for the will of his future mother-in-law, Hecuba, causes Achilles to retire from the field to his tent. Whereas in Helen's case sexual love is both the cause of betrayal and the basis of familial obligation, in Cressida's case the familial obligation becomes the cause of sexual betrayal. The importance of these bonds is illustrated most vividly when the course of the war ultimately rests upon the crucial choice allowed Helen between Menelaus and Paris. She chooses Paris because he "kisses better" (Pearson 3:309), and thus seals the fate of the great heroes on both sides.

In the fighting that follows, the Trojans gain a decisive advantage when they set fire to the Greek tents. Appealing to the family bond, Ajax persuades Hector "for Hesiones sake" (315) to quench the fire. The familial bond is also strong enough to dissuade Hector from fighting when Andromache tells of her prophetic dream (316–18). With the death of Margareton, family obligation is perceived exclusively in terms of revenge. With Hector's death, Troilus's desire for revenge makes him a second Hector or Hector's ghost that haunts the Mermidons. The familial bond between Hecuba and Hector becomes the basis for the Trojans' revenge upon Achilles, which will, in turn, result in the revenge of Pyrrhus. The sexual and familial bonds that motivate Greek and Trojan alike render their achievements consistently ironic rather than heroic. The final action of the play emphasizes the pervasive irony. Ajax, the greatest surviving warrior, is deprived of Achilles' armor, goes mad, and kills himself.

2 *The Iron Age.* Heywood's acknowledged compulsion to tell the whole history (Pearson 3:431) necessitated a division of 2 *The Iron Age* into two distinct parts: the first three acts depict the sack of Troy and the destruction of the house of Priam; the last two depict the fall of the house of Atreus and of all the Greeks, save Ulysses, who participated in Troy's fall. Despite this span of events and the shift of scene from Troy to Mycenae, the play is unified through the lust for revenge that motivates the action of both parts. 2 *The Iron Age* is Heywood's full-fledged revenge tragedy, replete with all of the conventions of that genre.[5] As the Machiavellian villain, Synon is developed into a major character. He not only devises the Trojan horse, gulls the Trojans into accepting it, and relishes the wholesale slaughter of Trojan women and children, but he survives to provide a satiric commentary on the aftermath in Mycenae. He is finally destroyed only because he meets his match in the Machiavellian revenger, Cethus, who masterminds the bloodshed of the second episode. In the characters of Pyrrhus and Orestes, Heywood plays out the convention of the revenge of a son for a father slain. Through the recurring pattern of requital and counter-requital and through the obvious analogues between characters of the two episodes, the playwright achieves thematic and structural unity.

The fall of Troy, the matter of the first three acts, is a full dramatization of the revenge of Pyrrhus as it is told in the player's speech in *Hamlet*. At the outset Pyrrhus resolves never to relent in his vengeance "till old *Priams* haires / Be dy'de in goare: till *Hecub's* reuerent lockes / Be gul'd in slaughter" (357). Penthesilia, the Amazon who seeks revenge for the death of Hector, is the first of Pyrrhus's victims. The death of Paris accomplished, Pyrrhus turns his wrath on all the women of Troy to ensure the murder of Polyxena. His blood lust is finally gratified in a masque-like, choreographed slaughter. Ulysses, Agamemnon, Synon, and Thersites are instructed by Pyrrhus to serve as audience to the bloody performance as Greeks are paired off with the helpless victims of the house of Priam (392). Synon, who habitually conceives of the fall of Troy as a grand tragedy (371, 379, 389), commends this bloody climax: "Why so, so, this was stately tragicall" (393). Sharing this aesthetic sensibility, Pyrrhus provides an epic catalogue of the death and destruction and concludes that "worlds to come / Shall Cronicle our pittelesse reuenge" (395).

Because of the pseudohistorical tradition that identified the founder of Britain as the grandson of Aeneas, Heywood, like most Renaissance writers, reflects a clear Trojan bias. The play's satirical perspective on the Greeks is evident not only in their anti-heroic slaughter of the helpless and in the reprehensible figures of Thersites and Synon, but also in the way Helen is reinstated. As Menelaus prepares to kill his faithless wife, Agamemnon intercedes: "Shee's Clitemnestras sister, for her sake / Hellen shall liue, and Kingly Menelaus / Receiue her into fauour" (387). He further justifies this intervention by reminding his brother that Helen was first taken from Sparta against her will. In light of what we have seen of Helen and are about to see of Clytemnestra, Agamemnon thus portrays himself as the ultimate fool. True heroism and wisdom, on the other hand, are to be found in this iron age only among those distant ancestors of the new Troy. Hector's ghost appears to Aeneas not to elicit revenge but to assure Aeneas that Troy's fall is part of a providential plan, the end of which is "great Britaines Troy-novant" (384). This true chronicle, like all true chronicles of the Renaissance, affirms through the wisdom of Aeneas that "The Heauens haue hand in all things, to their pleasure / We must subscribe" (390).

The fall of Troy marks a significant decline in the already-fallen world of the iron age. As the scene shifts between acts 3 and 4 from the ruins of Troy to the decadence of Clytemnestra's court, we enter the world of Italianate intrigue where all of the sins of the past come home along with the Greeks. Cethus, the Machiavellian revenge-villain, avenges the injury of his brother by convincing Clytemnestra and Egistus of the necessity of killing Agamemnon. He then arranges for Orestes to discover the murder and to take his own revenge. The thematic concern with the family bond, so important to the events depicted in 1 *The Iron Age*, culminates here in the final episode as Orestes chooses between the conflicting obligations to his dead father and corrupt mother. Orestes' dilemma is resolved in revenge-play fashion by the appearance of his father's ghost and the subsequent enforcing of the patriarchal duty.

Up to this point, we are invited to see Orestes as Jove's minister of justice. Egistus acknowledges:

> Oh but *Orestes*
> His ey's to me like lightning, and his arme
> Vp heau'd thus, shewes like *Joues* thunder-bolt
> Aym'd against lust and murder.
>
> (418)

Here Heywood's aversion to revenge necessitates a radical alteration in the Sophoclean story of Orestes. As the Greeks return from Troy, Orestes has become officially betrothed to Hermione, Helen's daughter. Agamemnon, however, has promised Hermione to Pyrrhus as an acknowledgment of his martial feats. Delighting in this complication,

Cethus tells Orestes as he stands over the corpse of Clytemnestra that Hermione and Pyrrhus are at the temple for the marriage service. Indifferent to the sacrilege accompanying his revenge, Orestes rushes into the temple, stabs Pyrrhus, and (with no sense of irony) declares,

> Priam before the holy Alter fell,
> Before the Alter bid thy life farewell.
> (427)

In the confused scuffle that follows Orestes and Pyrrhus — the two sons of fathers slain — kill each other. When the brawl ends, only Ulysses lives to provide the epilogue. Helen, overwhelmed by the carnage and by the awareness that she was the ultimate cause of all this strife but even more depressed by the sight of a few ugly wrinkles on the face "That launch'd a thousand ships from Aulis gulfe" (430), strangles herself.

Descending from the Arcadian pastoral exploits of the golden world, through the harmonious comedy of the silver world, through the tragedy of the brazen world, we finally come to rest in the satirical irony of this iron world.

Love's Mistress: or, The Queen's Masque

The Ages were, in many ways, excellent preparation for the theatrical triumph of Heywood's golden years, *Love's Mistress: or, The Queen's Masque*. The first three *Ages*, with their mythological characters, metamorphoses, dumb shows, descents from heaven and ascents from hell, spectacular properties, fireworks, and pastoral masques, bear a close relation to the court masque.[6] The first three of the seven pageants that Heywood wrote from 1631 to 1639 for the installation of the Lord Mayor of London also offered the playwright a rehearsal of devices for *Love's Mistress* in that they were mythological allegories requiring the services of a master of scenery and special effects, Garrett Christmas.[7]

The audience for which the masque-play was intended, however, was radically different to that for which Heywood wrote *The Ages* and the Lord Mayor's pageants. As the title suggests, *The Queens Masque* was performed in 1634 before King Charles I and Queen Henrietta Maria at Denmark House to celebrate the king's birthday. The success of the work is evident in the fact that, according to the 1636 title page, it was performed before royalty three times within eight days. In the address to the reader Heywood generously acknowledges that the suc-

cess of his "Dramatick Poem" resulted in large part from the magnificent sets and inventions provided by Inigo Jones. *Love's Mistress* is an
elegant synthesis of masque and play, and it provides us with an example of and a definitive statement about the importance of the audience to the kind and quality of the dramatist's achievement.

Even more than a statement about the collaborative relationship between playwright and audience, Heywood's masque is his chief defense
of poetry. *Love's Mistress* consists of a frame, the debate between Apuleius and Midas (or Art and Ignorance) over the value and nature of
Art. Within this frame, Apuleius presents his play of Cupid and
Psyche as proof not only of Midas's "treason 'gainst the *Muses* Majestie"
(Pearson 5:93), but also of the fact that "All true Poets raptures are
devine." Apuleius's mythological drama of the soul's pursuit of immortality and beauty is periodically interrupted by the recalcitrance of his
long-eared audience. Declaring that he cares "for no such toyes," Midas
must be entertained with the visual spectacle of a series of rustic dances
or antimasques. The allegorical play within of Cupid and Psyche is also
interrupted by the antics of Midas's bastard son, the clown Coridon.
This complex structure consisting of frame, play within, and comic
counterpoint or antimasque is unified through the prevailing pattern
of metamorphosis. To his primary source, Lucianus Apuleius's *The
Golden Ass*—which also contains as a narrative inset the story of Cupid
and Psyche—Heywood added the character of Midas because his metamorphosis provides an analogue of contrast to the metamorphoses of
Apuleius himself and Psyche.

Midas and Coridon reflect the tyranny of ignorance and bad taste
with which Heywood as playwright for the masses was habitually forced
to contend. Midas can be kept awake during Apuleius's play only by
the intervention of a series of dances. Apuleius, the playwright-persona, acquiesces to the limitations of his asinine audience: "Art sometimes must give way to ignorance" (119). This apology calls to mind the
Prologue to *The English Traveller*, in which the poet declares that for
once his art will not give way to the popular demand for those devices
used to bombast out a play. Midas's failure as an audience is an essential
failure of the imagination that prevents his entering the dramatic illusion. After seeing the beautiful and mysterious marriage of Cupid and
Psyche, Midas complains,

> . . . thou bring'st heere on the stage
> A young green-sicknesse baggage to run after

> A little ape-faced boy thou tearm'st a god;
> Is not this most absurd?
>
> (106)

His aesthetic blindness is demonstrated later by his choice of Pan's song over Apollo's (124–27). Coridon, Midas's bastard son, makes clear that the father's inadequacies are hereditary. Coridon's contempt for love is matched by his contempt for poets who "maintain" the god of love (113). Through his reductive vision, the poet's creative achievement is reversed as Homer's heroes become farmers, bakers, and butchers in a bout of cudgels (113–14). Midas's and Coridon's love of the material at the expense of the intellectual and the spiritual, as well as their literalism that denies the power of the imagination, make them the perfect embodiments of an unfit audience — of, that is, the mysomusoi[8] and the poetaster.

Apuleius's opening lines announce that the play's action is metamorphosis. As a kind of Faustian overreacher, Apuleius was transformed into an ass because his brain "aym'd at inscrutable things" as he attempted to pry "into Heavens hidden mysteries" (91). His account of his pursuit of forbidden knowledge, his fall, and his restoration through "the selfe same power / That calls all humane wisdome foolishness" establishes an analogy with the Christian myth of fall and redemption, as well as with the Cupid and Psyche myth as it is allegorized by Apuleius. Newly "retransform'd," Apuleius seeks "the way to Helicon" and the Muse's temple, where he must perform a sacrifice. The connection between his retransformation, the muses, and the intended sacrifice is vague at this point, but it becomes clear in the play he offers to Midas. The story that Apuleius chooses to tell Midas through his play is obviously a corrective to the materialism and retrograde metamorphosis of Midas; but it is also, as Apuleius says, "a story of mine owne" — that is, a self-reflexive story in addition to a story of his own creation. The following analysis will indicate the structural and thematic relationships between frame, myth, and comic episodes.

The play within begins with the pilgrimage of Psyche and her family to the Oracle at Delphi. This pilgrimage reminds us that Apuleius too is traveling to make a sacrifice to the muses, whose dance is governed by the harp of Apollo, god of poetry (94). Apollo tells of Psyche's fall that will result from a kind of forbidden knowledge, specifically from a form of perception: "his serpents face / If shee behold, she must see hell" (95). Psyche, like the poet, will survive this fall to be "retransform'd" and to achieve immortality. The fate of the poet, like that of

Psyche, depends upon vision: both succeed or fall on the basis of how and what they see. Venus, who according to Apuleius is lust, attempts to circumvent the metamorphic ascent of Psyche by affecting her perception. She tells Cupid,

> Make her in Love, but let her proud eyes doate
> On some ill-shapen drudge, some ugly foole.
>
> (98)

Cupid considers this command — "Shall Psiches beautious eyes gaze on base love?" — and resolves instead to nourish the inner eye of her soul. Transported from the purgatorial rock to Cupid's bower, where she is feasted with celestial pleasures, Psyche understands the error of her literal-minded sisters who expect to see the serpent:

> No serpent sure
> Lurkes in this pleasant bowre: my ear drinks sounds
> Of heaven-tun'd Instruments.
>
> (101)

Her prelapsarian vision of truth underscores the basic platonic concept, discussed at length by Jackson I. Cope, that "the ear is the eye of the soul."[9] As a personification of mankind's soul in the process of discovery and investment, Psyche is inclined toward hubristic dependence upon physical sight. She tells the celestial echoes, "oh let Psiche see your eyes" (102). Her joy in Cupid would be complete if "To this sweet voice, could I enjoy the sight" (103).

Midas, whose ass's ears are emblems of his failure to perceive through the eye of the soul, interrupts at this point with his corresponding refusal to "see out the play." He is appeased with the opportunity to "view [his] own infirmity" in the dance of the asses. Midas's lack of inner sight is further defined by his literal-mindedness. Every detail of the allegory must be explained to him because in his eyes Psyche is but a "young green-sicknesse baggage" and Cupid is only "a little ape-faced boy." Although Midas's perfect dullness contrasts sharply with the poet who "pries into Heavens hidden mysteries," and with Psyche, "the ambitious soul affecting heaven" (107), the three dramatic characters share the experience of a retrograde metamorphosis.

With the second act Heywood-Apuleius presents Psyche's temptation in terms of perception. Diverted from their first attempt to pry into the mystery of Psyche's husband, her sisters, Astioche and Petrea, realize that "Her husband is no serpent as twas said" (110). In a sense, they become the serpent as they use "the magicke of [their] tongues" (111) to deceive Psyche. With their second visit to the bower they tell her that they have seen a serpent entering the gate. Placing her faith in the eyes of her sisters, Psyche accepts the false vision and agrees to "cut his skalie throat" (118). Learning nothing from the play he watches, Midas, like Psyche, longs to see with his eyes. Apuleius explains that celestial raptures are never "Subject unto weake, and fleshy eye" (120). From his own experience Apuleius sounds the warning note: "Oh, who dares prie into those misteries, / That heaven would have conceal'd" (120).

The comic episode between the first and second visit of Psyche's sisters provides an analogue to the false vision that denies the divinity of Cupid and thus results in an enlightenment and a fall. Reducing the power of love to mere lust and folly, the clown Coridon explains that Cupid's power derives from "A company of pittifull fellowes call'd Poets" (113). His reductive vision in which Homer's gods and heroes are demythologized derives from what Cupid calls "a dull and brainlesse eye." The consequence is a comic fall: Coridon is struck by Cupid's birdbolt and falls in love with the ugly Amaryllis. From here he falls even further—into a frenzy of bad versifying (115). Coridon's fate, to fall in love with the first ugly creature he sees with his "fleshy eye," is the fate Venus intended for Psyche.

Coridon's faulty vision and fall are followed by Psyche's epiphany and fall. Psyche's sin of accepting or crediting a false vision is emblematically represented by the razor and the lamp she carries as she approaches the bed of the sleeping god. Enlightenment is immediate:

> Malitious sisters, I your enuy see,
> This is no serpent, but a Deite.
> (121)

The lamp that facilitates the "fleshy eye" betrays her. As the hot oil falls upon the sleeping Cupid, Psyche cries, "Ah me, thou envious light, what hast thou done?" (121). She is instantly transformed in the eyes of her husband-god as he awakens:

> What hellish hagg hath drop't this scalding oyle
> On Loves Caelestiall shape?

The god's curse brings a terrible alteration that mirrors Psyche's false vision of the serpent. Cupid tells Boreaus, "Lay waste and barren this fair flowrie grove, / And make this Paradise a den of snakes" (123).

Again, as in act 2, the myth is interrupted by a comic episode that provides an analogue both to the frame and to the myth. The clown tells of a chance encounter between Pan and Apollo and of their debate over whether Pan's pipe or Apollo's harp yields the better music. This debate, analogous to the one between Apuleius and Midas in the opening frame, will be resolved by a sample of the artist's creation. As in the frame, Midas will serve as audience and judge of the creative endeavor. But to perceive the beauty of Apollo's song Midas must see with the eye of the soul, something he has never been able to do. He thus awards the prize to Pan and is cursed by Apollo. Ugly cacaphony will now sound throughout Arcadia; heavenly harmony will be heard no more:

> Henceforth be all your rurall musicke such,
> Made out of Tinkers, Pans, and Kettle-drummes;
> And never hence-forth may your fields be grac'd
> With the sweete musicke of Apollo's lyre.
>
> (127)

Arcadia's loss of Apollo's lyre corresponds to Psyche's loss of the celestial raptures of Cupid's bower. Psyche's fall, signified by her metamorphosis into an ugly old hag, corresponds with Apollo's curse upon Midas:

> Midas, for thee, may thy eares longer grow,
> As shorter still thy judgement, dulnese, and dotage,
> Bee onely govern'd with those reverend haires;
> Let all like thee, that as they grow in time,
> Decay in knowledge, have that old mans curse,
> To be twice children.
>
> (127)

Psyche responds to her fall with an appeal to Cupid for pardon and mercy, and with humble and patient submission to the wrath of Venus. Her patience, coupled with mercy and assistance from Cupid, transforms the punishment of Venus into a rite of purification. Psyche's first spiritual labor, to sort the mixture of five grains into five piles of one kind, is accomplished by the ants. Apuleius explains to Midas that the grains are kinds of sins; the ants are "recollections" through which the sins are sorted "To pay to each indebted Penitence" (146). Psyche's second labor, to fill a vial from the rivers of hell, is accomplished with the assistance of Jove's eagle and is also glossed by Apuleius:

> A Violl fill'd with true repentant teares,
> And that she cannot fill, nor fetch from thence,
> But by the Eagles help, Heavens providence.
>
> (147)

Psyche's final ordeal, to descend into Hades and receive from Proserpine the box of beauty, is a test of obedience to and faith in the word of Cupid which protects her against illusion. Cupid provides the essential defense against hell's illusion because "the sound of hell wakes pitties eye" (142). He cautions Psyche against a repetition of her fall:

> Receive the box of beauty and be gon,
> Which still keep shut, let not thy daring eye
> Behold the wealth that in the boxe doth lie.
>
> (143)

Between the repentance and final ordeal of Psyche comes another comic episode of Coridon. Totally repentant, he reveres the "great god Cupid" (143) and the poets. His punishment for blasphemy against both is to be so troubled with a poetical itch that he scratches out endless rhymes, ballads, songs, sonnets, odes, and madrigals "till they bleede againe" (143). His ugly Amyrillus has been metamorphosed by "the eyes of poetry." A living lesson in perspective, he tells the swain, "say shee bee a foule beast in your eyes, yet shee is my Syren." Not content with the metamorphosis of his own eye, he resolves to steal the box of beauty from Psyche and apply its contents to himself and to the ugly Amyrillus. The clown's resolve to possess the power within the box is relevant not only to Psyche, but also to Apuleius. Cope points out that the clown's intended theft calls to mind that in Heywood's source Apuleius's metamorphosis "was accomplished by the stolen witch's salve, which he applied to himself in the hope of attaining the power of celestial flight."[10]

In Hades, Psyche avoids the temptation of Oblivion and Idle-folly and, most important, pride. Invited as the wife of Cupid to sit beside Queen Proserpine, Psyche responds,

> Psiche is Cupids out-cast, and his scorne,
> And therefore sits thus low, and thus forlorne.
>
> (149)

The one irresistible temptation, however, is the beauty in the box. Watching over this second fall, Cupid again shows mercy in acknowledging the limitations of her sex (152). What could not be gained by looking into the box is gained by drinking from the Eucharistic cup. The gods,

> Who taking a joynt pitty of her wrongs
> Gave thir consent, and then Great *Iove* himselfe
> Call'd for a cup of Immortallitie
> Dranke part to her, and Psiche quaff't the rest,
> At which, deformite forsooke her quite.
>
> (158)

The mercy shown by the gods to Psyche she, in turn, shows to her cruel sisters as she intercedes on their behalf (158). This grace, a manifestation of Psyche's own divine vision, signifies her perfect transformation.

We can return now to the earlier assertion that the fate of the poet, like that of Psyche, is defined by vision. As the poet aspires toward divine mystery — toward Truth and Beauty — he too must see with the eye of the soul and not with the "fleshy eye." With the eye of the soul he can perceive the "Idea or fore-conceit" wherein, as Sir Philip Sidney explains in his own defense of poetry, "the skill of the artificer standeth."[11] The idea or fore-conceit of Apuleius's play is apparent in his allegorical gloss. Psyche's story is his own in that the poet's presumptuous self-reliance results in a retrograde metamorphosis. He can be re-transformed from ass to poet only by grace: "the self same power / That calls all human wisdom foolishness." Apuleius's fall and redemption, like Psyche's, affirms for the artist the necessity of patience and humility, as well as a faith in the grace that comes to all. Through divine inspiration, a form of such grace, the eye of the soul beholds the divine. Thus, the nature of the poet's perception — blind Homer's being the supreme example — justifies Apuleius's assertion that "all true Poets raptures are divine."

The divinity of the poet is manifest in his capacity to reveal the divine within the ordinary or familiar appearance. In Cope's words, this play, like *The Ages*, makes clear that "Poetry makes every history into myth."[12] This is the process of the maker who creates a golden world — as well as a silver, a brazen, or an iron one. In *Love's Mistress*, Heywood's defense of poetry and of his own dramatic endeavors, we are invited to see the myth and the fore-conceit beneath the surface of his plays; otherwise, we too become Midases. The artist's trust in the inner eye of our discerning is expressed in Apuleius's final words to Midas:

But there's an understanding that hath depth
Beyond thy shallow non-sense; there's a wit
A braine which thou want'st, I to that submit.
                                        (159)

Chapter Seven
Conclusion

From his early dramatic endeavor, 1 and 2 *Edward IV*, through the culmination of his long career in *Love's Mistress*, Heywood presents a homogeneous, Christian vision of human experience expressed in the recurring myth of mankind's fall and redemption. He consistently presents the drama of the wayward, deluded, disobedient soul. In its various forms as the prodigal son-husband, the faithless wife, the idealistic gentleman, or the mythological psyche the soul progresses toward an understanding and acknowledgment of the redeeming power of love. Heywood's plays are thus the extended text of "love's school." As the fall results from a misplaced, ill-conceived, or falsely perceived love, so redemption derives from the gift of divine love and from the proper imitation of it in human relationships. Since divine love manifests itself in forgiveness, proper imitation precludes the all-too-human responses of hatred and revenge. Tests, trials, temptations, and ordeals shape the drama of those who fail or succeed in love's school. Virtue consists of patience, loyalty, and faith in a providential order that assures justice. Like his nondramatic works, the plays are a testimony of the author's simple Christian convictions.

As the history plays clearly illustrate, Heywood's political perspective is equally orthodox and serves to reinforce the Anglican Tudor-Stuart establishment. But within his affirmation of the established temporal order and authority is also a refreshing assertion of the dignity and potential of the ordinary man. This quality distinguishes Heywood, along with Dekker, from the aristocratic bias of the better-known playwrights of the age. Heywood's celebration of the common man is reflected in his paramount objective: to educate his middle-class audience.

With an old-fashioned optimism founded in Sidney's *An Apology for Poetry*, Heywood reaffirms the humanist belief in the reforming and transforming power of poetry. For Heywood as for Sidney, it is poetry's capacity to delight as it instructs that enables it to subsume and transcend history and philosophy: "What hath not Homer done, to make his name / Live to eternity?" But it is Heywood's insistence upon the power of poetry upon the stage that distinguishes him from the earlier apologist. Although *The Ages* and *Love's Mistress* confirm the divinity of poesy, Heywood writes not *An Apology for Poetry* but *An*

Apology for Actors. The key to Heywood's altered emphasis is found, nevertheless, in the work of his predecessor. Sidney defines poesy as "a representing, counterfeiting, or figuring forth—to speak metaphorically, a speaking picture—with this end, to teach and delight." When, however, he refers here to poesy as "a speaking picture" he is indeed speaking metaphorically. In *An Apology for Actors* Heywood's chief defense of the theater is based on his perception that drama makes literal Sidney's metaphor. In other words, through the medium of acting, art becomes quite literally a speaking picture, and the result is the altered reality of the audience. Heywood's lifetime commitment to the stage derives from his conviction that, of all the arts, drama is unique in its power to move to ethical action. He tells us in *An Apology for Actors* that

so bewitching a thing is liuely and well spirited action that it hath power to new mold the harts of the spectators and fashion them to the shape of any notable attempt. (B4^r)

To achieve this bewitchment and subsequent transformation, however, it must seem as "if the Personator were the man Personated." The dramatic illusion, in other words, must be lifelike. All plays, not just comedies, must be "the imitation of life, the glasse of custome, and the image of truth" (*An Apology for Actors*, F2^v) if they are to move the audience to ethical action. Heywood's effectiveness, like that of any dramatist, lies in his ability to give to his Christian vision a local habitation and a name, or, more specifically, to give to his characters the breath of life. This ability might be best defined as the art of realism, and Heywood's achievement as a dramatist of real, domestic life has long been acknowledged.

Nevertheless, except for *A Woman Killed with Kindness*, Heywood's plays have generally been ignored. The essays of Freda Townsend on Heywood's multiple plot structure, of Norman Rabkin on *The English Traveller,* and of Jackson Cope on *Love's Mistress* are the rare exceptions to this pattern of neglect. Careful reading of Heywood's dramatic canon reveals an artistic achievement that makes this neglect all too Midas-like indeed. What has never been sufficiently recognized is the diversity of and, in many instances, the excellence of his contributions to all the established dramatic genres of the Renaissance. His four history plays contribute substantially to our understanding of the kind, as well as provide a representative Renaissance perspective on two important monarchs, Edward IV and Queen Elizabeth. His comedies best illustrate the diversity of his talent. The pure delight of romantic love and high adventure in 1 *The Fair Maid of the West* makes this play the quintessential specimen of its kind and a worthy tribute to the golden years of Elizabethan daring. The comedies of prodigality and patience, *How a Man May Choose* and *Fortune by Land and by Sea*, affirm an equally noble human spirit, but within the context of the everyday existence shared by the audience. A tour de force of Plautine farce, *The Wise-Woman of Hogsden* deserves to be ranked with the best of its kind, yet this play has been totally ignored. The consequence of such neglect is the false conclusion that Heywood was capable of nothing more than a crude and clownish wit. His temperament and vision were not well suited to the Fletcherian tragicomedy or Cavalier mode. Nevertheless, he did adjust to the new mode well enough to produce one first-rate play of this kind, *The English Traveller.*

However one finally assesses the aesthetic value of Heywood's plays, it must be acknowledged that it would be difficult to find another dramatist whose plays are equally representative of the richness and variety of Renaissance drama. In this respect, Heywood takes his place beside Shakespeare—and without the usual deference. From the late 1590s until the closing of the theaters he was a major force—an actor, a shareholder, a nondramatic poet, and the most prolific of all playwrights. No other playwright reflects as well as Heywood the taste of the average playgoer or the substantial skill required to gratify that taste. How can we afford to ignore him?

Notes and References

Chapter One

1. A. M. Clark, *Thomas Heywood: Playwright and Miscellanist* (1931; rpt. New York, 1967), pp. 1–5. Unless otherwise indicated, biographical information comes from this authoritative work, hereafter cited as Clark.

2. *Oenone and Paris*, ed. Joseph Quincy Adams (Washington, D.C., 1943), p. v.

3. Quoted by Clark, p. 12.

4. *The Fair Maid of the West, Parts I and II*, ed Robert K. Turner, Jr. (Lincoln, Neb., 1967), pp. xi–xii.

5. Clark, p. 68.

6. Louis B. Wright, *Middle-Class Culture in Elizabethan England* (1935; rpt. New York, 1958), pp. 486–90.

7. Clark, p. 92. Unfortunately, there is neither a modern nor a facsimile edition of this work. For a summary of its contents, see Frederick S. Boas, *Thomas Heywood* (London, 1950), pp. 105–23.

8. For a recent account of the Puritan attack upon the stage and Prynne's role, see Philip Edwards, *Threshold of a Nation* (Cambridge, 1979), pp. 17–37.

9. *The Hierarchie of the blessed Angells* (Amsterdam, 1973), pp. 207–8.

10. Robert Grant Martin, "A Critical Study of Thomas Heywood's *Gunaikeion*," *Studies in Philology* 20 (1923): 160–83, provides a valuable catalog of Heywood's reading. Martin notes (p. 176) that Heywood is to be credited for the first citation by an English writer of the Italian text of Dante's *Paradiso*.

11. *An Apology for Actors (1612) by Thomas Heywood, A Refutation of the Apology for Actors (1615) by I. G.*, ed Richard H. Perkinson (New York, 1941), [E4v].

12. Clark, pp. 287–94. Studies subsequent to Clark's refute the argument that Heywood is responsible for interpolations (if indeed there are any) in *The Jew of Malta*. See Leo Kirschbaum, "Some Light on *The Jew of Malta*," *Modern Language Quarterly* 7 (1946): 53–56; also Robert Ford Welsh, "Evidence of Heywood's Spellings in *The Jew of Malta*," *Renaissance Papers 1962* (1963), pp. 3–9; and J. C. Maxwell, "How Bad is the Text of *The Jew of Malta*?" *Modern Language Review* 48 (1953): 435–38.

13. Clark, p. 191.

14. Allan Holaday, "Thomas Heywood and the Puritans," *Journal of English and Germanic Philology* 49 (1950): 192–203.

Chapter Two

1. Irving Ribner, *The English History Play in the Age of Shakespeare* (1957; rpt. London, 1965), p. 19.

2. Leonard F. Dean, "Bodin's *Methodus* in England before 1625," *Studies in Philology* 39 (1942): 164.

3. Ribner, *English History Play*, p. 8.

4. E. M. W. Tillyard, *Shakespeare's History Plays* (1944; rpt. New York, 1962), p. 362.

5. Otelia Cromwell, *Thomas Heywood: A Study in the Elizabethan Drama of Everyday Life* (1928; rpt. Hamden, Conn., 1969), pp. 159–62; also Clark, pp. 15–16.

6. Cromwell, *Thomas Heywood*, pp. 154–55; Michel Grivelet, *Thomas Heywood et le Drame Domestique Élizabéthain* (Paris, 1957), p. 365, hereafter cited as Grivelet.

7. Grivelet, p. 365.

8. See L. C. Knights, *Drama and Society in the Age of Jonson* (London, 1937), pp. 30–140.

9. Grivelet, p. 137.

10. The ballad cited by Cromwell (p. 156 n12) and Grivelet (p. 365) as an important source may be found in *Reliques of Ancient English Poetry*, collected by Thomas Percy, ed. Henry B. Wheatley, 3 vols. (Philadelphia: Sonnenschein & Lowrey, 1890), II: 268–73. For a discussion of the many versions of the Shore story, see Samuel M. Pratt, "Jane Shore and the Elizabethans: Some Facts and Speculations," *Texas Studies in Literature and Language* 2 (1970): 1293–1306. The sources for the historical episodes of parts 1 and 2 are Holinshed and Stow, and for the Hobs episode, a ballad to be found in Francis James Child, *The English and Scottish Popular Ballads* (1898; rpt. New York: Folklore Press, 1956), 5: 67–87.

11. Felix E. Schelling, *The English Chronicle Play* (1902; rpt. New York, 1964), pp. 144–46, notes Heywood's alterations in Holinshed and Stow's account: the character of Shore in the Falconbridge rebellion is substituted for Bassett, and the roles of Spicing and Jocelyn are substantially developed.

12. Ribner, *English History Play* (p. 275), notes that Heywood eliminates all the details in Holinshed that do not reflect favorably upon England and the King.

13. *If you Know not Me, you Know Nobody Part I*, ed. Madeleine Doran (Oxford, 1935), pp. v-xi.

14. *If you Know not Me, you Know Nobody Part II*, ed. Madeleine Doran (Oxford, 1935), pp. v-vii. All citations from Parts I and II are from the Doran editions, with line references cited parenthetically.

15. Doran, Part I, p. xi.

16. For a discussion of the idealization of Elizabeth during and after her reign, see Elkin C. Wilson, *England's Eliza* (Cambridge, Mass.: Harvard University Press, 1939); Roy C. Strong, *The Cult of Elizabeth* (London, 1977); and Frederick S. Boas, *Queen Elizabeth in Drama and Related Studies* (London: Allen and Unwin, 1950).

17. Georgianna Ziegler, "England's Savior: Elizabeth I in the Writings of Thomas Heywood," *Renaissance Papers 1980* (1981), pp. 29–39.

18. R. G. Martin, "The Sources of Heywood's *If you Know not Me, you Know Nobody*, Part I," *Modern Language Notes* 39 (1924): 220–22.

19. *The Acts and Monuments of John Foxe* (1843–44; rpt. New York: AMS Press, 1965), 8: 609.

20. According to Cromwell, *Thomas Heywood* (pp. 50–51), and Grivelet (p. 337), the sources for this bizarre potpourri are the chronicles, particularly Stow, and a popular narrative of old Hobson.

21. Louis B. Wright's emphatic generalization about Heywood—"Unstintingly he praises chastity and condemns license"—simply will not hold up in this case. See Wright's *Middle-Class Culture*, p. 643.

22. Knights, *Drama and Society*, pp. 250–53.

23. Ribner's assertion that "Hobson is an obvious imitation of Simon Eyre in Dekker's *Shoemaker's Holiday*" (p. 223) does not do justice to the originality of Heywood's creation.

Chapter Three

1. Although authorship of *The Fair Maid of the Exchange* remains uncertain, Karl E. Snyder, *A Critical Edition of The Fair Maid of the Exchange by Thomas Heywood* (New York, 1980), pp. 2–22, presents an argument that suggests that the play belongs to this category of Heywood's comedies.

2. Cromwell, *Thomas Heywood*, , pp. 44–47; *Thomas Heywood's The Four Prentices of London, A Critical, Old-Spelling Edition*, ed. Mary Ann Weber Gasior (New York, 1980), pp. vii–xv. All citations are from the Gasior edition with line numbers given parenthetically.

3. Gasior, pp. xvii–xxiii.

4. Ibid., p. xxxii.

5. Clark suggests 1609 or 1610 as the date of composition (p. 110). Ross Jewell, "Thomas Heywood's *The Fair Maid of the West*," *Studies in English Drama*, First Series, ed. Allison Gaw (New York: D. Appelton, 1917), p. 67, favors 1604.

6. *The Fair Maid of the West, Parts I and II*, ed. Robert K. Turner (Lincoln, 1967), pp. xi–xiv. All quotations and line references from Parts I and II are from this edition. Grivelet, p. 360.

7. Clark, p. 329.

8. William Carew Hazlitt, *Lectures Chiefly on the Dramatic Literature of the Age of Elizabeth* (London, 1820), p. 77.

9. From the third dedication, addressed "To All Noble and Brave Spirited Gentlemen, with the excellent and vertuously disposed gentlewomen in generall," as quoted by Marilyn L. Johnson, *Images of Women in the Works of Thomas Heywood*, Jacobean Drama Studies 42 (Salzburg, 1974), p. 48.

10. Turner, *Fair Maid*, p. 35 n51.

11. Norman Council, *When Honour's at the Stake* (London: Allen & Unwin, 1973), p. 24.

12. For an account of the Islands Voyage, see Turner's Appendix A, pp.

198–99, and Lytton Strachey, *Elizabeth and Essex* (New York: Harcourt Brace, 1928), pp. 147–48.

13. Clark, p. 110.

14. Turner, *Fair Maid*, p. xviii.

15. *How a Man May Choose a Good Wife from a Bad*, ed. A. E. H. Swaen (Louvain, 1912), pp. vi-xiii. Swaen's argument for Heywood's authorship appears to have convinced everyone but Otelia Cromwell, p. 200. Clark is apparently so convinced that he does not even raise the issue. Grivelet finds Swaen's attribution "decisive" (p. 362). All quotations and line numbers are from the Swaen edition, hereafter cited as Swaen.

16. Swaen, p. xlii.

17. Muriel Bradbrook, *The Growth and Structure of Elizabethan Comedy* (1955; rpt. London, 1962), p. 37.

18. Sylvia Feldman, *The Morality-Patterned Comedy of the Renaissance* (The Hague, 1970), pp. 16–24.

19. Alan C. Dessen, "The Moral as an Elizabethan Dramatic Kind: An Exploratory Essay," *Comparative Drama* 5 (1971): 154.

20. Ibid., pp. 146–47.

21. Marvin T. Herrick, *Tragicomedy* (1955; rpt. Urbana, 1962), p. 228. Herrick explains that the Christian Terence was created by sixteenth-century humanists who presented serious moral argument, often from the Bible, through the dramatic structure and conventions of Terence. The plays were thus a synthesis of native morality and mystery plays and the New Comedy. A favorite subject of these academic dramas was the prodigal son (pp. 37–46, 61–62).

22. Swaen, pp. xii-xvi, and C. R. Baskerville, "Sources and Analogues of *How a Man May Choose a Good Wife from a Bad*," *PMLA* 24 (1909): 711–30.

23. Baskerville, "Sources and Analogues," p. 717.

24. A. M. Clark, "Thomas Heywood's *Art of Love* Lost and Found," *Library*, Series 4, 3 (1922): 221.

25. *Clark*, p. 81 n4.

26. Ibid., p. 50.

27. Mowbray Velte, *The Bourgeois Elements in the Dramas of Thomas Heywood* (1922; rpt. New York, 1966), p. 114, assigns to Rowley the Forrest scenes of act I and the pirates' execution scene, act V, scene 1. *A Critical Edition of Fortune by Land and by Sea*, ed. Herman Doh (New York, 1980), pp. 3–10, supports Velte's attributions through a study of the use of colons. Nevertheless, Doh acknowledges that "Most opinions do not stray from Fleay's comment that he could not trace Rowley's hand in *FLS*" (p. 3). All quotations and line references are from the Doh edition.

28. Clark, p. 213.

29. Doh (pp. 32–37) favors the 1607–09 dates primarily because an earlier date would be unlikely if one assumes Rowley (born 1585) had a share in the play.

30. Doh, p. 40.

31. Although Doh does not mention the influence of revenge plays upon *Fortune by Land*, his notes point out numerous echoes from Shakespeare's

plays written before Elizabeth's death.

32. The history of these two Elizabethan pirates is told in Holinshed, in ballads, in tracts, and even in a 1639 pamphlet by Heywood called "A True Relation of the Lives and Deaths of the two most Famous English Pyrats, Purser, and Clinton." See Doh, pp. 12–31.

33. Cromwell, *Thomas Heywood*, pp. 169–70.

34. *Vincentio Salviolo his Practice* (1595) codified the practice of dueling for the period. Touchstone in Shakespeare's *As You Like It* seems to have this work in mind when he defines the fixed stages of a quarrel that culminate in the "Lie Direct" (V. iv. 65–77). Compare *The Fair Maid of the West*, Part I (II. iii. 51), and Turner's note.

35. Compare lines 194–236 and *The Spanish Tragedy*, II. v, especially the first passage of additions.

36. Knights, *Drama and Society*, p. 248; also cited by Doh, p. 44.

37. Doh, p. 51.

38. *A Critical Edition of Thomas Heywood's The Wise-Woman of Hogsdon*, ed. Michael H. Leonard (New York, 1980), p. 7. Subsequent quotations and line references will be from this edition.

39. Clark, p. 165.

40. Leonard, pp. 5–6.

41. Clark, p. 245.

42. Leonard, p. 11.

43. Leonard agrees with George F. Reynolds that the wise-woman places her hidden audience behind and perhaps alongside a curtain at the back of the stage, perhaps within the enclosure (p. 232). See George F. Reynolds, *The Staging of Elizabethan Plays at the Red Bull Theater 1605–1625* (New York, 1940), p. 109.

44. The fact that Hogsdon was known to the Jacobean audience as a district for wise-women is suggested by Jonson's opening to *The Devil is an Ass*. Satan ridicules Pug's enterprises: "Some old Ribibe [old woman] about Kentish town / Or Hogsden, you would hang now, for a Witch" (I. i. 16–17). Quoted by Fran C. Chalfant under "Hogsden" in *Ben Jonson's London: A Jacobean Placename Dictionary* (Athens: University of Georgia Press, 1978).

45. *Gunaikeion*, pp. 414–15; also cited by Clark, p. 66.

46. Because *The Late Lancashire Witches* seems to have been conceived primarily by Brome rather than Heywood, I have not dealt with it. For a discussion of this collaborative endeavor, see Catherine M. Shaw, *Richard Brome*, Twayne's English Author Series 290 (Boston, 1980), pp. 108–17. A new edition of the play with an extensive introduction is now available: *An Edition of The Late Lancashire Witches by Thomas Heywood and Richard Brome*, ed. Laird H. Barber (New York, 1979).

47. Clark, p. 128.

48. Velte, *Bourgeois Elements*, p. 85.

49. Grivelet notes the highly questionable morality of *A Maidenhead Well Lost* and attributes this deviation from Heywood's usual rectitude to his effort to write in the Fletcherian mode (pp. 157–58).

Chapter Four

1. Henry Hitch Adams, *English Domestic Or, Homiletic Tragedy 1575–1642* (New York, 1943), pp. 1–2. Also Peter Ure, "Marriage and the Domestic Drama in Heywood and Ford," *English Studies* 32 (1951): 200–1.

2. Clark, pp. 36–37.

3. T. S. Eliot, *Selected Essays* (New York, 1932), p. 150. Eliot's essay on Heywood first appeared in the *Times* (London) *Literary Supplement* in 1931 and is obviously influenced by Clark's study.

4. Freda L. Townsend, "The Artistry of Thomas Heywood's Double Plots," *Philological Quarterly* 25 (1946): 97–98; *A Woman Killed With Kindness*, ed. R. W. Van Fossen (Cambridge, Mass., 1961), pp. xxvii–lviii. Quotations with scene and line references are from this edition.

5. Eliot, *Essays*, pp. 157, 158.

6. Van Fossen (pp. xvii–xxvii) observes that the subplot derives from Illicini's Sienese novel about the Countess Salimbene through Bandello and Belleforest to William Painter's *Palace of Pleasure*. The source for the main plot is not known for certain but may again reflect Heywood's familiarity with Painter.

7. Townsend, "Artistry," pp. 101–3.

8. John Canuteson, "The Theme of Forgiveness in the Main Plot and Subplot of *A Woman Killed With Kindness*," in *Renaissance Drama*, n.s. 2 (1969), pp. 123–41. David Cook, "*A Woman Killed With Kindness*: An Unshakespearean Tragedy," *English Studies* 45 (1964): 363, sees "the actions as related in terms of charity rather than chastity."

9. Cook, "An Unshakespearean Tragedy," p. 363.

10. Townsend, "Artistry," p. 101.

11. The most familiar example of the wordplay this relation occasioned in the Renaissance is Hamlet's opening line, "A little more than kin, and less than kind." Other significant examples can be found in *King Lear* where kin/kind prove anything but kind.

12. Van Fossen, p. xxviii, and Townsend, "Artistry," p. 117.

13. Otto Rauchbauer, "Visual and Rhetorical Imagery in Thomas Heywood's *A Woman Killed With Kindness*," *English Studies* 57 (1976): 204.

14. Van Fossen, p. xxix.

15. A. G. Hooper, "*A Woman Killed With Kindness*, Scene XIV: Sir Charles's Plan," *English Language Notes* 11 (1974): 184.

16. Van Fossen, p. xl.

17. Cook, "An Unshakespearean Tragedy," p. 354, asserts that the characterization is "strikingly modern"; Canuteson, "The Theme of Forgiveness," p. 124, argues for an "instinctive reaction" to the play; Margaret B. Bryan, "Food Symbolism in *A Woman Killed With Kindness*," *Renaissance Papers 1973* (1974), pp. 15–17, reads Frankford from a perspective of depth-psychology.

18. Alfred Harbage, *Shakespeare and the Rival Traditions* (New York, 1952), pp. 205–6; Clark, p. 234.

19. Cromwell, *Thomas Heywood*, p. 54.

20. Ure, "Marriage and the Domestic Drama," pp. 206–7.

21. Van Fossen, p. xlvii.

22. Louis B. Wright, "Male Friendship Cult in Thomas Heywood's Plays," *Modern Language Notes* 42 (1927): 510.

23. Hardin Craig, *The Enchanted Glass* (1939; rpt. Oxford, 1966), pp. 128.

24. Rauchbauer, "Imagery," p. 204 n10.

25. Fredson T. Bowers, *Elizabethan Revenge Tragedy, 1587*–1642 (Princeton, 1940), p. 225. See also Van Fossen, p. xxxi.

26. Wright, *Middle-Class Culture*, pp. 204–8.

27. Adams, *English Domestic or, Homiletic Tragedy*, p. 151.

28. Eliot, *Essays* p. 157.

29. Ibid.

30. Hallett D. Smith, "*A Woman Killed With Kindness*," *PMLA* 53 (1938): 147.

31. Robert B. Heilman, *Tragedy and Melodrama* (Seattle, 1968), p. 213.

32. Adams, *English Domestic or, Homiletic Tragedy*, p. 159.

33. As quoted by Townsend, "Artistry," p. 102.

34. Cook, "An Unshakespearean Tragedy," pp. 366–72.

35. Fusion of horse and rider here prefigures the centaur Nessus who steals Hercules' bride in Heywood's *The Brazen Age*. For a similar image of horse and rider, see Shakespeare's *Rape of Lucrece*, ll. 705–7.

36. The "swift sandy glass" is but one of many images, verbally and visually presented, that are drawn from or at least have conspicuous correspondence in the emblem books of the Renaissance. Heywood's images of hearts and hands, Fortune's wheel, the lute, falconry, angels, card or chess games also suggest this influence.

37. Rauchbauer, "Imagery," p. 208.

38. Cecile Williamson Cary, " 'Go Breake This Lute': Music in Heywood's *A Woman Killed With Kindness*," *Huntington Library Quarterly* 37 (1974): 120.

39. Cook, "An Unshakespearean Tragedy," p. 37.

40. See John B. Friedman, *Orpheus in the Middle Ages* (Cambridge, Mass.: Harvard University Press, 1970).

41. Compare Livy, I. 47-II. 13.

42. *The Rape of Lucrece*, ed. Allan Holaday (Urbana, 1950), pp. 30–31. All quotations and line references in the text are from this edition.

43. Clark, p. 48.

44. Holaday, pp. 5–18.

45. A. M. Clark, "Reviews," *Review of English Studies*, n.s. 3 (1950), p. 286.

46. Clark, p. 47, notes that Valerius "may have suggested to Beaumont the equally jolly Master Merry-thought who actually sings one of the songs in Heywood's appendix."

47. The last three lines of this speech occur in Q1-Q4 but not in Q5, the 1638 edition.

Chapter Five

1. Madeleine Doran, *Endeavors of Art: A Study in Form in Elizabethan Drama* (1954; rpt. Madison, 1964), pp. 191–92.

2. Ibid., p. 193

3. Ibid., p. 198.

4. Eugene M. Waith, *The Pattern of Tragicomedy in Beaumont and Fletcher* (1952; rpt. Hamden, Conn., 1969), p. 143 n2.

5. William Painter, *The Palace of Pleasure* (2d ed., 1575), Tome II, Novel IV; ed. Joseph Jacobs (1890; rpt. New York, 1966), pp. 176–208. All quotations and page references are from this edition.

6. *The Captives; or the Lost Recovered*, ed. Alexander Corbin Judson (New Haven, 1921), p. 9. All quotations and line references are from this edition.

7. Ibid., p. 10.

8. Ibid., pp. 17–23.

9. Carolyn Prager, "Heywood's Adaptation of Plautus' *Rudens*: The Problem of Slavery in *The Captives*," *Comparative Drama* 9 (1975): 119.

10. Ibid., p. 119.

11. Townsend, "Artistry," pp. 112–14.

12. Clark, p. 113, prefers 1624 as the date of composition. G. E. Bentley, *The Jacobean and Caroline Stage* (Oxford, 1956), IV, 65–66, prefers to date the play around 1627.

13. Clark, pp. 119–20.

14. Adams, *English Domestic Or, Homiletic Tragedy*, p. 173.

15. Clark, p. 238.

16. Grivelet, pp. 187–88. In his subsequent article "The Simplicity of Thomas Heywood," *Shakespeare Survey* 14 (1961): 60, Grivelet notes the irony of Geraldine's love for Mrs. Wincott and demonstrates various thematic connections between the main and subplot.

17. Keith Sturgess, *Three Elizabethan Domestic Tragedies* (Baltimore, 1969), p. 8, classifies *The English Traveller* as domestic tragedy.

18. Norman Rabkin, "Dramatic Deception in Heywood's *The English Traveller*," *Studies in English Literature* 1 (1961): 1–16.

19. Ibid., p. 1

20. Townsend, "Artistry," pp. 114–15.

21. Clark, p. 164.

22. Grivelet, p. 386.

23. Clark, p. 164.

24. Algernon Charles Swinburne, *The Age of Shakespeare* (London, 1908), p. 230.

25. Clark, pp. 246–47.

26. For a discussion of this Platonizing fashion, see Alfred Harbage, *Cavalier Drama* (1936; rpt. New York, 1964), pp. 36–38.

27. Ibid., p. 41.

28. Ibid., p. 35.

29. Ibid., p. 39.

30. Waith, *Pattern of Tragicomedy*, p. 143 n2.

Chapter Six

1. Clark, pp. 63–64.

2. J. Q. Adams, "Shakespeare, Heywood, and the Classics," *Modern Language Notes* 34 (1919): 336; Clark, p. 65.

3. Clark, p. 222.

4. Reynolds, *The Staging of Elizabethan Plays*, p. 9. Reynolds conclusively refutes the suggestion by Joseph Q. Adams, *Journal of English and Germanic Philology* 10 (1911): 330, that the editions of these plays were published for closet reading and thus do not reflect conditions of actual performance.

5. Robert Grant Martin, "A New Specimen of the Revenge Play," *Modern Philology* 16 (1918): 1–10, identifies the last two acts of 2 *The Iron Age* as a somewhat self-contained playlet fitting the pattern of the revenge play. He does not appear to recognize the extent to which the first three acts also fit the pattern. The shadow of *Hamlet* is everywhere in this play, and there is no reason to believe, as Martin does, that Heywood's play predates Shakespeare's.

6. Clark, p. 222.

7. Ibid., p. 116.

8. Sir Philip Sidney's term for the poet-hater in *An Apology for Poetry*, ed. Geoffrey Shepherd (New York: Barnes and Noble, 1973), 121. Clark's argument (pp. 138–42) that Midas and his bastard are allusions to William Prynne and his literary offspring, *Histriomastix*, is quite convincing.

9. Jackson I. Cope, *The Theatre and the Dream* (Baltimore and London, 1973), p. 184. See Cope's excellent discussion of the play's statement about the relationship between sight and sound and its relevance to the dramatist's art.

10. Ibid., p. 188.

11. *An Apology for Poetry*, p. 101.

12. Cope, *The Theatre and the Dream*, p. 193.

Selected Bibliography

BIBLIOGRAPHIES

Donovan, Dennis. *Elizabethan Bibliographies Suppliments II: Thomas Dekker, Thomas Heywood, and Cyril Tourneur.* London: Nether Press, 1967.

Logan, Terence P. and Denzell S. Smith. *The Popular School: A Survey and Bibliography of Recent Studies in English Renaissance Drama.* Lincoln: University of Nebraska Press, 1975.

Rauchbauer, Otto. "Thomas Heywood: An Annotated Bibliography, 1967 — " *Research Opportunities in Renaissance Drama* 18 (1975): 45-50.

Ribner, Irving. *Tudor and Stuart Drama.* Goldentree Bibliographies. New York: Appleton-Century-Crofts, 1966.

Rider, Philip E. "Thomas Heywood: A Supplementary, Annotated Bibliography, 1966-1975." *Research Opportunities in Renaissance Drama* 19 (1966): 33-36.

Tannenbaum, Samuel A. and Dorothy R. Tannenbaum. *Elizabethan Bibliographies.* 10 vols. 1939; rpt. Port Washington, N.Y.: Kennikat Press, 1967.

PRIMARY SOURCES

An Apology for Actors (1612) by Thomas Heywood, A Refutation of the Apology for Actors (1615) by I. G. Edited by Richard H. Perkinson. New York: Scholars' Facsimiles, 1941.

The Captives; or the Lost Recovered. Edited by Alexander Corbin Judson. New Haven: Yale University Press, 1921.

The Dramatic Works of Thomas Heywood. [Edited R. H. Shepherd for John Pearson] 6 vols. 1874; rpt. New York: Russell & Russell, 1964.

A Critical Edition of the Fair Maid of the Exchange by Thomas Heywood. Edited by Karl E. Snyder. New York: Garland, 1980.

The Fair Maid of the West, Parts I and II. Edited by Robert K. Turner. Lincoln: University of Nebraska Press, 1967.

A Critical Edition of Fortune by Land and by Sea by Thomas Heywood and William Rowley. Edited by Herman Doh. New York: Garland, 1980.

Thomas Heywood's The Four Prentices of London, A Critical, Old-Spelling Edition. Edited by Mary Ann Weber Gasior. New York: Garland, 1980.

Gunaikeion: or, Nine Books of Various History Concerning Women. London: A. Islip, 1624.

The Hierarchie of the Blessed Angells. Amsterdam: Theatrum Orbis Terrarum, 1973.

How a Man May Choose a Good Wife from a Bad. Edited by A. E. H. Swaen. Louvain: A. Uystpruyst, 1912.

If you Know not Me, you Know Nobody Part I. Edited by Madeleine Doran. Oxford: Oxford University Press, 1935.

If you Know not Me, you Know Nobody Part II. Edited by Madeleine Doran. Oxford: University Press, 1935.

Oenone and Paris. Edited by Joseph Quincy Adams. Washington, D.C.: Folger Shakespeare Library, 1943.

The Rape of Lucrece. Edited by Allan Holaday. Urbana: University of Illinois Press, 1950.

Troia Britanica: OR, Great Britaines Troy. Amsterdam: Theatrum Orbis Terrarum, 1974.

A Woman Killed with Kindness and The Fair Maid of the West. Edited by Katherine Lee Bates. Boston: Heath, 1917.

A Woman Killed with Kindness. Edited by R. W. Van Fossen. Cambridge, Mass.: Harvard University Press, 1961.

A Critical Edition of Thomas Heywood's The Wise-Woman of Hogsdon. Edited by Michael H. Leonard. New York: Garland, 1980.

An Edition of The Late Lancashire Witches by Thomas Heywood and Richard Brome. Edited by Laird H. Barber. New York: Garland, 1979.

SECONDARY SOURCES

1. Books

Adams, Henry Hitch. *English Domestic Or, Homiletic Tragedy 1575–1642.* New York: Columbia University Press, 1943. Still the best study on this subject and particularly useful for the historical context of Heywood's plays.

Bentley, Gerald Eades. *The Jacobean and Caroline Stage.* 7 vols. Oxford: Clarendon Press, 1941-68. Definitive source of information and companion to E. K. Chamber's *Elizabethan Drama.* On Heywood, Bentley generally defers to the authority of A. M. Clark.

Boas, Frederick S. *Thomas Heywood.* London: Norgate, 1950. An extremely brief description and discussion of exemplary nondramatic and dramatic works. Boas offers generous quotations from non-dramatic texts that are not readily available.

Bowers, Fredson T. *Elizabethan Revenge Tragedy 1587–1642.* Princeton: Princeton University Press, 1940. The authoritative study on this subject, which notes Heywood's innovation regarding the revenge pattern.

Bradbrook, Muriel C. *The Growth and Structure of Elizabethan Comedy.* 1955: Reprint. London: Chatto and Windus, 1962. Excellent study of the origins and distinguishing characteristics of the genre. Sees Heywood as representative of the popular school of playwrights who wrote for the stage, not for the printed page.

Clark, Arthur Melville. *Thomas Heywood: Playwright and Miscellanist.* 1931: Reprint. New York: Russell and Russell, 1967. The authorizative source for information about Heywood's life and canon. So scholarly and thorough that the reader is sometimes lost in the maze of details. Does not adequately acknowledge Heywood's aesthetic achievement.

Cope, Jackson I. *The Theatre and the Dream.* Baltimore: Johns Hopkins University Press, 1973. An excellent study of the epistemological significance of Renaissance metaphors of theater and dream. The discussion of Heywood's imagery of sight and sound in *Love's Mistress* is a superb corrective to the reductive approach to Heywood.

Craig, Hardin. *The Enchanted Glass.* 1939: Reprint. Oxford: Basil Blackwell, 1966. Indispensable study of Renaissance assumptions about cosmology, religion, science, psychology, logic, and literature. The chapter on Renaissance psychology is particularly relevant to Heywood.

Cromwell, Otelia. *Thomas Heywood: A Study in the Elizabethan Drama of Everyday Life.* 1928: Reprint. Hamden, Conn.: Archon Books, 1969. Discusses Heywood's skill with domestic themes and ordinary people, but does not credit him with much aesthetic sophistication.

Doran, Madeleine. *Endeavors of Art: A Study in Form in Elizabethan Drama.* 1954: Reprint. Madison: University of Wisconsin Press, 1964. The best study of dramatic kinds and techniques; defines the poetics of Renaissance drama.

Edwards, Philip. *Threshold of a Nation.* Cambridge: Cambridge University Press, 1979. Examines the close relationship between politics and plays and charts the rise, triumph, and decline of the theater through its dependence upon the crown.

Eliot, T. S. *Selected Essays.* New York: Harcourt, Brace, 1932. Seriously underestimates the achievement of Heywood.

Feldman, Sylvia D. *The Morality-Patterned Comedy of the Renaissance.* The Hague: Mouton, 1970. Discusses *How a Man May Choose* as the prototype of morality-patterned plays involving a fall, repentance, and forgiveness.

Grivelet, Michel. *Thomas Heywood et le Drame Domestique Élizabéthain.* Paris: Didier, 1957. Demonstrates Heywood's importance as a playwright of domestic life and provides a useful appendix of his canon, including dates, sources, and plot summaries.

Harbage, Alfred. *Cavalier Drama.* 1936: Reprint. New York: Russell & Russell, 1964. Discusses trends in the drama during the Caroline and Commonwealth periods and the early years of the Restoration. Particularly useful for information on the influence of the court of Henrietta Maria upon the plays of the Caroline period.

_____. *Shakespeare and the Rival Traditions.* New York: Macmillan, 1952. Defines the separate repertoires and distinctive characteristics of the public and private theaters. Also provides valuable information on the different acting companies and their audiences.

Hazlitt, William Carew. *Lectures Chiefly on the Dramatic Literature of the Age of Elizabeth.* London: Stodart & Steuart, 1820. Reinforces the assessment of Charles Lamb by paying tribute to Heywood's "beautiful prose put into heroic measure."

Herrick, Marvin T. *Tragicomedy.* 1955: Reprint. Urbana: University of Illinois Press, 1962. Traces the history and development of the form beginning with the classical background and continuing through the seventeenth century.

Heilman, Robert. *Tragedy and Melodrama.* Seattle: University of Washington Press, 1968. A provocative essay on the distinguishing characteristics of tragedy and melodrama. Sees *A Woman Killed* as a generic malformation.

Johnson, Marilyn L. *Images of Women in the Works of Thomas Heywood.* Jacobean Drama Series 42. Salzburg: Salzburg University Press, 1974. Illustrates that Heywood is generally kindly disposed toward his female characters and that his views of women are fundamentally conventional.

Knights, L. C. *Drama and Society in the Age of Jonson.* London: Chatto & Windus, 1937. Traces the social and economic revolution that came with the rise of capitalism as reflected in the drama.

Lamb, Charles. *Specimens of English Dramatic Poets, who lived about the Time of Shakespeare.* 2 vols. London: Longman et al, 1808. Describes Heywood as a "prose Shakespeare."

Leggatt, Alexander. *Citizen Comedy in the Age of Shakespeare.* Toronto: University of Toronto Press, 1973. Defines the various kinds of citizen comedy set in a middle-class milieu and distinguishes between plays written for and those written about the middle class. Heywood's belong to the first category.

Reynolds, George F. *The Staging of Elizabethan Plays at the Red Bull Theater 1605–1625.* New York: Modern Language Association of America, 1940. Discusses the staging of many of Heywood's plays and stresses the special effects required by such works as *The Ages.*

Ribner, Irving. *The English History Play in the Age of Shakespeare.* 1957: Reprint. London: Methuen, 1965. Defines and traces the development of the genre; sees Heywood as instrumental to the genre's decline through the intrusion of romance matter.

Schelling, Felix E. *The English Chronicle Play.* 1902: Reprint. Haskell House, 1964. Traces the origin, development, and decline of the chronicle play and notes Heywood's introduction of highly sentimental scenes into this kind of drama.

Shaw, Catherine M. *Richard Brome.* Twayne's English Authors 290. Boston: G. K. Hall, 1980. Discusses the Brome-Heywood collaboration, *The Late Lancashire Witches,* and attributes the virtues of the play to Brome.

Strong, Roy C. *The Cult of Elizabeth.* London: Thames and Hudson, 1977. A beautifully illustrated study of portraits and pageantry that contributed to the establishment of the myth of Elizabeth.

Sturgess, Keith. *Three Elizabethan Domestic Tragedies.* Baltimore: Penguin, 1969. An edition of *A Woman Killed with Kindness, A Yorkshire Trag-*

edy, and *Arden of Faversham,* with a good introduction on domestic tragedy.

Swinburne, Algernon Charles. *The Age of Shakespeare.* London: Chatto & Windus, 1908. Contains an appreciative discussion of several Heywood plays.

Tillyard, E. M. W. *Shakespeare's History Plays.* 1944: Reprint. New York: Collier Books, 1962. An excellent study of the philosophical context in which Shakespeare and Heywood wrote their history plays.

Velte, Mowbray. *The Bourgeois Elements in the Dramas of Thomas Heywood.* 1922. Reprint. New York: Haskell House, 1966. Stresses the limitations of Heywood's plays as a reflection of the tastes and values of his bourgeois audience.

Waith, Eugene M. *The Pattern of Tragicomedy in Beaumont and Fletcher.* 1952. Reprint. Hamden, Conn.: Archon Books, 1969. Defines the distinctive characteristics and origins of the tragicomedy of Beaumont and Fletcher.

Wright, Louis B. *Middle-Class Culture in Elizabethan England.* 1935. Reprint. New York: Cornell University Press, 1958. Indispensable study that emphasizes the importance of Heywood to an understanding of middle-class Elizabethan culture.

2. Articles

Beck, Ervin. "Terence Improved: The Paradigm of the Prodigal Son in English Renaissance Comedy." *Renaissance Drama,* n.s. 6 (1973), pp. 107–22. Sees the pattern of rebellion against but eventual return to the values of the preceding generation within the larger context of redemptive comedy.

Berry, Lloyd. "A Note on *A Woman Killed With Kindness." Modern Language Review* 58 (1963): 64–65. Argues that Scene ii constitutes a "burlesque parallel" to Scene i.

Bryan, Margaret B. "Food Symbolism in *A Woman Killed With Kindness." Renaissance Papers 1973* (1974), pp. 9–17. Sees the pattern of the fall through the images of voracity.

Canuteson, John. "The Theme of Forgiveness in the Main Plot and Subplot of *A Woman Killed With Kindness." Renaissance Drama,* n.s. 2 (1969), pp. 123–41. Argues for a modern "instinctive" reaction to the characters and situations of the play.

Cary, Cecile Williamson. " 'Go Breake This Lute': Music in Heywood's *A Woman Killed With Kindness." Huntington Library Quarterly* 37 (1974): 111–22. Excellent analysis of music imagery as part of the play's concern with moral order.

Clark, Arthur Melville. "Thomas Heywood's *Art of Love* Lost and Found." *Library* series 4, 3 (1922): 210–22. Traces the history of Heywood's early translations of Ovid.

Cook, David. "*A Woman Killed With Kindness*: An Unshakespearean Tragedy." *English Studies* 45 (1964): 353–72. A superb argument for the human, three-dimensional nature of Heywood's characters and for the play as a tragedy of ordinary people.

Dessen, Alan C. "The Moral as an Elizabethan Dramatic Kind: An Exploratory Essay." *Comparative Drama* 5 (1971): 138–56. Explores the term "morall" as it applies to sixteenth and seventeenth-century plays. Examines Heywood's use of the term in *An Apology for Actors.*

Forker, Charles R. "Shakespeare's Histories and Heywood's *If you Know not Me, you Know Nobody.*" *Neuphilologische Mitteilungen* 66 (1965): 166–78. Shows the influence of *Richard II* and *Henry V* on Heywood.

Grivelet, Michel. "The Simplicity of Thomas Heywood." *Shakespeare Survey* 14 (1961): 56–65. Demonstrates that the relationship between main and subplot is anything but simple, particularly in *The English Traveller.*

Hardison, O. B. "Three Types of Catharsis." *Renaissance Drama*, n.s. 2 (1969), pp. 3–22. Heywood's *Apology for Actors* provides an excellent example of the Renaissance theory of "moral" catharsis in which a member of the audience is compelled to confess his guilt after seeing his crime mirrored on stage.

Holaday, Allan. "Thomas Heywood and the Puritans." *Journal of English and Germanic Philology* 49 (1950): 192–203. Counters Clark's argument that late in life Heywood became a Puritan.

Holstead, W. L. "Dekker's *Cupid and Psyche* and Thomas Heywood." *English Literary History* 11 (1944): 182–91. Presents passages in Heywood's *Love's Mistress* and Dekker's *England's Parnassus* that are almost identical and concludes that these were first part of Dekker's contribution to *Cupid and Psyche* (ca. 1600) and later borrowed by Heywood.

Hooper, A. G. "*A Woman Killed With Kindness*, Scene XIV: Sir Charles's Plan." *English Language Notes* 11 (1974): 181–88. Argues that Sir Charles never intends to prostitute Anne but counts on the courtesy of Acton.

Levin, Richard. "Elizabethan 'Three Level' Play." *Renaissance Drama*, n.s. 2 (1969), pp. 23–37. *A Woman Killed* is an example of drama that presents three distinct levels of society through three classes or kinds of characters.

Martin, Robert Grant. "A Critical Study of Thomas Heywood's *Gunaikeion.*" *Studies in Philology* 20 (1923): 160–83. Presents an amazing catalog of works that Heywood read or was at least familiar with.

_____. "A New Specimen of Revenge Play." *Modern Philology* 16 (1918): 1–10. Sees the last two acts of 2 *The Iron Age* as fulfilling A. H. Thorndike's definition of revenge tragedy.

Prager, Carolyn. "Heywood's Adaptation of Plautus' *Rudens*: The Problem of Slavery in *The Captives.*" *Comparative Drama* 9 (1975): 116–24. Notes Heywood's sensitivity to the political and moral issue of slavery.

Pratt, Samuel M. "Jane Shore and the Elizabethans: Some Facts and Speculations." *Texas Studies in Literature and Language* 2 (1970): 1293–1306. Traces the history and appeal of the Jane Shore story, but does not do justice to Heywood's contribution.

Rabkin, Norman. "Dramatic Deception in Heywood's *The English Traveller.*" *Studies in English Literature* 1 (1961): 1–16. Excellent discussion of the theme of appearance and reality and of audience manipulation.

Rauchbauer, Otto. "Visual and Rhetorical Imagery in Th. Heywood's *A Woman Killed With Kindness.*" *English Studies* 57 (1976): 200–10. Sees a series of allegorical emblematic images that enrich the play's meaning.

Smith, Hallett. *"A Woman Killed With Kindness." PMLA* 53 (1938): 138–47. Answers T. S. Eliot's depreciatory view of the play by demonstrating the moral integrity and accountability of the characters.

Townsend, Freda L. "The Artistry of Thomas Heywood's Double Plots." *Philological Quarterly* 25 (1946): 97–119. Corrects the mistaken assumption that Heywood was careless about plot structure and affirms the aesthetic sophistication of the playwright.

Ure, Peter. "Marriage and the Domestic Drama of Heywood and Ford." *English Studies* 32 (1951): 200–16. Emphasizes the importance of marriage in domestic drama and makes clear the similarities between Heywood and Ford in their treatment of the tragic consequences of a breach of marriage vows.

Wright, Louis B. "Heywood and the Popularizing of History." *Modern Language Notes* 43 (1928): 287–93. Argues that Heywood was a serious literary craftsman profoundly committed to patriotic teaching.

————. "Male Friendship Cult in Thomas Heywood's Plays." *Modern Language Notes* (1927): 510–14. Notes that the friendship between Frankford and Wendoll is as important as the marriage between Frankford and Anne.

Ziegler, Georgianna. "England's Savior: Elizabeth I in the Writings of Thomas Heywood." *Renaissance Papers 1980* (1981), pp. 29–39. Traces Heywood's obsession with Elizabeth as the defender of the Protestant faith.

Index